Angela

Strategic Advertising

Strategic Advertising
A practitioner's handbook

Judith Corstjens

Heinemann Professional Publishing

To Marcel

Heinemann Professional Publishing Ltd
Halley Court, Jordan Hill, Oxford OX2 8EJ

OXFORD   LONDON   MELBOURNE   AUCKLAND   SINGAPORE
IBADAN   NAIROBI   GABORONE   KINGSTON

First published 1990

© Judith Corstjens 1990

British Library Cataloguing in Publication Data
Corstjens, Judy
  Strategic advertising
  1. Advertising
  I. Title
  659.1

ISBN 0 434 90244 6

Printed and bound in Great Britain by
Billings Ltd, Worcester

Contents

Preface

It is commonly said that the advertising environment is becoming tougher, and with good reason. Media and production costs are rising in real terms and the overall volume of advertising is increasing. The spread of video recorders and remote control encourage zapping, while media options proliferate. On the consumer side, the stereotyped consumer, the two-parent, two-child family, is dying out. Worst of all, as consumer markets mature and the lead times given by innovation shrink, companies often find themselves marketing virtually identical products or services.

Taken together, these trends add up to mean that ads now have to shout louder, appeal more strongly or seduce more subtly than in the past, to give the same return on investment.

Advertising companies feel this pressure, they want their ads to work harder, and often interpret this as a need for originality and impact. They demand ever greater 'creativity' from their ad agencies.

The immediate effect has thus been a greater striving for excellence in agency creative departments. This translates into sharply increased demand (and salaries) for creative people with proven track records, and a high turnover of creative directors.

However, it is also natural to react by looking for new and richer sources of inspiration for the (scarce and expensive) creative talent. To ask whether it is possible to provide the creative teams with better briefs, which put them ahead in their race to the best creative solutions.

This means cultivating the expertise and creativity of the executives who develop advertising strategy. It means encouraging them to experiment with subtler and more intelligent use of information on the consumer.

And that is where this book comes in. This book is about techniques for involving the end consumer in the advertising development process. It is about handling more complex marketing data and using more subtle thinking to generate better strategic ideas to hand over to the creative people. The overall objective is to enable advertising strategists to give their overtaxed creative colleagues a head start in producing advertising which works harder.

Planning

In the UK 'cultivating the expertise and creativity of the executives who develop advertising strategy' has led to a new type of agency function, and to an extent, a change in attitudes, which go under the title of 'planning'.

Planning is really a new name for the process by which advertisers and their advertising agencies try to understand their public and develop advertising which affects that public. As such, planning has existed for as long as advertising. The current interest is not due to its invention, but to its formalization as a specialized function within agencies, and to the increased emphasis these agencies manage to place on developing advertising with, and for, the end consumer.

Planning was first introduced in the UK in the late 1960s, and since then the majority of top British agencies have adopted it. Saatchi and Saatchi London claims a planning department numbering 30*; six of Y & R's thirty-two board directors are planners†. The wave of new agencies set up in the late 1980s all opted for a distinct planning function.

Interest is growing outside the UK as well. In the US Ogilvy & Mather have introduced planning and Young & Rubicam and J. Walter Thompson are using their UK experience to develop planning in several of their offices internationally. Chiat Day (US) adopted the radical policy of hiring a significant number of experienced, UK-trained planners to head up planning departments in San Francisco, Los Angeles, Seatle and New York. In Europe, Paris has become the most involved after London, with six agencies currently experimenting.

The purpose of this book

The inspiration for this book was my experience of having worked in one of the agencies (Boase Massimi Pollitt) which helped to originate the concept of planning in the late 1960s, and then of being involved in the introduction of a planning approach in two larger agencies (D'Arcy McManus and Masius, as it then was, in London, and Boulet Dru Dupuy Petit, in Paris), each very different in outlook and working practice.

The essence of the task was to train and encourage executives to apply the many techniques and theories which exist for developing effective advertising.

Campaign, 20 November 1987.
†*Campaign*, 5 February 1988.

In doing this, it became apparent that the books available on advertising development are generally too remote from the everyday task to help in the actual day-to-day advertising strategy decisions. There is a distinct lack of books written for practitioners which give practical help on questions such as 'finding an advertising strategy', 'writing a creative brief', 'assessing the effectiveness of advertising before it runs' and 'evaluating its success afterwards'.

This book is different from others on advertising development because it is written for advertising professionals and not for academia. It concentrates on practical, usable theories, presented in a straightforward, non-technical way. It provides a readable and usable handbook for executives involved in the development of advertising. It tackles problems right through to the point of application. It details practical ways of finding marketing and advertising strategies, with checklists and thinking frameworks. No book can actually have ideas for you, but this book gets as near as a book can to helping you find solutions to typical advertising problems.

Is this book for you?

This book is for you if you ever spend time chewing a pencil, wondering what to say in your advertising, or agonizing over whether the advertising you have produced was, or will be, effective.

It will be interesting to students or others interested in a career in advertising, as an introduction to the real challenges faced daily by advertising managers and executives.

Believing that a book is only as useful as it is readable, I have tried to make it lean and fun, as well as informative. I hope you get some ideas as you read, but just as much, I hope you find it amusing enough to justify the effort of reading.

Judith Corstjens

Acknowledgements

Many colleagues and clients have helped and taught me but none more so than Ross Barr and Chris Cowpe at BMP, Andrew Roberts at Masius and Jean-Marie Dru at BDDP. It was Jean-Marie who originally started me on this book by suggesting that I try to write out all the techniques I applied, almost subconsciously, to developing advertising.

Thanks to Professor David Aaker for finding time in a busy schedule to read sections of the book and provide thoughtful comments. Thanks to Professor Michel Brimm for constructive criticism so pleasantly put that I had no trouble in accepting practically all his ideas.

Heartfelt thanks to Edouard Demeire for launching me into wordprocessing and then for repeatedly rescuing parts of the text, suffering various degrees of lostness, from the bowels of my Amstrad PC.

I would also like to thank all the companies who have given permission for their material to be reproduced.

Last but most, thanks to my husband, Marcel, for his suggestions and his unfailing support and encouragement, without which this book would have been highly improbable.

Note

To save complication the following simplifications are used throughout.

Anything which might be the subject of advertising, be it corporation, political party, charity, service or whatever, is referred to as a product or brand. Any person to whom an ad might be addressed (e.g. employee, charitable contributor, stockbroker) is referred to as a consumer. 'Sales' is used to cover donations, votes or whatever response is required.

The terms 'advertising professional' and 'manager' are used loosely to cover all company and agency personnel who have responsibilities concerning the advertising budget.

Male pronouns are used to refer to unidentified humanoids. (Here I am in the company of Germaine Greer in her seminal book *The Female Eunuch*. The first line of the first chapter declares: 'It is true that the sex of a person is attested by every cell in *his* body.')

1 Introduction

The advertising market

The ad industry is a market like any other, with agencies producing advertising and selling it to their clients. There is scope for a variety of agencies positioned and differentiated to suit the needs and tastes of all the clients.

Unlike most other products, the 'quality' of advertising is notoriously difficult to evaluate objectively. It is next to impossible to make an objective measure of an agency's output, or even to define what is 'good' advertising. There remains considerable scope for a wide range of philosophies and approaches to survive in the advertising industry.

In developing advertising there are usually a number of somewhat conflicting objectives (on top of keeping to budgets and timing schedules). Clearly, the management in an advertising company wants advertising which is effective, but they also want work with which they feel comfortable and which they feel able to defend. They want to respect their company's self-identity, the opinion of their agency advisers and the tastes of their target audience. The work must be original and have impact, but management must minimize any risk of its failing.

Advertising agencies have to compromise between pleasing their clients, creating a shop window of high profile campaigns, winning creative awards and controlling their costs, as well as market effectiveness.

Given the uncertainty in any definition of excellent advertising, it is not surprising that the ideal varies markedly from client to client and agency to agency. In particular it is not true to assert that all advertising is produced and judged purely on the basis of its effectiveness against its primary target audience.

Alternative approaches to advertising development

In any established advertising company or agency there has to be a 'normal approach' to advertising development. This means a procedure of some sort for deciding the creative brief and then some accepted rule for judging whether an ad is 'good' or not. This 'normal approach' is upheld by usage even if it is never explicitly identified.

Since there can be so many different views of what constitutes good advertising, and this book is about producing that commodity, it is worth starting out by making explicit the assumptions which underlie the methods suggested in this book.

The approach adopted in this book could be called a *market-led* approach to advertising development. The idea is that advertising development is dictated single-mindedly by the market, and market effectiveness is the overriding criterion for judging advertising.

The approach is best defined in terms of its two key underlying beliefs:

1 *Message and creation* – an effective advertisement must always be based on two ideas working harmoniously together – an ad has to have something motivating to say (the strategic idea) and an intrusive, memorable and complementary way of saying it (the creative idea). The creative idea is the vehicle which carries the strategic idea which will influence the customer. The resulting challenge is to develop a strategic base for advertising and then ensure that the strategic aims are truly answered by the proposed creative vehicle. This 'creation plus message' view of an advertisement is not controversial, but the balance of emphasis between the two can vary along a considerable spectrum. There are agencies with an extreme philosophy of creativity who defend their position on the basis that an ad achieves nothing if it is not noticed in the first place (which is perfectly true, if not the whole truth). Conversely, there are agencies in the habit of producing stodgy but strategic advertising, often for well-established and well-marketed brands with large budgets, who point to sales effects to defend their approach (also with partial validity). A market-led definition recognizes two distinct tasks in advertising development -- strategic and creative goals must be achieved and be complementary, neither can dominate or exclude the other.

2 *Consumer research* – the second belief concerns the value and usability of consumer research. This applies equally to the development of the message (or advertising strategy) and to the creative vehicle. On a practical, cost-effective basis one has to accept that the future effects of a proposed advertisement are generally unmeasurable (this problem is discussed in detail in Chapter 5, on pre-testing). There is no scale, no instrument, no experiment that can predict the exact effects of an advertisement in

advance. However, this does not mean that advertising is simply unmeasurable. The second critical belief in the market-led philosophy is that in trying to make explicit the way the advertising is supposed to work, it becomes possible to use consumer research to assess the advertising in a relative (it is better to do this than that) or directional (the ad would be improved by changing such and such) sense. This applies both to the content, or message, part of the ad and to the creative, vehicle part. The resulting challenge is to develop more meaningful and sensitive procedures for testing and evolving creative work. It also means learning to react to the research results before production and media investments become too heavy, and learning to integrate the results into the judgements which still have to be made.

The above sounds something like a definition of good professional practice and must leave the reader wondering whether anyone, agency or advertising company, would openly admit to *not* espousing a market-led philosophy. Acknowledged or not, there certainly exist other approaches, and they can, in fact, be highly successful.

Advertising is one of those products which is bought by one party for its effect on another. Three players are involved in advertising development – the advertiser, who pays for it, the consumer, who forms its target, and the agency, for whom the advertising represents its reputation and corporate image (important for attracting both clients and personnel). Advertising is always partly developed with the consumer in mind, but in practice the other two players often have a much more major influence than is generally recognized.

The client-led approach

Some advertising companies have evolved a set of principles for their advertising which have been proven to work over a large number of years and a large number of brands. Examples that come to mind readily are Procter & Gamble or Mars. By following their advertising rules they know that they will produce advertising which works to their satisfaction, and which involves little risk. It has proven itself to be cost-effective. It is often calculated to be effective given a certain (large) size of budget.

The advertising produced tends to be criticized for being predictable (by definition) and dull. It is also criticized for being product-focused, rather than focused on the consumer's needs and feelings. However, many clients do understand their businesses and their customers, so this approach is not, in fact, ineffective in terms of the advertising produced.

In agencies which subscribe to the client-led approach the implicit system of ad development is based on subtly discerning the exact requirements of the client. This involves close client liaison by account management which enables the agency to discern exactly what the client really wants, in terms of the end product.

The task is then to translate this understanding into a brief, and eventually creative work, which is true to the client's original vision. After the work is presented it is evolved further according to the client's criticisms and suggestions.

The definition of a good ad is one that the client likes, feels comfortable with and would in fact have written himself with a bit of training in copywriting.

In the current advertising climate, where the need for creativity is becoming more and more pressing, this approach is losing favour. Even traditionally conservative clients are now inclined to criticize agencies which simply give them 'what they asked for'. 'Surprise me' is now much more the fashion.

However, the client-led approach has served many large and successful agencies for years, and there are still many clients who find this system fits best with their own organization and philosophy. As the paymasters of agencies are the advertisers and not the consumers, this client-led approach is quite logical from the agency's point of view.

The agency-led approach

At its most extreme this approach implies relying on a senior, often high-profile, advertising 'star' to define the strategy, creative brief or even complete creative idea, on the basis of his own nous, prejudice and experience.

This philosophy tends to judge an ad to be 'good' if it is 'creative'. This means it attracts attention and is admired within the advertising industry i.e. wins the incestuous industry awards.

This type of working practice helps to explain why advertising is such a 'people' business – even in a large agency this key role, being in fact the embodiment of how the agency works, may be held by just three or four star people.

Again, though this approach may be condemned by theorists, the practice may not be so flawed. Given that the 'star' is synthesizing as much information as possible, fed to him by his client, his juniors, and his own observations and experience, and given also that clients tend to exert a moderating influence on an agency's worst excesses, the results may often be pretty close to the mark.

The drawback here is the risk of big mistakes caused by overconfidence, exacerbated by the agency's preference for larger-than-life advertising which enhances the agency's image.

For agencies there is a second, practical drawback – as the agency grows such a methodology has trouble expanding. The three or four star people cannot take on more work indefinitely, and their reputations and charisma are unlikely to transcend international barriers when the agency wants to expand overseas. (Not everyone believes this – Frank Lowe, head of Lowe Howard-Spink and Bell UK, and a much respected '*star*' of the London ad scene, promised to sign-off personally all work produced by their new agency, Lowe Tucker Metcalf, when it opened in New York[1].)

The descriptions market-led, client-led and agency-led are, of course, caricatures, and no real agency is purely of one type or another. In practice all advertising is influenced by a mixture of market, client and agency opinion.

Nor was the above meant to be an argument in favour of a market-led approach – indeed in this context, it is worth pointing out a drawback of being market as against client or agency-led.

The market-led approach tends to ignore valid short cuts – taking the client's view or trusting the intuition of an experienced advertising professional are both pragmatic economies of time and effort. Market-led agencies have been known to consume an entire four-week pitch period painstakingly demonstrating that the client's original brief or the agency's first hunch was correct.

The importance of these definitions is simply to note the rather purist approach of this book. The ideas presented all assume adherence to a basically market-led approach.

Market-led advertising and creativity

The main interest in systematizing the advertising development process usually springs from the hope that it will improve the creative department's output, or at least help them find solutions more quickly and painlessly. However, if you flick through a magazine or watch TV for half an hour and pick out the ads you admire most, it is not always obvious what contribution strategic thinking has made to them.

The first point to make clearly and honestly, is that not all advertising strategy is complex or critical. There are situations where the key advertising task *is* the creative one. In the case, say, of an established, mainstream lager, or a popular child's breakfast cereal, nothing can replace that one great idea. In cases like these the creative team's own experience is quite sufficient for them to identify the only possible strategy, and they are basically on their own in the battle with the blank sheet of paper.

It is also important to say that strategic work never obviates the need for a bright creative idea – at the end of the day it is still left to the creatives to come up with the ad.

But there are ways in which the logical groundwork can help creative thinking. The first is in limiting creative thought to a small area. Having a more precise strategic goal leaves the creative team free to concentrate on the translation of the strategic idea into a distinctive creative idea. For example, when looking for follow-on ads in the Smash (instant mashed potato) campaign, the 'strategists' suggested two areas, 'nutritional content' and 'prestigious cooking' where Smash's image could usefully be improved. The resulting films used a Martian body-builder, and a Martian hostess preparing a dinner party. These ideas are totally to the credit of the creative people, but more creative time could have been wasted if they had had to think of a strategy or 'selling idea'. If the creative brief clearly defines the selling idea, the creative team can concentrate on finding a sparkling way of saying it. The creative task is made simpler, if not easier.

The other positive aid that can be given to the creative team by the strategic team is sorting out valuable nuggets of information from the mass usually available. This is something many creative people have got used to doing themselves, but it is often a logical-type task which can be delegated to the strategic team. Providing thoughts or hooks which give creatives toeholds or spring boards for thoughts is an important goal for the strategists. A nice little example is the technical detail 'Teflon coated not once, but twice' used in the Tower non-stick frying pan ads.

These two points give the positive ways that strategic thinking can help creativity. There are also pragmatic ways in which strategy helps to protect creativity. A clear strategy for an advertisement tends to reduce the impact of personal prejudice in judgement of the ad. If a controversial creative approach is proposed which clearly satisfies the strategy it is less likely to be chiselled away to nothing by the agency account team and client. The response is likely to be 'let's test it to see if it does what we intended' rather than 'forget it, I hate it'. Outlandish creative ideas are somewhat protected if they can take cover under a logically defendable strategy. On the whole, clarity breeds confidence and experimentation, whereas vagueness breeds fear and caution.

The second tenet, reliance on early experimentation with creative ideas, also reduces the sense of risk and increases the willingness to experiment. This is especially true in ads which take a somewhat irreverent or tongue-in-cheek attitude to the product being advertised. A television ad for Sony's compact disc in the UK refers laconically to 'an hour of Mozart out of a beer mat'. Not perhaps the most direct way to emphasize the superiority of a highly technological product, but one that was confidently chosen by Sony after testing with the projected target audience.

Continuous consumer feedback within an agency tends to breed a more realistic spirit towards advertising and the consumption of advertising. A realization that the typical viewer is going to be uninterested and cynical is often at the heart of the most creative advertising.

Market influence on the advertising development process

A typical version of the broad stages in the development of an advertising campaign is shown diagramatically in Figure 1.1. The steps which should involve input from the market are marked with an asterisk.

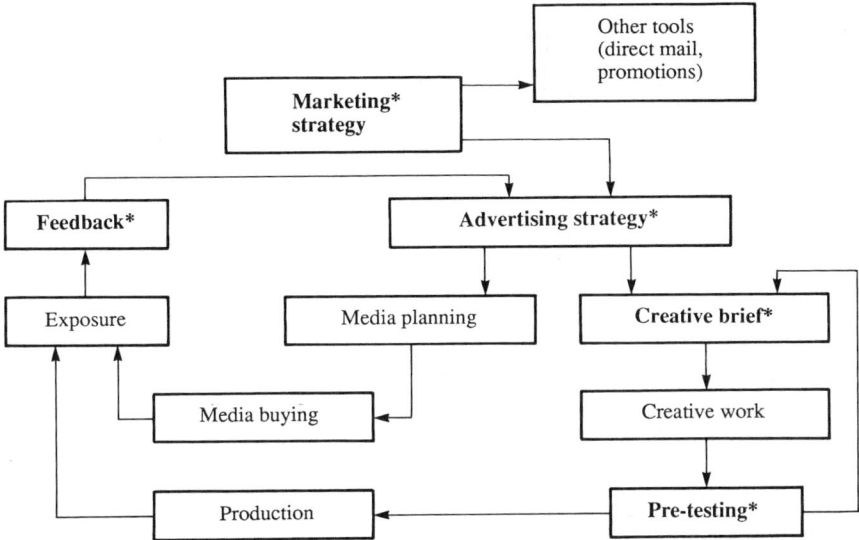

Figure 1.1   *The broad stages involved in producing an advertising campaign. The asterisks indicate the need for input from the market*

Simple as it is, Figure 1.1 immediately draws attention to an important analytical framework which underlies the advertising development process. This framework breaks an ad into discrete conceptual layers – marketing strategy, advertising strategy and the creative vehicle (see Figure 1.2).

In the abstract this separation seems almost trivial, but in practice, in discussions within the agency and between agency and client, a common language for these different layers allows much more precise analysis of an ad's strengths and weaknesses. For example, if an ad seems to be failing to affect its audience, at the simplest level there are three different types of explanation for its failure:

1 *Marketing strategy failing* – this happened at the launch of Prestel (Telecom's viewdata service) to the general public. Even when the advertising communicated the intended messages successfully, it failed to interest people in the product.
2 *Advertising strategy failing* – the failure of a striking press campaign for a popular knitting machine was traced back to the advertising strategy.

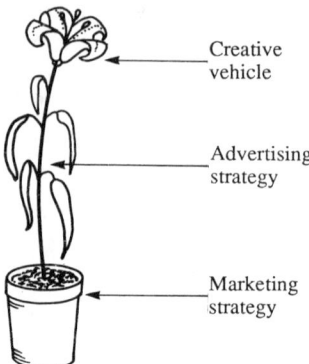

Figure 1.2   A whimsical representation of the three concepts which underlie effective advertising

The advertising idea was to show marvellous designer knit dresses, on slinky models, demonstrating the extremes of the machine's potential. The ads were noticed, liked, understood but their appeal was strongest for women who were least inclined to buy knitting machines.

3   *Creative vehicle failing* – the ad is ignored, misunderstood or rejected as advertising while the proposition/message is felt to be interesting and motivating once explained. One example of this is a building society who had two genuinely innovative products (one a link with a bank account and the other a clubby-type discount and promotions card). The initial creative approach tried to link these products with other great innovative ideas – the wheel, the telephone. The ads failed (and were never run) because the creative idea was a failure – it overiced the cake.

In some cases advertising strategy and creative vehicle are too intertwined to be analysed separately and the ad has to be perceived as an indivisable whole. However, in the majority of cases these distinctions are extremely useful. The separation of advertising strategy as a discrete task, undertaken before the creative brief is written, invariably leads to a better, clearer, more single-minded brief.

The stages which involve input from the market can be abstracted from Figure 1.1 and represented by the cycle shown in Figure 1.3. This diagram summarizes the specific market-led tasks, and gives a visual representation of marketing strategy as the driving force behind the whole ad development process.

Here it also serves as a visualization of the contents and organization of the next five chapters.

The following chapter deals with understanding marketing strategy. Understanding the product's marketing strategy is the first step towards producing effective advertising for the product.

Advertising strategy, its relationship to marketing strategy, its definition and techniques for finding one, are dealt with in Chapter 3. The translation of advertising strategy into creative brief is covered in Chapter 4, with the help of several examples of briefs.

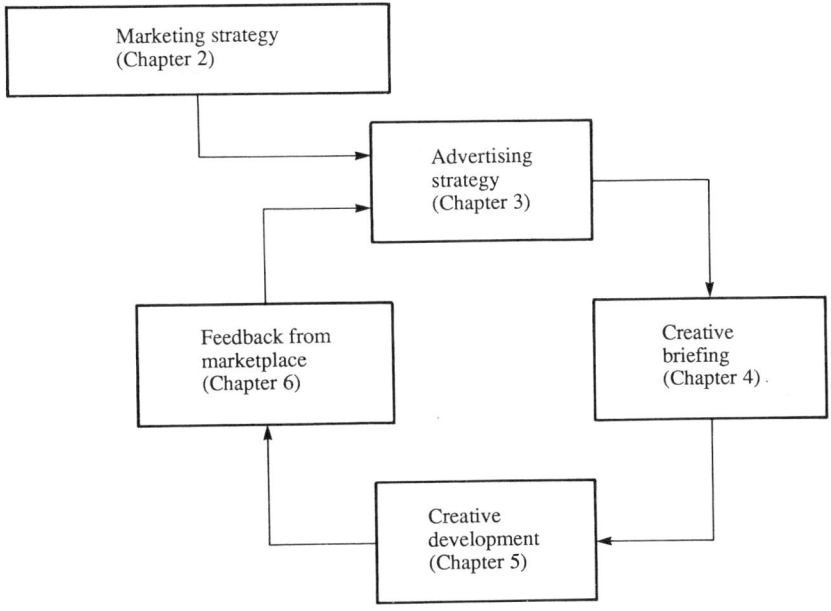

Figure 1.3   *The 'planning' cycle – input from the market on advertising development*

Chapter 5 investigates the controversial area of testing and developing creative work and the most valid objectives and methodologies when doing so.

Feedback from the marketplace, once the campaign has run, is an essential part of the market influence – only by keeping in touch with evolving consumer perceptions can the team hope to improve its market-sensitivity as time goes by. However, this area is fraught with problems to the extent that many advertising professionals do not expect advertising to be 'accountable'. The problems and possible solutions are discussed in Chapter 6.

Chapters 2 to 6, therefore, cover the tasks depicted in Figure 1.3. As such they form a day-to-day handbook for producing effective advertising.

References

1 *Campaign*, 23 January 1987, plus 'Comment Column', *Campaign*, 13
   February 1987.

2 Understanding marketing strategy

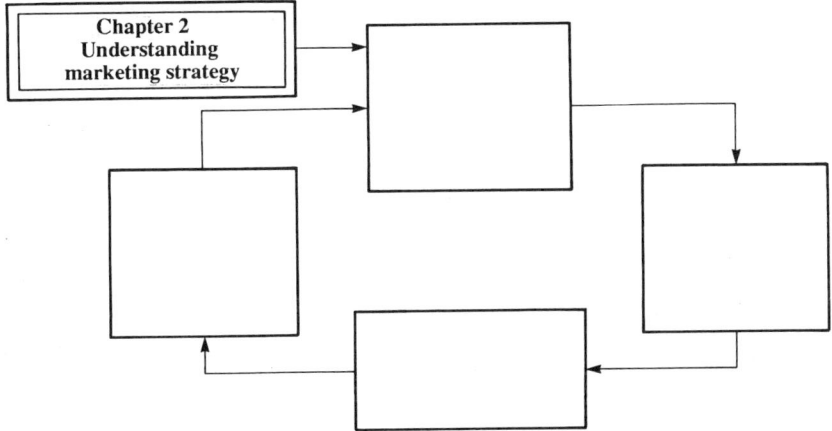

Chapter 2
Understanding
marketing strategy

The marketing concept

The key to success in business is to provide value in terms of the qualities which best satisfy the needs of the market.[1] The marketing concept is that the only sure route to sales and profits is to find out what people want to spend their hard-earned cash on and then devise a way of giving it to them. A marketing strategy is a company's idea for delivering the product that its consumers want.

The marketing strategy has to be clear and explicit before advertising development can begin. Sometimes it is already well understood, and the advertising company uses it to brief their agency. Sometimes the marketing strategy is not stated explicitly but already exists (as is often the case with an established product that is new to marketing and advertising). The task then is to discover and define the marketing soul of the product. In other cases, particularly with new products, or products which do not yet exist, a strategy has to be developed from scratch.

Definition of a marketing strategy

Marketing is the art of providing a product that certain people want to buy more than any other. A marketing strategy is one product's blue-print for how to be that most desired product, at least for a particular group of consumers.

Specifically, a marketing strategy consists of:

1   A defined group of people who form the *target market* for the product.
2   A *differential advantage* which makes that product the most appropriate to satisfy that target group.

These two elements together form the 'raison d'être' for the product. The product has a 'niche' or 'sense' in the consumer's world. It offers some solution, pleasure, association or symbol value not exactly matched by any competing product and which is valued, at least by a section of the public.

Some examples of successful marketing strategies illustrate this definition:

- **McDonald's Restaurants**
  Target: Budget-conscious families.
  Differential advantage: Quick service, clean surroundings and high-quality familiar food, mean that children are not a hassle. Value for money is also essential to attract this group.

- **Daff cars**
  Target: Older or reluctant drivers.
  Differential advantage: Automatic transmission, meaning no gear changing, in a modestly-priced car.

- **Bang & Olufsen hi-fi**
  Target: Affluent, image-conscious hi-fi buffs and snobs.
  Differential advantage: Chic, sophisticated image established by communication, supported by elegant visual presentation and product quality.

The group of people who form the target for the product is usually referred to as a 'segment' of the market, and dividing the market into such groups is called segmentation.

The differential advantage of a product is often defined in terms of its 'positioning'. Positioning suggests a reference to other objects – these can be the competition, or any other scale or frame of reference in the consumer's mind.

Positioning a product simply means identifying it in the consumer's mind with certain characteristics, associations, benefits or values particularly tied to that brand. It is always concerned with securing some sort of differential advantage.

The advantages of having a marketing strategy

Choosing a segment and a position for a product is a critical and long-term commitment. Any particular choice of segment and position implies kissing goodbye to many other segments and positions and hence to some potential sales. The choice is long term because a positioning is expensive and slow to establish and therefore uneconomical to change. So what are the advantages of having a marketing strategy?

Most purchases are made on a 'first past the post' type decision, rather like British elections. A product has to be first choice for some people and not everybody's second choice. By concentrating on one particular subgroup the marketer can design his product to match its needs more precisely than any of the competitive products. Conversely the company that succeeds in being everyone's second choice loses out to each of the 'targeted' brands.

For a graphic illustration of this theory in action consider the strategies used by aftershave brands. Looking through one edition of Esquire[2] one comes across an aftershave for men who want exclusivity – VIP Special Reserve by Giorgio (see Plate 2.1). Aramis are there promoting their Tuscany brand to romantic, sensitive types. The ad uses the line 'Lose yourself in Tuscany' and shows a wimpish guy looking lost on a roof overlooking Florence. Calvin Klein use a grainy close-up of an orgy to establish Obsession as the brand for that segment of men who like making love to three women simultaneously. However, there is not one brand targeted at 'all men' or 'the average man' with advertising bland enough not to alienate any group.

Research or sales results would tell which, out of exclusivity, romance or lasciviousness has most potential for attracting aftershave buyers. What is certain, without such information, is that any of these three positionings/ segmentations will be more effective than a marketing strategy which tries to appeal to 'all men'. The former three are better because they appeal to three common motivations each of which exist in significant proportions of men, while the latter would be likely to fall flatly between all groups. No manufacturer will get the whole market, and he who aims for everyone ends up convincing no one.

This same observation applies when testing new products and concepts – the 'top box' or 'most preferred' statistic is key. A new product development system offered by Volney Stefflre and his company Proteus uses 'percentage of people who prefer this product to their current favourite in the category' as the basis for predicting brand share. Initially this seems a rather drastic demand to make, but actually it is based on sound logic – what value being runner-up?

The second reason for choosing a specific segmentation and positioning is the need to concentrate marketing resources. Market research focused on the needs of the chosen segment, media effort bought against a certain group,

Plate 2.1   *Giorgio's VIP Special Reserve – this ad appeared in the same magazine as a dozen other ads for aftershave brands. Each brand has to find a unique appeal, based on the aspirations of their particular target audience or 'niche'. Putting together a collection of aftershave ads would in effect create a 'colour chart' of aftershave wearers' personalities*

advertisements which emphasize only certain key benefits, all enjoy efficiencies which allow smaller resources to stand up against larger resources spread across a wider front. A manufacturer who overextends his resources will lose out to competitors who have each focused their efforts. A segmentation strategy can enable a small brand to compete profitably against a larger one.

A third benefit which can in fact accrue to all competitors in the segmented market, is the reduction of competitive pressure. If competing companies tailor their efforts to different groups, the price competition between them will lessen, as consumers are less inclined to view all the products as substitutable. This is not necessarily a disadvantage for the consumer, who benefits from more exact satisfaction of his needs – the market becomes more efficient, providing greater 'value' to all.

In particular, if one manufacturer produces several products which can be substituted one for another, a segmentation strategy can reduce the competitiveness between his products and improve his profitability. The most extreme example of this is transportation companies (airlines, railways, buses etc.). By segmenting their markets on type of users (businessmen, shoppers, tourists) they can tailor products (first class, cheap day returns, off-peak discounts) to the needs and price sensitivity of each group. This type of policy optimizes both volume and profit while (hopefully) providing the type of service most valued by each group.

The key to finding effective segmentation strategies and the corresponding positionings is understanding the needs and motivations of consumers.

The needs or motivations exploited (or served, pandered to) by marketers are becoming increasingly complex and esoteric with the more basic consumer needs being largely satisfied in our rich Western societies. Distasteful though it may seem, if one contrasts this situation with that found in the poor two-thirds of the world, the next section examines current consumer 'needs', which form the raw material for our marketing strategies.

Needs and motivations

The fertile source of inspiration for the marketer and advertiser is the astonishingly wide, complex, varied and irrational area of consumer needs. Needs, in the broadest sense, covering all whimsical desires and conditioned aspirations, are fundamental to marketing. Only if people perceive needs can they be motivated.

The psychologist Maslow first had the idea of analysing and classifying human needs.[3] He categorized motivations into five types, from the most basic of food and shelter to the final, highest human goal of 'self actualization' (Figure 2.1).

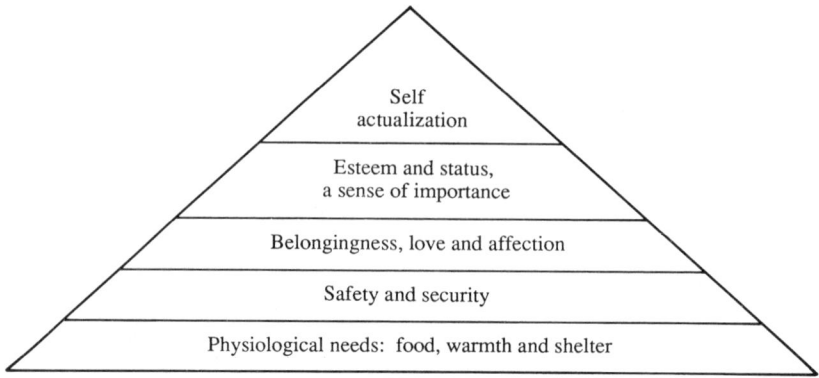

Figure 2.1   *Maslow's five levels of needs*

In Maslow's day there may have been a vague hope that as one rose through the triangle, one's needs would be nearer to being satisfied and would eventually (like the vertex of a triangle) disappear. However, as purchasing power increases it seems that consumers simply demand higher levels of satisfaction from each type of need and that each human activity is called upon to satisfy a more complex set of needs. Functional, physiological needs stretch to cover sun-drenched holiday, second car and swimming pool (i.e. these come to be considered simple, physical needs for a comfortable, healthy life). Food, far from simply providing sustenance is used to provide pleasure, health, excitement and even identity (vegetarianism) or prestige (strangely coloured vegetables).

Maslow may still be accurate on a broad scale, but the modern marketer needs a more functional analysis of the types of need that motivate today's consumers. There are, in fact, six basic types of need, or motivations, which drive consumption in our society.

Functional needs

These needs cover all the practical and functional, but none of the psychological and emotional benefits that consumers get from products. The typical claims in this area concern:

- Saving time, effort or money.
- Security, safety, health.
- Comfort, cleanliness, convenience.

They are based on functions or qualities of products (real or perceived), their effectiveness or price.

For years this was felt to be the key area for marketing strategy. Ads which use demonstrations, which concentrate on information about the product (including price) or which seem to be trying to argue or convince, are generally examples of this approach. Such strategies do not exclude humour or originality. The famous Araldite ad, where the car is glued onto the poster, promotes a simple functional benefit (see Plate 2.2).

Pleasure

The pleasure motivation is never quite as rational or objective as the functional need; the satisfaction given by one chocolate bar compared to another is hard to pin down.

People are forever seeking gratification: oral (taste, texture, quantity); sensual (softness, fragrance, beauty); mental (excitement, peace, romance, relaxation, amusement, nostalgia). Many frequently-purchased consumer goods such as foods and toiletries, are bought for these satisfactions.

The 'problem of pleasure' – providing and communicating ever-increasing levels of pleasure – stretches to exasperation the imaginations of R & D labs, marketing departments and ad agencies. Cadbury's (US) seem to be expressing this struggle when they write 'Indescribably Delicious' (registered phrase!) on the pack of their Almond Joy chocolate bar. A similarly exasperated line emerged from the UK promoters of fresh cream recently – 'Too nice for words'.

Communication needs

Marketers have long been conscious of the psychological needs of their markets. A large class of these psychological needs concerns identity – the need that people have to express themselves both to themselves and to the outside world.

To do this consumers do not require physical benefits from products, they look for products with *symbol values*. It is futile to approach a marketing solution for a bath additive, whisky or wristwatch in terms of product functions – the starting point has to be people, their personalities and their symbol needs.

The advertising strategy is an integral part of a symbol value product. Far from being 'salesmanship in print', this type of advertising actually creates something people want to buy. Without advertising, Levi 501s are just scraps of blue cloth (see Plate 2.3).

It also has interesting implications for targeting the media. There's no point in buying a Porsche if nobody else knows what it says about you. What a disaster to buy a diamond for a girl who hasn't been told what it means. The advertiser has to reach the friends and acquaintances of his potential buyers in order to create a true symbol. This is why glossy cinema advertising can

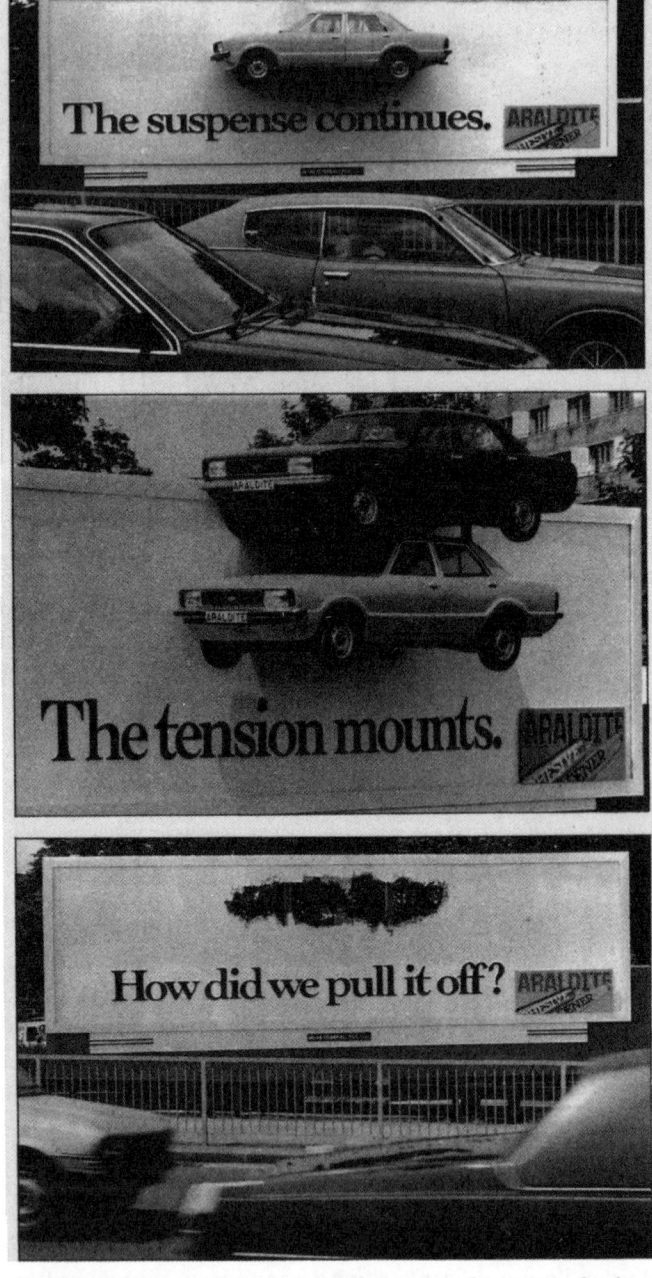

Plate 2.2   *Araldite – having an advertising strategy based on a simple physical property does not obviate the need for creativity. Nor does it inhibit creativity as Araldite here clearly demonstrates*

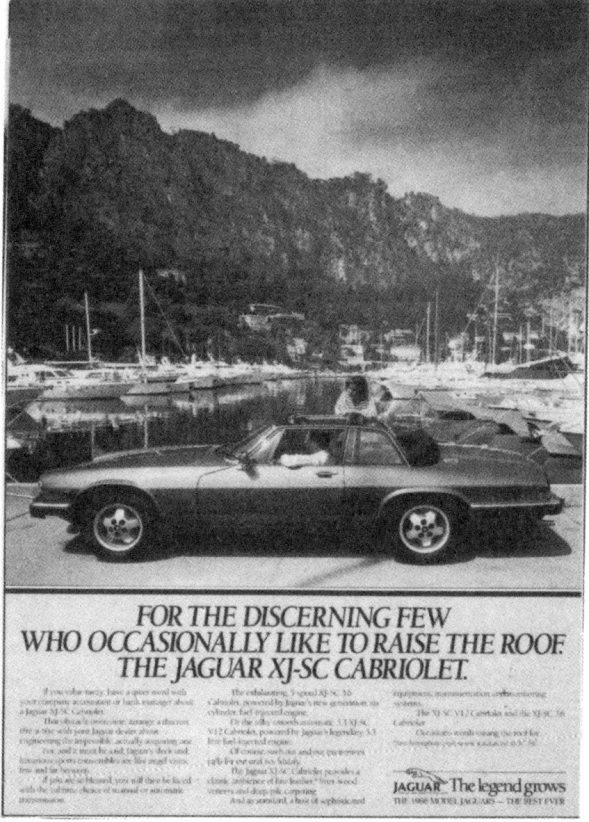

FOR THE DISCERNING FEW
WHO OCCASIONALLY LIKE TO RAISE THE ROOF.
THE JAGUAR XJ-SC CABRIOLET.

JAGUAR The legend grows

Plate 2.3 *Jaguar – advertising for 'symbol products' actually brings into being a means of communication. Products can say you are conservative, experimental, young or sophisticated. This is an intangible commodity that people want to buy*

be justified for a prestige car even though only a tiny fraction of the viewers will actually buy.

In developing marketing strategies based on communication needs it is useful to distinguish between self identity and image.

(a) 'Me→me' communication (identity)

Everyone has a picture of themselves, or more importantly, a picture of how they would like to see themselves. The products they consume, use or wear help them confirm this identity. Products can be marketed on the basis that they help their users feel sporty (LaCoste casual wear), up-to-date (Swatch watches), professional (Olympus cameras), sexy (gold) or successful (BMW cars).

A slightly different use of the desire to identify oneself, is also exploited by marketers. Oxo (beef stock cube) produced a series of exceptionally popular and memorable ads based on the idea of representing a real, as against the usual idealized, family. Viewers strongly *identify* with the reciprocal illtreatment among family members, and undoubtedly feel closer to the product as a result.

(b)   'Me→them' communication (image)

This is a well-worn marketing area, but its importance is still growing and there are always opportunities to use the motivation in new ways.

The classic benefit was to establish one's importance, class, wealth and success. Apparently, the decision to market the first Japanese version of the *Encyclopaedia Britannica* on the prestige of possession rather than its contents, led to one of the publishing coups of 1902.[4]

Attitudes change, and social groupings seem to have fragmented in recent years, increasing the range of 'me→them' symbol values, and the sophistication of the strategies which use them. Coolness, ecology mindedness, style or taste, youthfulness, friendliness, religiousness, sensitivity and even being hard-up are just some of the messages which people want to send to each other.

Tobacco marketing exploits this powerful area of motivations (despite the legal restraints which make it more and more difficult to do so) with boxes which are like miniature poster sites, advertising the user's tastes. Examples of symbol values in that field are:

- Rothmans (UK) – conservative, establishment, secure.
- Hamlet (UK) – relaxed and philosophical approach to life.
- Virginia Slims (US) – independent, liberated femininity (using the line 'You've come a long way baby').
- Winston (US) – sociable, unpretentious 'real' people.

By contrast, the anti-smoking lobby have usually preferred to adopt functional approaches, epitomized by lines such as: 'Haven't you coughed up enough' or 'More than 30,000 people die each year in the UK from lung cancer'. Perhaps the newer strategies which aim to make smoking seem down-market, dirty and anti-social will prove more (de)motivating.

Admiration

People like to associate themselves with great things and great people, albeit in a humble way. There is satisfaction to be had walking round the track of an empty Olympic stadium, walking where great athletes have trodden. It is a pleasure to read about statesmen, heroic acts or film stars.

People like to come closer to the things they admire. This is one of the best arguments for using stars to promote a product. Lux soap does not promise to turn you into a film star, nor to make people think you are a film star, but it is nice to know, as you lather yourself in your suburban bathroom, that you have just this much in common with Nastashia Kinski. Company chairmen appearing in their own ads may come under this category (e.g. Iacocca, for Chrysler, when he was something of a national hero or role model).

Admiration exists for art, emotion, wit and success which can all be beneficially associated with products. This is the logic behind sponsoring sports, theatre, art, even rubbish bins, and often the logic which inspires ads to be beautiful, witty, warm or clever.

This latter idea, that a sense of admiration can be created by the ad itself (such as the sixty-second mega-production for Apple Computer's '1984' Macintosh launch ad) is relatively subtle and new. It implies that a product can be differentiated on the basis of its association with its own (admired) advertising. In the Apple example the advertising itself was extravagant, confident, individualist and somewhat anarchistic. Thus the advertising itself becomes the competitive advantage or 'positioning' for the product. This is quite distinct from positionings which simply depend on advertising (such as Bang & Olufsen, mentioned above) to create their differential advantage (in that case a luxury, elegant image).

This technique is widely used in Japan, Britain and France, and, not surprisingly, such advertising often strongly reflects the respective culture. The best-known Japanese example is Parco, who use breathtaking and often impenetrably enigmatic visuals to attach a cachet to their commercial-cultural complex. Also noteworthy is the agency who is brave enough to apply the technique to itself. Kasugai of Nagoya City produce beautiful posters signed off with the agency name and, in very small print, the line: 'This poster is one of the imaginary poem series that we present to you every year with fresh feeling and wonderland atmosphere.' (See Plate 2.4.)

In Britain the visual brilliance of the surrealist posters for Benson and Hedges Gold cigarettes has created a whole genre, but the classic approach is wit. The wit of the multi-media campaign 'Heineken refreshes the parts other beers cannot reach', is an excellent typical example, though Guinness have used 'witty advertising to admire' for longer. The French admire beautiful people more than they admire wit (they may, in fact, enjoy sex more than laughter). This is why so many French ads feature women with legs too long to fit into the average TV screen, and a man who has trouble keeping his bow tie tied for the duration of a commercial.

Plate 2.4   *Kasugai – many agencies use logical argument (the most conservative advertising strategy!) in their house ads. Kasugai Advertising Company of Japan uses the same type of strategy as Benson and Hedges. Association with their own imaginative posters creates a positive image for the agency*

Altruism

People do have feelings of altruism and duty to various causes. The most obvious marketing on this need is, of course, for charities, but such feelings are also engendered in political advertising, recruitment (Your Country Needs You! – the famous ad in which Kitchener points his finger asking British men to go and fight Germans at the start of the First World War)* and even, occasionally, commercial products.

The go-ahead Bank of Scotland (UK) are currently (1987) marketing their Visa credit card by offering to donate £5 to a children's charity for each new subscriber, and to make a further contribution each time the card is used (see Plate 2.5). MasterCard are doing the same thing in the US, with the refinement of allowing the cardholder to choose from a selection of charities. Heinz have run similarly charitable schemes for returned labels.

Altruism can be a more integral part of the product as for refrigerators without ozone-destroying chlorofluorocarbons and washing powders without river-polluting phosphates.

Conversely, charities which always focus their appeals on an altruistic

---

* The same ad also offered a functional benefit and the greatest overclaim of all time – 'The war to end all wars'. The only motivating, *functional* benefit for selling war to a democracy is peace. The later US version 'I (Uncle Sam) want you for the US Army' dropped the claim itself, but the same idea ran through Woodrow Wilson's speeches.

Why should he care which credit card you use?

Children like Sam need your help.

They need it now, and they need it badly. Which is why your choice of credit card could be vital.

Because the new Bank of Scotland NSPCC Visa Card has been created with a particular object in mind.

To help children.

Children in need, in danger, and distress.

Last year, the NSPCC helped over 44,000 youngsters.

To some that meant the difference between life and death.

Which is why we've joined forces.

And why we're asking for your support.

For every one of these new Visa accounts opened, we'll donate £5 to the NSPCC.

But it goes a lot further than that.

Whenever you buy something with the card, you'll help the children too.

It's a splendid way of contributing.

You don't have to get into debt, or run up credit.

You don't even have to use your card more than you usually do.

Because every penny counts.

And with lots of people taking part, the sums will soon mount up.

They could easily top the million pound mark.

That's an awful lot of hope.

For very little effort.

So whether or not you already have a credit card, please return the coupon now.

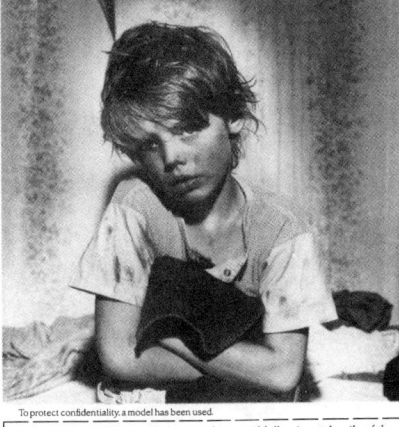

To protect confidentiality, a model has been used.

Please send me an application form and full written details of the new Bank of Scotland NSPCC Visa Card. I am over 18 years of age. Send to: Bank of Scotland Visa Centre, FREEPOST, Dunfermline, Fife KY99 5BR; or dial 100 and ask for FREEFONE Bank of Scotland.

First names _____
(Mr/Mrs/Miss/Ms)

Surname _____

Address _____

_____

_____

_____

Postcode _____ Tel. No. _____

Cardholders in England, Wales and Northern Ireland will benefit the NSPCC and, in Scotland, the RSSPCC

 **BANK OF SCOTLAND**
A FRIEND FOR LIFE  NSPCC VISA

Plate 2.5 *Bank of Scotland – the motivation of altruism is most commonly used to sell charities. However, the go-ahead Bank of Scotland have developed an appeal based on altruism for their commercial Visa Card operation*

segment of the population might do well considering whether they could appeal to less altruistically-motivated groups, by tackling motivations such as the pleasure of giving or the effect on one's self-identity. Comic Relief may have achieved this, allowing people to communicate something about their attitudes by wearing red noses and linking their image with having fun as well as charity.

Applying the motivations to marketing problems

In any given case not all six motivations will be relevant. For example, if a product is used exclusively in the home (e.g. toothpaste) there may be no viable strategies based on image. Toothpaste does not have the capacity to communicate 'me→them'. This explains why there is a market for expensive fountain pens (Waterman, Mont Blanc etc.) but attempts to launch similarly classy razors have failed.

Most of the motivations can be engendered directly or vicariously, i.e. consumers can be motivated not only for themselves but also for their loved ones: a mother wants to give pleasure or prestige to her children; a lover wants to reinforce the self-identity of his girlfriend etc.

This analysis of needs is offered as a practical tool, and is not put forward as a complete and perfect account of human needs (for example the strong and important impulse to procreate does not fit naturally into any of the categories and there is obviously an overlap between self-image and altruism). Its validity lies simply in its usefulness in developing marketing and advertising strategies. Its usefulness is illustrated in detail in the next chapter.

Figure 2.2 summarizes the six motivations, and illustrates them with stereotyped examples of their meanings to consumers.

Segmentation schemes and positionings spring, in pairs, from consumer needs and either may be discovered first. Segmentation is tackled first in this book as this maintains the focus on the consumer. The next section covers the definition of a viable segmentation and ways of finding one.

Segmentation

The concept is simple – segmentation is the art of grouping together people who share a certain need.

Segmentation by age, geography, personality or whatever is valid if, and only if, these variables differentiate a group in terms of their needs. This is what Saatchi's are getting at in their promotion of global marketing, when they say that the jogger in Central Park has more in common with the jogger in Les Jardins de Luxembourg, than with his neighbour in Harlem. If you

Functional	Me→them	Admiration
'In my everyday life I seek to save money, make less effort and avoid problems'	'I want people to think I'm cool, sexy and fun and so win their love, affection or admiration'	'I admire great sports-men and leaders of men, success and fame and enjoy feeling nearer to them'
Pleasure	Me→me	Altruism
'I like to indulge in the odd bar of chocolate and love the smell of clean sheets'	'I like to think I'm a kind, happy, sensible and thrifty sort of person, and quite nice looking'	'I am genuinely patriotic and charitable, I care that the world survives past my death and am upset when major acci-dents occur'

Figure 2.2   *A Summary of the six major types of motivation currently exhibited in affluent societies*

are a manufacturer of designer jogging shorts your segment might include executives from all major financial centres if they sense a common need for exclusive sportswear. Of course, segmentation schemes can be more or less attractive and one consideration will be reachability, which may involve geography (see Plate 2.6).

Criteria for segmenting a market

Market segmentation is based on the notion that consumers within a market have slightly different needs to each other or attach different importance to differing needs. These differences allow product offerings to be tailored more exactly to particular subgroups of the market.

Finding clear, efficient groupings within a market is, however, a com-plicated and often non-exact process. Ideally one would like to satisfy the following criteria:

1   *Differentiation* – the need identified should be common to all the members of the segment and should clearly differentiate them from the rest of the market. To justify a segmentation strategy on this criterion it is enough to show that some people in the market have, or attach importance to, a certain need while others do not.
2   *Importance* – the need is (or can be made to seem) important enough to create a significant added value for an offering which satisfies it. To fulfil this criterion it is necessary to show that the segment is sufficiently motivated by the perceived need to be swayed to some meaningful degree

CET INSTANT OÙ L'ÉMOTION SOUDAIN PREND LE PAS SUR LA FÊTE. OÙ VOUS ÊTES SEULS AU MONDE AVEC VOTRE BON-HEUR. OMEGA. POUR TOUS LES TEMPS FORTS DE VOTRE VIE.

OMEGA MARQUE TOUJOURS LES TEMPS FORTS. DES JEUX OLYMPIQUES. DE LA CONQUÊTE DE L'ESPACE. D'UNE VIE RÉUSSIE COMME LA VÔTRE. OMEGA CONSTELLATION. POUR VOUS DEUX.

Ω
OMEGA

Plate 2.6   *Omega – two ads, one in French, one in English. Often manufacturers find that their segment transcends national boundaries. The target for an expensive watch may include upwardly mobile executives in all major business centres if they sense a common need to flash prestigious jewellery from under their starched cuffs*

IT IS A MOMENT YOU PLANNED FOR. REACHED FOR.
STRUGGLED FOR. A LONG-AWAITED MOMENT OF SUCCESS.
OMEGA. FOR THIS AND ALL YOUR SIGNIFICANT MOMENTS.

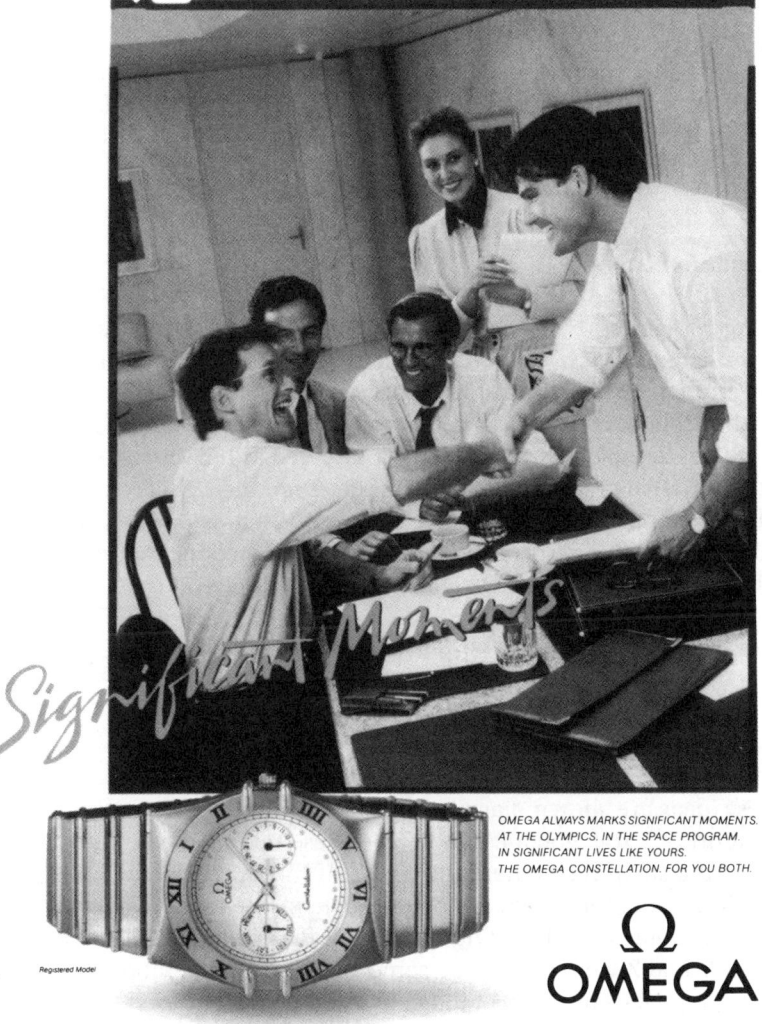

OMEGA ALWAYS MARKS SIGNIFICANT MOMENTS.
AT THE OLYMPICS. IN THE SPACE PROGRAM.
IN SIGNIFICANT LIVES LIKE YOURS.
THE OMEGA CONSTELLATION. FOR YOU BOTH.

Ω
OMEGA

Omega — Official Timekeeper of the Olympic Games, Calgary and Seoul 1988

Plate 2.6 (*continued*)

in their purchase decision. If this or the previous criterion is missing, the segmentation strategy is non-existent and a marketing strategy based on it is false.

3   *Size and reachability* – the segment is large enough to be profitable and is reachable (or better still, selectively reachable) through some media. This criterion is often more difficult to verify, particularly if the segmentation is based on a psychological need. Verification usually implies relating the need to an identifiable and measurable characteristic of the population. It is in assessing a segmentation's effectiveness on this third criterion that *segmentation bases* have their importance.

Segmentation bases

Defining a segment by its special needs or motivations makes perfect sense from the point of view of producing the right product and making a profit. However, in order to estimate how large the segment is, and how to reach it through media, it is usually necessary to identify a segmentation base.

Take, for example, a brand of yogurt targeted at health-conscious mothers as an alternative to the unhealthy snacks which their children demand. This 'need' can be related to demographic criteria such as age, sex and presence of children, possibly also educational level, socioeconomic group or type of housing. In this way demographic criteria could be used as a *segmentation base*.

Bases are useful if:

1   They correlate well with the (need) segment chosen.
2   They are efficient for selecting media.

These ideas are shown diagrammatically in Figure 2.3.

In Figure 2.3 the 'goodness of fit' is represented by the amount of overlap between the small rectangles X, Y and Z. If the shaded areas were the same size as X, it would mean that all the people in the target segment exhibited the demographic criteria defined and used the media being proposed. If the areas X, Y and Z were also of the same area the segmentation *base* would be 100 per cent efficient.

In this example (assuming that all the areas are drawn to scale) the demographic base does not seem to help much – medium Z covers about 30 per cent of the population, and only about the same proportion of X-type people.

The most commonly used segmentation bases are demographics, along with various usership (of product or brand) and ownership (such as freezer or microwave) data. On the whole, demographics score well in their appli-

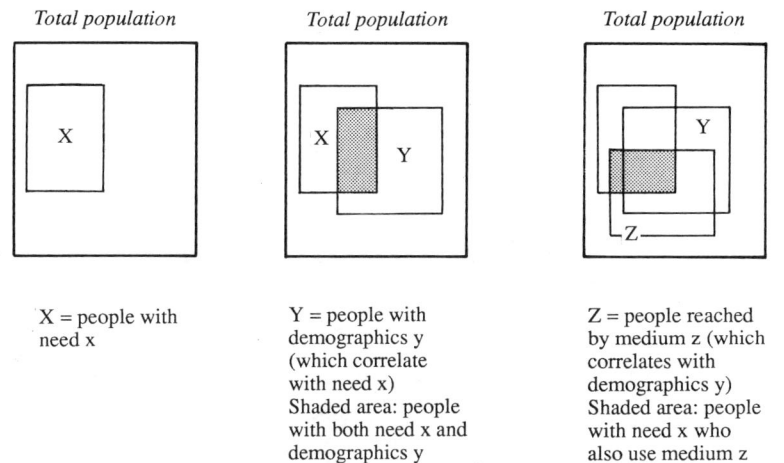

Total population   Total population   Total population

X = people with   Y = people with   Z = people reached
need x   demographics y   by medium z (which
                         (which correlate   correlates with
                         with need x)   demographics y)
                         Shaded area: people   Shaded area: people
                         with both need x and   with need x who
                         demographics y   also use medium z

Figure 2.3   *Diagrammatic representation of the effectiveness of Y as a segmentation base for X*

cability to media – major media all provide breakdowns of their audiences on those same demographics.

However, demographics are criticized for their failure to reflect qualitative differences between consumers. People of the same age and income, living next door to each other, do not necessarily share the same lifestyle and buying habits. These criticisms have led users and providers to wonder whether there could be a better method for capturing consumer segments and relating them to media use.

Psychographics and sociocultural groups

In recent years research companies, sensitive to the shortcomings of demographics, have tried to develop 'personality' or 'lifestyle' related measures. Hence 'psycho' as against 'demo' graphics.

At its simplest, this new thinking has led the British Market Research Bureau to introduce some psychological dimensions in its annual Target Group Index survey. This large-scale survey, carried out for media owners, has for many years related usage of a large selection of products to demographics and media use. Nowadays, respondents are asked not just their age, family size, income etc. but also some attitudinal indicators such as whether they 'like trying out new things' or 'prefer more traditional things'. This modification means that media buyers using the TGI can select a media

Swatch

Plate 2.7   *It is futile to approach a marketing solution for a symbol-value product in terms of its physical qualities or functions. The starting point has to be personalities which dictate people's symbol needs. Wristwatches which cost under £10 tell you the time; all others tell the world you are up-to-date (Swatch), a perfectionist (Rolex), young and in the swim (Timex), or sensuous (Citizen)*

Severiano Ballesteros. A strong mind is his secret. A strong watch his choice.

The Times called it "arguably the finest last round in the history of the championship".

The man who played it called it "the best round of my life". Then he added: "So far."

In winning his third British Open Championship, Severiano Ballesteros had displayed, once again, the qualities that have caused so many of his peers to regard him as the finest player in the world.

His game has always been noted for breathtaking drives and the kind of recovery shots that reveal a man who clearly does not recognise the word "quit".

Since Seve was nine years old, practising clandestine golf strokes after hours on his home Pedrena golf course, his sheer mental stamina has driven him on. Indeed, when someone asked him recently what he thought was the most important characteristic of a would-be champion, Ballesteros said promptly: "A strong mind."

This single-minded search for perfection is reflected in his choice of watch: a Rolex Day-Date.

It is a beautiful timepiece; but it is as tough and uncompromising as his game. "It is a very strong watch," he says. "No water or sand can get into it at all."

No wonder. Severiano Ballesteros' Rolex possesses an impenetrable Oyster case and self-winding movement.

Together, they ensure one thing: however tough the going, the tough will *keep* going.
ROLEX
of Geneva

THE ROLEX DAY-DATE CHRONOMETER IN 18CT. GOLD WITH THE PRESIDENT BRACELET. ALSO AVAILABLE IN 18CT. WHITE GOLD OR IN PLATINUM.

Rolex

Plate 2.7 (*continued*)

Timex

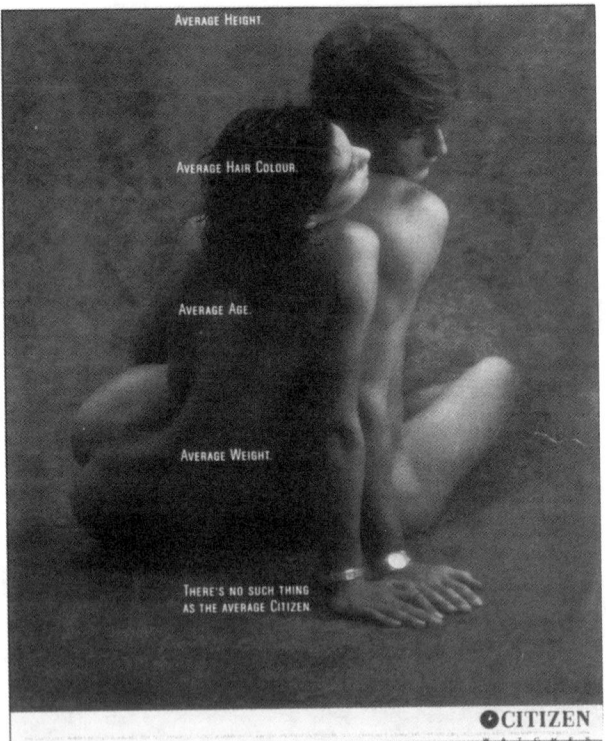

Citizen

Plate 2.7 (*continued*)

schedule which is skewed, for example, towards consumers who claim to be predisposed to trying new things.

At a more sophisticated level, SRI International (US) with their VALS system use detailed questionnaires covering lifestyle, attitudes and values to divide the US population into subgroups defined by their dominant motivation – need driven (survivors and sustainers), outer directed (achievers, belongers and emulators), inner directed (I-am-me, experientials and societally conscious).

The idea is to try to divide the population up into truer, more meaningful groups than 'aged sixteen to twenty-four' or 'white collar workers', which on the face of it, should not be difficult. The groups which are generated by these more complex methods are dubbed 'sociocultural', 'personality' or 'lifestyle' groups.

The way to measure the efficiency of new segmentation bases is to try them out in existing markets and see how well they discriminate between current-user segments. So, for example, do existing heavy, light and non-users of a product or users of different brands, belong to different psychographic groups? Similarly, do the psychographic groups differentiate well on current media use?

As it turns out, the classic demographics tend to do a better job of differentiating between product, brand and media use than do psychographics.

There are three main reasons why these personality measures fail to predict behaviour and choice accurately:

1   The usual research techniques are inadequate to capture the total personality. People exhibit contradictions – they can be both extrovert and shy, they can react differently in different situations or on different days. They are sincerely incapable of rating themselves objectively – in one psychological study[5] *all* respondents rated themselves as above average in their ability to get on with other people. Interesting information, certainly, but inaccurate data.
2   Personalities are so complex that they are extremely difficult to group sensibly. It is not for nothing that people are informally referred to as 'individuals'. Different personality dimensions will be important for different choices. For example, a segmentation for a cleaning product might concentrate on attitudes to cleanliness, housework and women's roles. A segmentation for savings schemes might focus on wealth, attitudes to the future and level of interest. Many consumers will be in the market for both types of product but there is no reason to suppose that the segment structure of the two should be the same.
3   Availability of money or physical needs often override personality issues. A man with modest means and four children is not going to buy a Ferrari, a woman with dandruff will use Head & Shoulders even if she's

psychographically 'I-am-me'. Demographics in fact carry much information relevant to means and needs, which reflects and links product use and media choice, even if it does not explain the causes as well as psychographics might.

In terms of usefulness as segmentation bases, psychographics have yet to prove their value. They do offer something valuable to the marketer, but it is in a rather different context, that of looking for segments, which is examined later.

Single source data

This is probably the most promising innovation for applying segmentation strategies in the future. The idea is to collect data from a single sample of the population on media use, product and brand use, ownership of durables, demographics, lifestyle and attitudes. The same group of people are asked questions in all these areas to create a multidimensional data base.

This data base would be stored on a computer and interrogated to provide tailormade stratifications of the population. For example, a pet food manufacturer might ask what proportion of women have at least one dog, no children and describe themselves as 'feeling reasonably well off these days'. He might be interested in some other data: How old are they?; Do they own freezers?; What brands of pet food do they buy at the moment?; What volume of the market do they account for? If he decides on the basis of this information to launch a range of frozen snacks for child-substitute dogs the computer can tell him how best to reach his target – where they live and what they read, watch or listen to.

The key difference between this approach and demo- or psychographics is that it creates a direct link between the factors which create the needs and media use. The availability of computer time now makes it possible for advertisers to really exploit such data.[6]

Finding a viable segmentation scheme

What segments exist, or could potentially exist in the market, and which one offers most scope?

The task is easiest if the product possesses a distinct difference (real or perceived) through its history, physical properties, or whatever. The segmentation task is then to identify the group of people for whom the difference is a benefit and understand exactly what motivates them.

In the case of new product development, spotting a viable segment is the key to long-term success and should dictate the specifications of the product. Mars (the chocolate manufacturers) observed this several years ago. They observed that their R & D laboratories could turn out products which scored higher than current top sellers in product tests, and yet when launched met with only moderate success or actual failure. This was a startling observation, since one would tend to assume that chocolate bars are chosen largely for their 'deliciousness'. Although trial is fairly easy to obtain for a new bar, the established bars are not pushed aside by the technically superior, novel products. Mars turned to favouring new product development led by lifestyle and consumer trends research, interpreted into a brief for R & D. Tracker, the nature bar, was one of the first results of this philosophy.

The most difficult, but most common, starting point for segmentation is, however, an existing product whose differences or distinct benefits are fairly marginal and provide little guidance in the search for a segment.

Here are four techniques for finding market segments, applicable even to products with no identified differential advantage. The methods are based on four distinct ideas:

1 *Behavioural segmentation* – examination of the 'natural' segments which already exist in the market.
2 *Benefit segmentation* – looking directly at the needs of different groups of consumers and the importance they attach to those needs.
3 *Psychographic segmentation* – partitioning a population by personality, attitudes or dominant drives and interpreting these groupings with respect to the market of interest.
4 *Decision-maker analysis* – who, within a group of decision makers, may be sensitive to a marketing approach?

Behavioural segmentation

This approach is used daily by research companies, marketing departments and advertising agencies, often without their being really conscious of it. The trick is to pick two or more groups of consumers who differ in their behaviour within the market, and then to compare them with the objective of understanding the motivations behind their different behaviour.

The most common example of this practice is probably the reflex that most qualitative researchers have to do focus groups among users and non-users of a particular brand or product. Comparison of the two groups often identifies the motivations of the segment already attracted to the brand or product.

Apart from the brand user/non-brand user split, there are many other 'natural' segments which can be exploited in the same way. The market may be structured on individual brands, but it is more often divided up between groups of brands. These 'natural' groupings can be discerned by using brand switching or dual-usage analyses. If distinct groups of consumers show up in this way (e.g. a healthy vs sweet division in the cereals market; a premium vs standard vs value structure in the whisky market) it may be more revealing to carry out the comparison between users of different groups of brands. Nor need the comparisons be limited simply to user/non-user. Each of the following are useful in the appropriate situations:

- Trialists vs non-trialists.
- Repeaters vs lapsed users.
- Heavy users vs light users.
- New users vs established users.

In each case the subject may be a product, a class of products, a particular brand or a group of brands.

The comparison may be done through qualitative research, but since these behavioural (or usage) segments are frequently captured in standard quantitative surveys, a quantitative analysis is readily actionable in many cases.

Media-sponsored surveys, usage and attitude studies and diary panels usually relate usage to demographic information (age, sex, region, presence of children, income etc.). Often they also link usage to cognitive data such as awareness of brands, image of brands and preference scores, and to consumption data (who, when, for what occasion). This type of data is straightforward to collect if it is not available on record.

The analysis is also simple to effect. The data is arranged into cross-tabulated tables analysing the behavioural segments by the demographic, cognitive or consumption statistics. By comparing across these tables, hypotheses begin to emerge as to the causes behind the behavioural segments.

An example of this type of analysis was undertaken for a fast service restaurant. The behavioural groups examined were heavy users, light users, non-users who had tried and non-users who had never tried. Comparisons between the four groups showed that:

1   Attitudes towards the restaurant were equally and strongly positive among heavy and light users, but strongly negative among non-users, both trialists and non-trialists.
2   The main difference between the heavy and light users was not in age or presence of children, but in the range of occasions for which they used the restaurant.

The marketing strategy at the time had been to dispel the negative perceptions and promote trial among non-users. After the above analysis, it became obvious that encouraging a wider range of usage occasions among current *light* users would be a much easier way to push up sales. This meant a new target segment.

The results of this type of analysis are often hypotheses which need to be investigated in greater depth, usually by qualitative methods. For example, by comparing users/non-users of an 'all-purpose' cleaning product it was noticed that the brand mostly appealed to people over a certain age. Focus groups were recruited among young users, old users and young non-users. This research concluded that the key difference was that the younger generation had grown up exposed (through television) to the idea of a specialist product for each cleaning task and planned their purchase and use of cleaning products on this premise. To an extent, the brand was facing a genuine middle-aged crisis, but it was helped by a repositioning on the idea of the multispecialist, demonstrating a range of uses for which the product could be seen as a specialist.

Benefit segmentation

Examining behavioural segments will not reveal all the (need) segments which exist in a market – two people might easily behave in the same way (e.g. use the same product) for different reasons. Similarly, behavioural segments will not reveal segments which could exist in the future, but whose members currently 'make do' with being part of a larger segment for lack of a proposition which suits them more perfectly.

The idea of benefit segmentation is based directly on the definition of segmentation. The aim is to measure the differing importance attached to differing needs among a representative sample of the market, and then to regroup the market according to the results. In other words, benefit segmentation groups together consumers according to which benefits are important to them in a given market.

The classic example of such a segmentation, energetically pursued by marketers, is the toothpaste market – brands aim for the fresh breath segment, the no-caries segment, the white teeth segment, the nice taste segment or various combinations of these benefits.

Intuitively the approach seems ideal because it promises to provide exactly the data required – which consumers want what from a product, the blueprint for a perfectly marketed product. The problems arise in the practice, in the consumer's ability to identify, articulate and quantify his needs and the difficulties in handling such data. It may be difficult to group the consumers meaningfully or to trade off the importance of their different needs.

The difficulties intensify as the benefits become more psychological – it is easier for consumers to evaluate rational, functional qualities than to evaluate emotional, subjective ones. Needs in a personal computer might be size of memory, speed, reliability, type of operating system and price, which are all reasonably concrete constructs. Needs in a whisky will involve elusive constructs such as quality, pretentiousness, attractive bottle and a sociable image, while price will play a much more complex role.

If the situation is one where the consumer can distinguish and quantify his needs he can be asked to do so directly, for example, by rating attributes on a five-point importance scale. This is not possible if the consumer is unable to untangle his motivations or to make conscious his decision process. Safety must be an important attribute for an airline, but can an air traveller give a sensible response to the construct 'safety' in a survey? How do people handle this issue? Perhaps in real life he would never dare to think consciously about the safety issue.

Often it is not clear even to the decision maker how he adds up or makes compromises between various benefits. Hence more subtle ways of uncovering the consumer's true priorities have been developed for use in these more complicated situations.

Conjoint analysis

Also known as trade-off analysis, this technique involves presenting the consumer with a range of choices, usually presented as descriptions written on cards and asking him to rank the cards in terms of his personal preference.

For example, a manufacturer developing a new brand of bleach has in mind various possible benefits and is interested to know which appeal most strongly and the size and characteristics of the interested segments. He presents 400 bleach purchasers with twenty-four show cards permutating the following characteristics: three levels of price; liquid vs viscous; chlorine vs pleasant pine smell; standard vs double strength.

A typical card would say: 'A liquid bleach with a pleasant pine smell and double bleaching power sold at price x' and each bleach buyer would have to sort twenty-four cards into an order representing his preferences, trading-off the appeal of each description against the others. (A greater number than twenty-four permutations can be handled, without extending the sorting task, by working out various rotations of a subset of the cards, between the respondents. This does however point to one limitation of the method.)

This data can be processed using a suitable computer program[7] to work out what value or 'utility' each consumer attaches to each option of each variable (viscosity, pleasant smell, double bleaching power, the three price levels). The output is a series of 'utility' curves indicating the value rendered by the different values of the variable being considered. An example of the type of results provided by conjoint analysis is shown in Figure 2.4. These charts can be plotted for individuals, the whole sample aggregated together, or subgroups chosen from the sample.

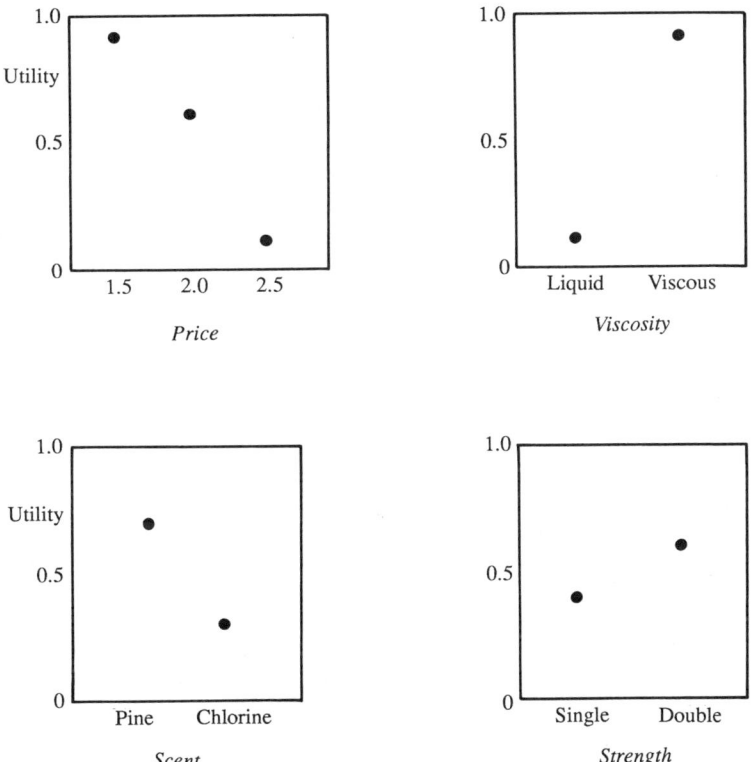

Figure 2.4 *Print out from a conjoint analysis showing the utilities attached to the four variables (utilities can be compared across graphs). The change from liquid to viscous is worth the most to this (or these) consumers, while double strength seems to mean little. Note also the kink in the price curve.*

Preference regression

This is another sophisticated approach for getting at the values consumers attach to attributes. In this method the consumer is asked to rate competitive products against a battery of pre-selected attributes. These ratings are then compared with his preferences for these products (either stated or estimated from his past purchasing habits) to derive the importance which he attaches (perhaps subconsciously) to each attribute. That is to say, the 'importances' are calculated via a regression analysis which explains his preferences in terms of his perceptions of the products.

The attributes have to cover all aspects which affect consumer preference, without being unworkably numerous, and they have to be described (probably using only words) in such a way as to be readily and unambiguously understood by all respondents. Generating such a list of attributes is a considerable challenge and is discussed in more detail under the heading 'Eliciting the attributes used to evaluate the competition' later in this chapter.

Preference regression does at least give a warning if important attributes have been omitted, as the level of explanation achieved by the regression analysis will be unsatisfactory. For example, if one of the attributes which influenced washing powder purchase was the shininess and brightness of the packaging, but this was not appreciated consciously by purchasers or the researchers, the regression on to the incomplete list of attributes would indicate that a factor was missing. However, this information might come rather late, and the identity of the missing attribute might yet remain a mystery.

There are also other, more technical limitations with this method. There are few markets where consumers can give meaningful ratings on more than a handful of brands, whereas to be statistically sound the number of rated brands should (ideally) exceed the number of attributes. The solutions proposed to overcome the problem are far from perfect and also make the methods rather 'black boxy', for the non-technical user.

Conjoint analysis and preference regression both aim to overcome the consumer's difficulties in describing the importance he assigns to different attributes. However, another practical problem has to be solved before benefit segmentation becomes possible. This is the problem of aggregating the data from a number of respondents.

One solution is simply always to work with the data at a disaggregated level, trying out different combinations of benefits and seeing how the individuals, as recorded on the computer, each react. Then the reactions can be aggregated to give brand share or preference.[8]

However, for the purposes of a segmentation strategy as described above, consumers have to be clustered together to form homogeneous segments, according to the benefits or bundles of benefits which interest them most. Only then can the results be used to direct strategic thinking.

For example, the bleach manufacturer would like to know that there was a highly price-motivated group who did value strength and a separate group who were less motivated by price and were indeed interested in a pleasantly-scented product. These groups could then be identified on segmentation bases such as demographics, and also against any other data collected in the survey, such as current brand preferences or relevant attitude measures.

Individuals all have different priorities, giving different patterns of trade off and generating different preference models, and the task of grouping people together will not usually have a unique solution.

In fact, the mathematical tools (factor analysis, cluster analysis) which are used to create the groups can lead to some pretty arbitrary results. The groups found may not be consistent over time (unfortunate if your target group disappears from one survey to the next!) and may not be unique – another grouping, giving a different set of segments, may be almost as valid from the point of view of the mathematical tools. Which of the alternative solutions should be chosen as the basis of the marketing strategy?

Despite the practical difficulties in its implementation, the basic idea of investigating people's needs directly, and grouping them according to these needs is a sound and useful one. It works best for product areas where benefits tend to be somewhat functional and the consumer decision process relatively straightforward.

Psychographic segmentation

Benefit segmentation is most useful for products which offer rational, functional benefits. When the method is applied to symbol value products, the results tend to become somewhat tenuous. Psychographic segmentation is based on the idea of answering people's 'communication' or 'symbol' needs and is applicable for emotional and symbol benefit products.

This approach is less quantified than the previous two methods, but its great strength, in a world where ideas and inspiration are at a premium, is its ability to suggest potential segments which do not yet exist.

The use of psychographics (lifestyle groups, personality types, sociocultural groups) as a segmentation base was reviewed above, with a rather negative conclusion – psychographics are often not as good as simple demographics for identifying groups which buy certain things and for revealing their media habits.

When choosing a segmentation base one uses the simple criterion of level of discrimination – which system best isolates different usership or media using groups. It is not important that the base fails to reveal *why* the groups do these things. The fact that young people (sixteen to twenty-four) buy jeans, does not explain why they buy them, nor what advertising should say to attract them. Still, in planning media, media used by young people may well be the most efficient policy.

When looking for need segments for products whose benefits are their symbol values, psychographics come into their own. It is necessary in such cases to segment consumers on their self-images, their me→them communication needs, or their interests (e.g. music, sport) and then to reflect these in the product's image, rather than to think in terms of the product and the benefits it could (physically) supply.

The 'Pepsi generation' concept is based on widespread identification with youth, energy, music and Tina Turner, and not, *a priori*, with any functional benefit consumers or a marketing department would naturally associate with the product itself.

Although psychographics might misclassify individuals into the wrong groups, or move respondents from group to group on different days or different surveys, the overall feelings and trends picked up by such a study are likely to reflect real characteristics in a society. In terms of getting an idea for a segment it is more important to know that *an attitude exists in a society than to know exactly who is in the segment*. It is also of secondary importance to be able to link them with media use, though this will have to be done eventually.

Here, as an illustration, are the groups that a French research company used to describe French society in its reaction to the economic crisis (La Crise) of the 1980s:

	(%)		(%)
Action orientated	13.4	Entrepreneurs	10.0
		Militants	3.4
New materialists	26.4	Utilitarian	7.9
		Good citizen	10.6
		Wait and see	8.3
Laid back	17.5	Liberal	5.8
		Dilettante	5.7
		Profiteer	5.8
Retrogressive	20.1	Conservative	5.1
		Moralist	6.5
		Responsible	8.5
Ego-centred	22.5	Bluffer	6.5
		Defensive	7.3
		Cautious	8.7

The detailed descriptions for each group give overall outlook on life, attitudes to authority, social aspirations, main interests, ideas of 'style', demographic tendencies and typical media use.

For example, the 'utilitarian new materialist' is described as:

Living in a closed family-orientated circuit, restricted by their resistance to change. Very modest means, often isolated or rural environment, increasingly cut off from society at large by La Crise and modernization.

Anxious and pessimistic with respect to La Crise, they are above all concerned to hold on to what they have, to manage their affairs with caution while having faith in the care and protection of the state, or their company. Old-fashioned and 'naturalist' they distrust new experiences and innovation.

Loyal and cautious consumers who demand a great deal of service and personal attention, and respond best to advertising which is familiar, friendly and traditional.

Demographic tendencies – towards women, up-age and frequently retired, often living alone. Often economically inactive, incomes are very modest and level of education and culture is low. Socially isolated, main media contacts are television (local news programmes, gameshows, soaps), local papers, needlework magazines, television guides.

Not perhaps a likely target for a record company, but a political party might be interested.

The detailed descriptions usually also link the groups with current products or product characteristics that appeal to them. Alternatively, it is necessary to guess at the likely values that the group would espouse. What analgesic would suit the moralists? What coffee for the cautious? What make-up for the militants? What shampoo for the good citizen? Or the question can be: Which of these groups has aspirations not catered for by the current brand images?

Since advertising professionals tend to belong exclusively to one small subgroup, such studies help to remind the team of the true composition of their society, and help them recall the existence of large buying groups who are low profile in terms of media attention.

The psychographic approach generates possible segmentations but measuring and assessing the opportunities has to be quantified separately. The technique is not precise (the percentages are best interpreted as weights of importance of these attitudes rather than actual numbers of people) and the link between claimed attitudes and actual behaviour (e.g. between desiring a healthy lifestyle and changing eating and exercise habits) is not always direct.

Parallel markets

One related, and similarly 'soft' method for finding segments deserves to be mentioned here. It is possible to generate ideas in the image area by drawing parallels with other 'symbol' markets. For example, by looking at the segments (represented by brands) in the perfume market it may be possible to generate parallel concepts for the aperitif market. Gerry Moira, advertising wit, has observed analogies in packaging between cigarettes and boxed chocolates;[10] Terry's All Gold = Benson & Hedges Gold, Black Magic = John Player Special, Milk Tray = Embassy filter, but has he thought of inventing new chocolate products on this basis?

Decision maker analysis

This approach can lead to radical change in the marketing target, with similarly radical results. The method is based on the simple observation that the assumed buyer may not be the sole, or even the major, decision maker.

A brand may steal a march on its competitors by turning its attention to another decision maker who has, as yet, been ignored by the marketing effort. Women influence the choice of the family car, children dictate about 50 per cent of breakfast cereal purchasing, lorry drivers are capable of lobbying for the most comfortable truck cabin, and secretaries for a preferred word-processor. The first advertiser to recognize such a relationship has the added advantage of flattering his chosen audience.

The research for this approach is easily carried out once the possibility is recognized. Once the alternative decision makers have been identified, qualitative or quantitative research can easily be designed to reveal their particular needs and priorities.

Positioning

Positioning is the other half of marketing strategy. Positioning refers to the 'position' that the product will take in the mind of the target segment. The positioning does not exist *within* the product or within the marketing strategy – it exists in the consumer's mind (or not at all).

The term 'positioning' is almost synonymous with differential or competitive advantage, as the purpose of any positioning is to bestow a differential advantage on a product. The terms image and brand personality are also used to describe positioning strategies of particular types.

The positioning of a product serves as the guiding principle in the whole marketing programme. The clarity of its definition is crucial to ensure that all elements of the marketing effort are consistent and synergistic. As a result, the positioning task is as often a question of understanding what the product really is for its consumers, as imagining what it could be.

When is a differential advantage not a differential advantage?

It is not uncommon for marketers to be deluded about their product's competitive edge. A true differential advantage is:

1   *Perceived to be unique* – the whole game is about differentiating the product from the mass of others, but it is worth noting that uniqueness in itself is insufficient. The marketers 'real world' is the hazy world of consumer

perceptions, and only when the difference is established in that world of perceptions is it real in the marketing sense. If one compares the specific gravity (i.e. alcoholic strength) of the major UK lager brands with consumer perceptions of alcoholic strength, there is in fact a weak, inverse relationship. The one that is perceived to be 'probably' the strongest isn't, and the one that is has therefore lost out. Uniqueness alone is not enough and indeed, physical uniqueness is not essential.

2   *Important to the target market* – the difference must motivate and not simply differentiate. Quaker's Sugar Puffs, for example, is unique in that it is the only children's cereal made from whole grains of wheat, puffed up. However, in the consumer's mind this technical difference counts for little – in function and even taste the product is not unique. A 'difference' may be motivating in one area but not in another. Tradition might sell beer but not yoghurt, brand familiarity might increase the appeal of a washing machine but not a perfume, being perceived as 'smart' might help a whisky but not a brand of milk. This criterion underlines the relationship between positioning and segmentation – only by understanding the motivations of the target segment can an important, motivating positioning be developed.

3   *Sustainable* – the classic example of an ephemeral differential advantage is low price. Low price can be a very powerful differential advantage and can form the basis of a highly successful strategy if a company is able to sustain it. However, at any point the competition can wipe out the entire advantage, simply by dropping their prices. Tjaereborg, a direct mail tour operator, had a very successful launch, offering genuine savings of 10 per cent on package holidays, through cutting out the travel agents. A year later they found themselves without any competitive claims. Frequently, Japanese companies enter a market with a low price strategy and then trade up to a more sustainable advantage once they have created volume sales. This happened with motorbikes. In the 1960s they entered the market with cheap copies of European models. During the 1970s they became reliable and then fast. Since about 1980 they have been producing technological masterpieces offering not only silky smooth handling and hair-raising power but, finally, spectacular styling. Often lifestyle or emotional benefits are more sustainable than physical or functional ones. Any cigarette manufacturer can launch a low tar brand, but establishing a brand for would-be cowboys would now look sham.

When a product does have a unique, motivating differential advantage it will inevitably attract me-toos attacking its uniqueness or competitors trying to establish the greater importance of their benefits. In this situation defending and sustaining the existing differential advantage often becomes the preoccupation of marketing and advertising.

The key steps in positioning a product

The idea of a product positioning depends on the existence of some frame of reference used by its consumers. An obvious place to start the quest for a positioning is by discovering the relevant frame of reference.

'Frame' has rather two-dimensional overtones but the frame of reference may be unidimensional or multidimensional. Battery manufacturers have to slog it out on the single dimension of longevity (see Plate 2.8). By contrast, consumers perceive cars on any number of complex social, sexual and functional aspects.

The logical steps for discovering and defining the consumer frame of reference are as follows:[11]

1 Identify the product's competitors.
2 Determine how the consumer compares and evaluates these various competitors (including the product to be positioned).
3 Determine how the product and each of its competitors is perceived in terms of the constructs determined at (2).

Identifying competitors

It may be that the closest competition in product terms is not the most useful in terms of developing a meaningful frame of reference for the positioning.

Syndicated market research (for example Nielsen or IMS) usually define markets for their own purposes on the basis of 'similar products' and have a habit of imposing their choice on the whole industry. A marketer who bucks the given definition has the problem of reprocessing the data in order to monitor his redefined market, but he should not feel constrained in the first instance from developing his own view of what market he is in.

Here is an example of a revealing redefinition:

The 'tea-totaller's' tale

Tetley's tea bags were introduced to the UK from the US in the early 1950s. As the only tea bag (other teas being sold 'loose') Tetley initially had 100 per cent of 'their' tea bag market. By the early 1980s, all the major loose tea brands had launched bag versions and Tetley's share had fallen to around 25 per cent. Since the tea bag market was growing by 5 or 6 per cent per year, Tetley's management were happy to hold on to share and grow at the market rate. However, this did not happen. Tetley's share fell year by year, despite their disproportionately high advertising investments (a fact they liked to point out to their agency).

One of these tells you it's fresh without having to sniff it.

Now every new pack of DURACELL® batteries has a freshness date. So you can be sure that DURACELL batteries not only come to you fresh, but stay that way for up to three years after we make them. It's all part of the LIFEGUARD system.

BEST IF INSTALLED BY
DEC 90

So if you want to be sure you're buying fresh batteries, buy DURACELL batteries. In fact, why not buy a dozen.

Introducing LIFEGUARD.
A fresh idea only from Duracell.

Duracell batteries US

Plate 2.8 *Some products, such as cars, are perceived on a multitude of dimensions, and consumers differ markedly in their wants. Some markets are almost uni-dimensional and the brands have to slog it out on one attribute. Study these three battery ads and work out what research shows consumers want from their batteries (continued overleaf)*

Duracell batteries UK

Mazda batteries France (TV) – an authoritarian nanny is accused of stopping her ward playing with his little toys. As fitting punishment she is sentenced as illustrated, for the duration of a 'Mazda'

Plate 2.8 (*continued*)

Then someone had the idea of adding together Nielsen's two tea markets (tea bags and loose tea) and showed that Tetley's overall share of the *static* 'total' tea market was completely stable.

The 'growth' in the tea bag market was caused by a systematic drift from loose tea users – and Tetley was the only brand not to have a counterpart brand in the loose market. Apart from explaining a worrying situation, the redefinition of the competition served to highlight an opportunity for Tetley to attract loose tea users as they went through the transition to bag use.

Like human beings, no product is indispensable, and this idea provides the key for unpeeling the layers of competition. If product x did not exist, what would consumers buy/use/do instead? There are two ways of posing the question:

1   *Directly* – if x had not been available, what would you have bought instead or equivalently and more concretely, what other products did you consider buying when you bought x?
2   *Indirectly* – for what occasions or type of use do you buy x? What other products could you use on those occasions, or for that type of use?

Both questions can be asked over and over again, either with the same sample or with a change of respondents, to get at the second and third degrees of competition. Clearly, the first use gives the closest, most direct competitors and so on.

Land-Rovers may be considered alongside sports cars by extrovert drivers, summer holidays may compete with decorating the house for time and the annual savings. All food products compete at a 'share of stomach' level since humans are limited in the number of calories they can consume. At the limit, any food they accept has to push another off their menu. Similarly, all leisure products eventually compete for time and all durables for money.

Eliciting the attributes used to evaluate the competition

Comparisons are a powerful tool for eliciting dimensions on which consumers perceive and evaluate products. In what way are these two products similar?; In what way different?; Which of these three products is the odd man out? – Why?; What aspects would you think about if you were choosing between these products?

People tend to give the most obvious answers first and frequently focus on physical features to start with. The trick in investigating the full range of dimensions is to continue to stimulate the respondents' interest and imagination beyond their initial, rather automatic responses.

No attribute list for a consumer product is complete unless respondents have been led to consider and compare the competitors in such a way as to generate dimensions which cover:

- *Product attributes* – physical, functional, price, quality.
- *Usage* – for what occasions, in what type of situations.
- *Users* – type of users, their reasons for choice.
- *Personality* – if this product was a person what (or who) would it be like? For example is the product mean or generous, feminine or masculine, indulgent or austere?
- *Analogies* – if this product was a car, a country, an animal, what would it be?

The latter, more bizarre suggestions (called 'projective' techniques) are neither more nor less important than the physical or usage attributes. They illuminate and shade the picture obtained. In some markets they have little significance while in some classic marketing areas such as beer (where brand managers are incapable of identifying their own brands in blind taste tests) the user/personality/image dimensions are key.

Of course such an approach will overelicit in the first instance, and a huge list of constructs will be generated. This list has to be reduced before being used further. Whether this is done judgementally or via correlations and factor analysis is a matter of taste and resources, but the objective is to keep representatives of all the constructs which help people differentiate products, while reducing redundancy and overlap to a minimum. (Note that the attributes generated here provide the type of input required for the benefit segmentation studies described on page 40.)

Determining how the competitors are perceived

At this stage the key dimensions on which the products are perceived have been elicited and the list has been reduced as far as possible to minimize duplication. Respondents can then simply be asked to rate the products with which they feel familiar on the dimensions defined.

If many attributes have been used it becomes difficult to summarize and comprehend the information. Using a computer it is possible to extract the *principal components* of perception, which will be a combination of several, related dimensions, and plot these as a two-dimensional *perceptual map*. In many cases, two or three principal components account for a large proportion of the differences perceived between products. This suggests that consumers actually use rather simpler rules for discriminating between products than the normal huge arrays of attributes suggest. An example of a typical output from the above type of exercise is shown in Figure 2.5.

The method just described sounds very reasonable, but it is fair to ask whether most consumers can respond meaningfully when asked whether a washing powder is 'caring' or an insurance company is 'fatherly', even though these dimensions may form a real part of their choices. Consumers are not used to articulating such feelings, even to themselves. It is often more natural to have a holistic or general feeling about a product which may be difficult or meaningless to decompose.

There are alternative methods (known collectively as non-metric multi-dimensional scaling techniques) for mapping out the relative positions of products, which avoid the pre-selection of attributes and the necessity to burden the consumer with the effort of decomposing his global perception onto the given constructs.

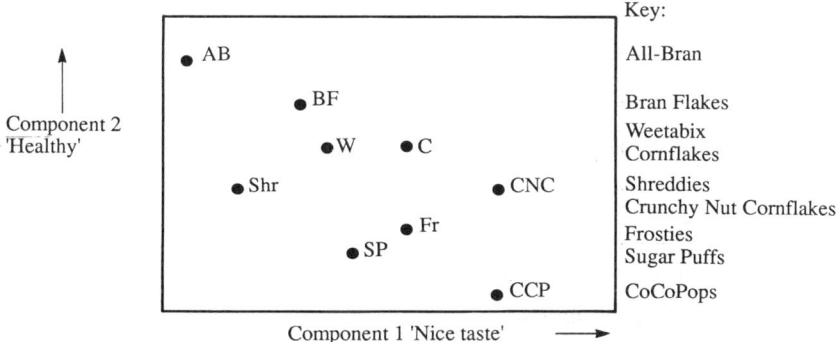

Figure 2.5   *A perceptual map produced for the cereal market on two principal components. The two components are weighted averages of attributes monitored in the survey. Examining the attributes which make up the components suggests appropriate descriptive labels, as shown*

Non-metric MDS techniques

Consumers are simply asked how different they perceive the various competitors (known to them) to be. The answers can be estimated differences, say on a scale from one to nine, for each pair of competitors, or respondents can rank a set of show cards, each containing the names of two competitors, according to how similar or dissimilar they find them. Cards comparing each competitor with the 'ideal' can be added to produce an ideal point on the final map.

Feeding these data into a suitable computer program[12] will give two dimensional maps showing projections of the product positions. The results would look something like Figure 2.6. The program also indicates the number of dimensions needed to explain the differences between the competitors. This is given in terms of how good an explanation can be given, using one or two dimensions, how much a third improves it etc.

The dimensions are not named and the user has to decide what dimensions are being depicted, and the rotation of the axes. For example, if the products were food stores, one dimension might deal with all the aspects of good value – cheap, not for luxury purchases, reasonable quality for the price, for money-conscious housewives, thrifty etc., while another all aspects of convenience – parking, checkout queues, instore canteen, for people in a hurry, modern and so on. The user has sketched in his estimate on Figure 2.6.

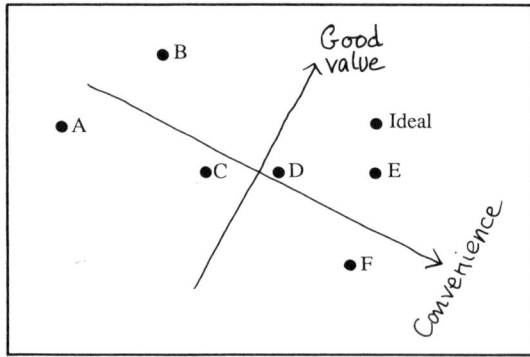

Figure 2.6   *Typical print out from a non-metric MDS program. The user has to work out what it means. Here the user has sketched in his estimates*

However the perceptual map is constructed, the next problem is to aggregate the data from a number of consumers. Unless all consumers have similar perceptions and ideals the data cannot be averaged – this loses the information needed for a viable segmentation and positioning. Respondents need to be clustered according to their ideals. Then separate perceptual maps, with separate ideal points, can be produced for these more homogeneous subgroups, or segments.

Clearly these positioning studies converge with the segmentation studies discussed above and they would often form part of the same research. Rating products on attributes is used here to understand their competitive positions relative to one another, while in the segmentation studies the objective was to relate these positions to consumer preferences and thereby understand what different groups of consumers were looking for in the market.

This parallel development of information for positioning and segmentation is a natural consequence of the dual nature of marketing strategy.

Choosing a positioning

The analysis proposed so far will provide:

1. A list of dimensions (functional, user and personality) via which the consumer perceives the product and its competitors.
2. The positions of the competitors on these dimensions, relative to each other and to the ideal points for various segments.
3. The ideal points which give clues to areas of the perceptual map likely to appeal to significant numbers of consumers, especially if no products currently lie near.

The marketing team's understanding of their market is, as such, enviably complete, but as yet a positioning has not been chosen. At this point imagination has to take over from mechanical analysis, but there are still some guidelines and pointers which can help direct the search.

Start with the positioning discovered

For any existing, established product the current positioning has to be the starting point. The most realistic, cheapest, most attainable and lowest-risk strategy to consider is the one that develops the existing strengths of the brand. The further one aims to change a positioning, the lower the chance of success and the higher the chance of confusion – this is one reason why it is well to discover where the brand is initially, rather than picking a positioning out of the blue.

Respect reality

Reality may mean the company reputation, the physical delivery of the product, the promotional resources available.

A breakfast cereal with a high sugar content is ill-advised to go for too healthy a positioning – even if the ideal points show potential for such a move. Attracting interest from consumers who are motivated enough to read the ingredients list and who will then reject the product, wastes effort which could be directed to people who would appreciate the sweetness. Strategies at odds with reality can even be counterproductive. A slimming or health magazine could pick on the product for trying to be deceptive.

Keep it simple

The risk in more complicated positioning statements is that they end up communicating nothing.

Positionings also need to be consistent. If they use several attributes, the attributes should be complementary. The sporty but practical car, the gentle but effective analgesic and the cheap but high-quality shoes all have to spend more to establish their positionings to overcome dissonance and disbelief.

An alternative to positioning – changing the map

The discussion so far has centred around the idea of positioning a product on a given frame of reference. However, in situations where the product is already strongly positioned there are a few alternative marketing strategies based on shifting the frame of reference itself, shifting the competition, or changing the competitive structure.

Changing the frame of reference

A successful differential advantage has to be perceived as important by its target audience. This can itself suggest a type of marketing strategy – that which aims to promote not a difference *per se*, but the importance of a difference. This means altering the importance consumers attach to different attributes, in fact changing the perceptual map. Hence if a product is perceived as cheap, one alternative might be to make it seem acceptable and intelligent to buy cheaply. 'C'est demodé de payer cher' – it's old-fashioned to pay more than you need to – says a French fashion store. Volvo, conscious of its established characteristic 'solidly built' has tried to increase the value placed on security by exploiting feelings for the family's safety (see Plate 2.9).

Plate 2.9   *Volvo (cars, UK) – Volvo often uses its advertising to position its cars on the attribute 'build strong, safe cars'. Alternatively, its advertising concentrates on changing the frame of reference by increasing the perceived importance of safety. At one stage Volvo even tried to develop 'resale value' as a factor in the car buying decision*

When the US Surgeon Generals announced that dietry fibre had been proven to contribute to cancer prevention, Kelloggs jumped in with All-Bran ads which introduced a 'helps avoid cancer' dimension into the breakfast cereal frame of reference. This dimension, of course, strongly favoured the extreme position already occupied by All-Bran.

In effect these strategies aim to bring the ideal point towards the product's established position, rather than to move the product towards the ideal point (where the competition are probably converging). Making your real differences important rather than moving to where all the market is going is also a strategy for sustaining a differential advantage.

Denigrating the opposition

This is often an alternative to praising oneself, though the pitfalls of consumer distaste, legal restrictions and possible retaliation need to be carefully considered. Sometimes humour can help to carry it off, as with Wendy's Hamburgers 'Where's the beef' campaign or the Democratic Party's jibe 'Would you buy a used car from this man?' against Vice-President Nixon in 1960, or in the UK, the Conservative Party's pun 'Labour isn't working', used in the election campaign in 1979.

Using a fighter brand

Finally, rather than shifting the positioning of a successful brand to parry the attack of a competitor, it may be possible to launch or reposition another brand. Typically, the new brand is positioned close to the competitor, but more distant from the first brand. This stops the competitor shifting his position too drastically, for fear of losing his own users (see Figure 2.7).

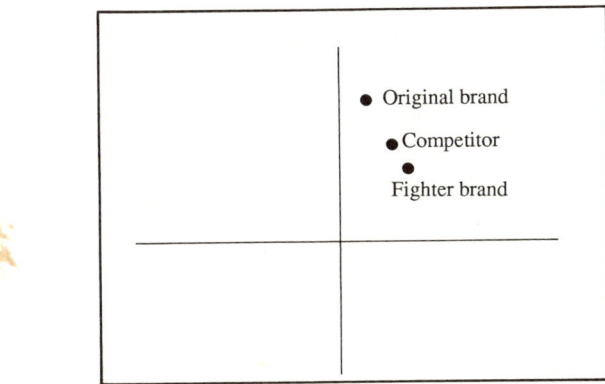

Figure 2.7   *Positioning a new, fighter brand to squeeze the competitor while minimizing take from the original brand*

Meanwhile it saves the original brand from a need to reformulate or reposition which might alienate a proportion of its current users.

Coca-Cola company claim that their 'New Coke' is a fighter or attack brand, sweeter and smoother, which copes with Pepsi's appeal to younger drinkers and saves them from having to adjust the Classic Coke's traditional positioning and taste.

This type of strategy may also be appropriate when there is a technological change in the market (such as washing powder to liquid detergent) which will appeal to a proportion of the original brands users. It is also used as a way to deal with price competition. Rather than dropping the price of the main brand to hold on to the price-sensitive fraction of users, a value brand is introduced which fights the competitor on price. The original brand thus continues to collect its premium price from its loyal or quality conscious users.

This chapter has summarized the main features of marketing strategy, and the guidelines for finding one. The next chapter looks at the development of an advertising strategy, based on these foundations.

Notes and references

1   Peters, Thomas and Waterman, Robert (Jr), *In Search of Excellence*, Harper & Row, 1982.
2   *Esquire*, vol. 109, no. 2, February 1988.
3   Maslow, A., *Motivation and Personality*, Harper and Row, 1954.
4   Kanehisa, Tching, *La Publicité au Japon*, Maisonneuve & Larose, 1984.
5   Peters, Thomas and Waterman, Robert (Jr), *op. cit.*, p. 56.
6   In the UK, Central TV provides a service of this type, called ADLAB.
7   MARKPACK, a multifunction package of marketing programs from the consultancy company Prism (France).
8   This is the approach used in the market simulation model SANDPIPER, marketed by Alan Frost International (London).
9   CCA is the research subsidiary of Havas – these groups are taken from a survey called *Les Nouveaux Socio-Styles*, 1984–85.
10   *Campaign*, 18th December 1987, p. 39.
11   This section was influenced by Aaker, David A. and Shansby, Gary J., 'Positioning Your Product', *Business Horizons*, vol. 25, no. 3, May–June 1982.
12   MARKPACK, *op. cit.*

3   Advertising strategy

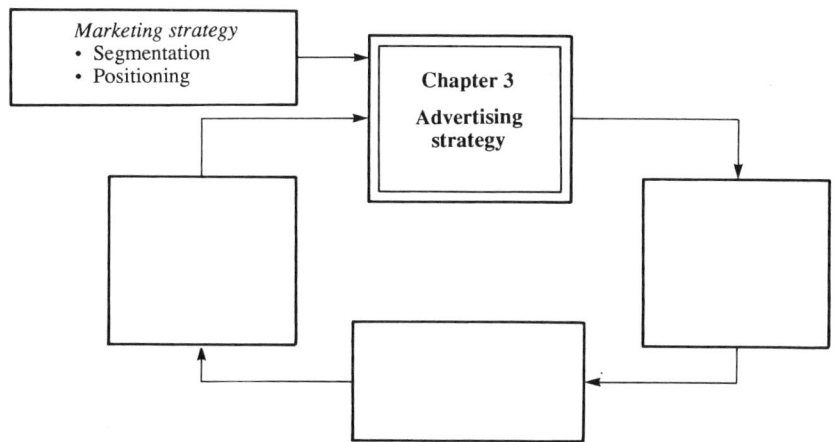

Definition of an advertising strategy

There can never be a single answer to the question 'How does advertising work?' because advertising as an idea, is as wide and varied as the concepts 'persuasion' or 'communication'. Examples of successful advertising range from classified ads to filmed scientific experiments, from posters simply showing the product's pack to surrealist extravaganzas where the product hardly appears at all. Nobody would try to argue that these advertisements all work in the same way.

However, in any particular case it is essential to develop a clear view of how that advertising is going to work. This is the challenge accepted when setting out to write an advertising strategy.

The role of an advertising strategy is to define what specific marketing task the advertising will perform and how it will achieve that task.

Advertising strategy is really one coherent idea about how the advertising is going to work. Like marketing strategy, it can be conveniently broken into its component parts.

Setting an advertising strategy involves answering four interrelated questions:

- *What* is the advertising going to do? (Role)
- *Who* is the ad going to do it to? (Target)
- *How* is it going to do it? (Content)
- *Where* and *when?* (Media)

The advertising strategy is a step away from marketing strategy towards creative work, a step nearer the production of an original creative idea, and a step towards the real world.

Marketing strategies communicate between marketing specialists. They use marketing concepts, jargon and shorthand. Advertising strategies, by contrast, need to be consumer-orientated and specific (not 'an image' but 'what image'). Above all, they must contain the germ of an advertising idea, a clever twist, an insight which begins to suggest the personality and feeling of the final ad.

Before examining the definition of advertising strategy in detail, it is useful to run through an example which we will refer back to later.

An illustration of the move from marketing strategy to advertising strategy: McClan Whisky's launch in France

The essentials of the marketing strategy can be summarized:

Objective: McClan's aims to become a volume brand in the standard sector, alongside Ballantines and Johnny Walker.

Positioning: A typical mainstream whisky, neither up-market, nor value, attributed with the central whisky values (listed separately) and a specific personality within the codes of the French whisky market (serious, status).

Segment: Regular whisky drinkers, currently buying the standard brands mentioned above. Looking for good value but neither the prestige of a premium nor the money saving of a value brand.

The marketing strategy dictated the 'what' of the advertising. To create:

- Awareness, familiarity.
- An image – a real whisky with a distinct personality, clearly within the values of the French whisky market (serious, status, luxury).

The marketing strategy defined the 'who' in a quantitative sense – regular whisky drinkers meant men and women aged twenty-five to fifty, upmarket, urban and 'socially active'. Two alternative psychographic targets were generated from qualitative research among this quantitative target:

Who 1:   Not sure of their own ability to judge quality of whisky, feel uninformed in this area (as compared, say, to wine), feel a need to reassure themselves. Look to advertising as a justification for their choice.

Who 2:   Open and enquiring. Perceive themselves as appreciating a wide range of modern culture (art, music ... even advertising!) and to have a desire to express themselves creatively and socially.

The respective 'hows' had to be in sympathy with these targets, and able to deliver the 'what':

How 1:   McClan is the whisky for people with the maturity to discern the true values in life. This is the brand for those who choose the authentic and true over the ephemeral and gaudy, those who value 'being' over 'having', who make their choice according to their own tastes and not to impress other people. A character campaign, projecting an image of the typical McClan user, fitting this description (c/f Marlboro cigarettes or Charlie perfume).

How 2:   McClan embodies the spirit of France today, the 'new adventurers' (this group was the name of a psychographic group identified by the research company Cofremca). Although dynamic and aspirational, their ambition is directed to a full and varied experience of life, self-expression and appreciation of art and culture and not towards the goals of social standing or political power. An evocative visual campaign, exploiting the physical elements of the brand which already evoke positive images among French whisky drinkers – the name (short, sharp, powerful), the golden label, the distinctive bottle shape, the red typography (a visual campaign c/f Benson and Hedges cigarettes, Anais Anais perfume).

Media: Luxury magazines were chosen (television being banned for spirits), since they offered colour and a prestige environment. The balance of luxury, high status and 'arty' magazines was to be skewed according to the target audiences described.

Each of these strategies was translated into a creative brief and creative work. Eventually, it was the creative work based on the second of these ideas that ran.

The role of advertising (What?)

Advertising is communication – simply words and images. The only useful definitions of the role of advertising recognize this simple fact and set a task which can be directly fulfilled by advertising.

Advertising can:

- Generate awareness, familiarity, curiosity, top-of-mindness.
- Inform, demonstrate, argue, claim.
- Create images, associations, personality, feeling.

Even limited to the tasks achievable with words and pictures, the range of advertising objectives is pretty wide. In the McClan example the role was described as generating awareness, and legitimacy by way of an image and personality consonant with a mainstream whisky.

The yogurt whose marketing strategy (see Chapter 2) was to target health-conscious mothers with a positioning as an alternative to snack food, could choose various roles or 'whats'. It could suggest the product as a solution to the snack problem, in contrast to other snack-food competition, or could use either argument or emotional reassurance to establish this particular brand of yogurt as the most appropriate for such usage. This decision will clearly influence the other three, the 'who', the 'how' and media.

It is worth just noting here that the 'what' of an advertisement is often not very exciting or imaginative. It is often pretty mundane 'what' an ad should do, as is the case for the yogurt. The twist and excitement is yet to come – in the 'who' and 'how'.

The advertising target (Who?)

The term 'advertising target', and even more the mnemonic 'who' is in a sense misleading. The problem is that they both suggest a number of clearly-defined individuals. In fact, target really refers to a potential desire which can be touched by the advertising. A target is a desire or feeling that is common to a proportion of consumers some of the time and which advertising can exploit.

To illustrate the importance of this seemingly rather hair-splitting definition, consider the fact that the targets of any group of closely-competing brands are going to cover largely the same group of people. If the targets are literally defined by 'who' (actual physical people) they will all be exactly the same. The real differences in brands' targets has to be the different feelings or attitudes in the (same) people's heads.

This definition is consistent with the reality about brand loyalty. A grocery brand which accounts for over 30 per cent of its users purchases in that product field can pride itself on high loyalty. Most consumers, in most product fields, divide their purchases over several brands. In this way a woman might be both an Ariel buyer and a Persil buyer, and in the target audience for the advertising for both brands. She has a variety of needs from a washing powder, and it is these various needs that the two detergents target.

In the McClan example the quantitative definition given by the marketing strategy was regular whisky drinkers. In fact most standard whiskies will be aiming at these same people, but while competitors play on the need for social status, on authenticity or the night-club image, McClan has to find other feelings and motivations which also affect choice. The advertising strategies have to capture some other motivation, widely present in this group, which can be touched by advertising. The two options selected were the need for reassurance in the absence of knowledge ('the mature choice'), and the desire to express an artistic, cultured but dynamic outlook through their choice of whisky ('the new adventurers'). The two resulting targets sound very different, but they may cover largely overlapping groups in terms of actual people.

The key to defining the advertising target is to understand what it is in a person that makes them susceptible to the product. Something in their situation, personality or the way they see themselves makes them open to this product's offer at least some of the time. The more three-dimensional, detailed and closer to the truth the description, the better eventually for helping the creative team.

Age, sex, socioeconomic group and region are all useful for the media decision, but in terms of producing the actual advertising they rarely contribute. A complete list of names and addresses would be of no value at all.

D'Arcy McManus & Masius (as they were at the time) used to use an amusing example to drive home this point:

A rather unsuccessful account director came home one night to find his fourteen-year-old son sporting a pink, Mohican-style haircut. Without a moment's strategic reflection, the father yelled: 'Get that hair back to normal (*message*) or I'll beat the living daylights out of you (*support/reason why*).' The next night he got home to find his son's hair unchanged: 'Did you not hear what I told you? (*recall test*). Did you not understand? (*comprehension*).' The son had, but his behaviour and intentions had not been influenced in the slightest. What had gone wrong?

The answer was, of course, that despite the father's complete knowledge of *who* his target was, he had failed to understand his son's *beliefs*. These were, in fact, that anything his Dad hated must be okay and that if his father tried to hit him, his mother would intervene.

The essence of defining the target is understanding what makes them tick.

The content (How?)

If your objective is to appear modest it is crass simply to shout out that you are. This is the challenge of creative strategy.

The advertising strategy contains the idea of the ad, the idea that is to be animated by the chosen creative vehicle. The 'how' part of the strategy contains the twist that unites the target and the objective into one coherent advertising concept. A plausible 'how' for somebody wishing to appear modest might be to praise a lesser rival.

Studies exist which aim to list the different types of 'hows'. For example, Book and Cary[1] listed thirteen types: story line, problem/solution, logical argument, demonstration, testimonial, spokesman, special effects/mood, slice of life, suspense, satire/humour, analogy, fantasy and, finally, personality.

Unfortunately, even if such listings do achieve appropriate labels, they offer little help in generating original, or even workable, hows. Story line, logical argument, cartoon character, spokesman etc. give little guidance for creating a new ad, where the question is *what* story, *what* logical argument or *what* character.

Finding that original and motivating something demands a creative solution. The 'what' may be quite banal e.g. 'remind users how much they enjoy eating Yuk chocolate' but the 'how' has to have a twist. The McClan example gives a good illustration of 'hows' which suggest very specific routes for delivering the 'what'. No rules exist for finding a good 'how', but later in this chapter we examine a series of techniques that help in the search.

Media choice

The advertising budget always limits what the advertising can achieve. Some studies suggest that consumers are bombarded (as the cliché goes) with around 5,000 advertising messages a day. The media decision is driven by this fact – the increasing difficulty in buying a piece of the consumer's undivided attention.

Media choice and type of advertising have to be considered together, by both the strategy and media teams. Media planning is too important to simply follow ad strategy.

There are six major media issues which have to be decided in relation to, and at the same time as, the overall advertising strategy.

1 *Appropriateness to the advertising task*

The task of the advertising is always the number one determinant of media choice. The type of message, the need to explain or demonstrate, the need for visual representation or for sound, for prestige, intrusiveness, repetition, continuous presence etc. often dictate the choice of media. However, there is usually some margin for adjustment and the relationship has to be two-way. To optimize the effect of media within the budget, media planners have to be allowed to use the margin of flexibility which often exists in terms of alternative advertising tasks.

2 *Appropriateness to the target*

The advertising target should be defined not only in demographic terms (which are only ever a guide) but also in terms of needs, attitudes and behaviour. If this is the case, the media can be planned in terms of finding people with the right attitudes, or in the right mood at the right moment.

It is very difficult to put a value on catching a respondent in the right mood or at the right time. It is difficult to estimate the correct premium for an ad appearing among sympathetic editorial or to quantify the belief that certain media are paid greater attention than others. If one magazine is offering the same man at a lower price, it takes some courage to choose another more expensive publication for one of these 'qualitative' reasons. The more media planners are involved in strategy decisions, the better their judgement is likely to be, and the greater their scope to exploit these qualitative aspects of media.

3 *Level of concentration*

Resources can be spent on a broad campaign touching as many people as possible, or concentrated, so that a smaller audience is heavily exposed. Concentration can take place geographically or in time, creating a relatively intense presence for say, a day, week or month. Concentration can also be achieved by dominating one medium, even down to one publication or one television series. Apple computers favour this latter 'media domination' policy.

Concentration can mean efficiencies in media buying, and the decision to concentrate the media is again part of overall advertising strategy which can affect choice of advertising objective, target and message.

4   *Relative inter-media value*

The values is given by traditional media fluctuate and change relative to each other and every medium has a point where it is no longer cost-effective for a brand. It is up to media planners to make sure that advertisers are aware of the advantages of flexibility (which often means the worth of media other than television) and the need to permutate different media according to the value being offered.

Demand from advertisers has led to many new ways to speak to the consumer. Direct mail has become more viable with better data handling, and new opportunities, from parking meters to warehouse roofs near airports come on stream each year. To benefit from these opportunities it is necessary to understand what types of messages are possible in different media, and *be willing to change advertising strategy*, according to the media situation.

5   *Synergy with the environment*

Often called creative media planning, this is more than simply putting travel ads in the travel pages of a newspaper. The idea is to augment the paid-for advertising by latching on to something featured in the media, or some intrinsic aspect of a medium. The topicality and cleverness then become an integral part of the campaign (see Plate 3.1).

Heineken beer have a reputation for exploiting humorous media stories, by getting a version of their highly adaptable 'Heineken refreshes the parts other beers cannot reach' campaign alongside the relevant news item, at extremely short notice. In this way when a Russian submarine was marooned on a Swedish sandbank, the ad had it being floated free with the help of a can of Heineken.

Seiko advertised James Bond's watch during the appropriate James Bond movie and John Player Special (Black) cigarettes use posters which make puns on their environment – 'Hump black bridge' on a billboard next to a hump back bridge, 'Tail black' alongside a reliable traffic jam spot etc.

One other variable is important, for a different reason.

6   *Scope for testing*

Much of the information needed for the decisions mentioned above will not be available, and the choices are simply made on judgement. Only by building in the right type of variability in the media plan can information on the effects of these decisions be created for the future. For example, the decision to use bursts or drip schedules on television – if identical actions are carried out everywhere, and repeated over time, little information will be generated

Scottish and Newcastle Breweries (beer, UK)

Virgin Atlantic (airline, UK)

United Rum Merchants, UK

Plate 3.1 *The idea of creative media planning is to augment the paid for advertising by latching on to some intrinsic aspect of the medium or its environment. The topicality and cleverness become an integral part of the campaign*

for the next round of decisions. This topic is discussed in more detail in Chapter 6.

If these six issues are going to get the attention they deserve, the media specialists have to be brought into the advertising development process at an earlier stage than has been usual in the past. Media planners have to get involved in a two-way discussion in advertising strategy meetings at the point where objectives, target and message are still being decided.

Good media buying means being able to negotiate knowledgeably with media owners, and being able to recognize and take opportunities that are appropriate to the task in hand. A media buyer who has been involved in the strategy decision is in a strong position in both these respects.

How does advertising work?

The preceding section defined and illustrated the idea of an advertising strategy. All very worthwhile, of course, but the problem is not usually recognizing one, but finding one in the first place. This section tackles the all-important question of finding an advertising idea.

The marketing strategy gives the blue-print for how the product should be promoted. Frequently the role of the advertising is to establish or reinforce the positioning defined in the marketing strategy. However, it is the nature of the consumer decision involved which indicates *how* advertising is likely to work in a particular market. The consumer's decision determines how the positioning task should be approached – with detailed information, a simplistic claim, feelings or associations?

The consumer's decision

Understanding how consumers make their choice in whatever the product field, is usually an excellent starting point for developing advertising strategy.

The earliest attempts to model the consumer decision were the '*hierarchy of effects*' models put forward during the 1950s. The idea was that consumers moved through different stages in their nearness to buying a product, and that advertising worked by helping to move them through those stages. Most of the models are remembered via acronyms – AIDA is one of the best known, standing for Awareness-Interest-Desire-Action (see Figure 3.1).

AIDA was one of several alternative formulations of the theory – the models became more convoluted and subtle but the key characteristics remained the same. They were all based on a sequential, single-track model and their stages could be broken up into three main sections – a 'learning' phase, a 'feeling' phase, and finally a 'doing' phase.

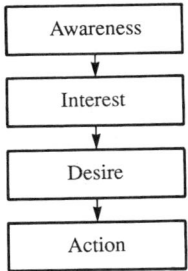

Figure 3.1   *The hierarchy of effects model known as AIDA*

The best-known model appeared in 1961 from Lavidge and Steiner[2] and clearly demonstrates these three states (see Figure 3.2).

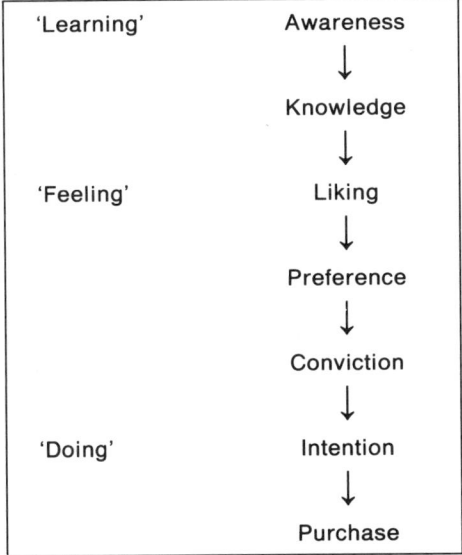

Figure 3.2   *Lavidge and Steiner's heirarchy of effects model illustrating the three broad steps typical of this theory.*

These theories are now widely disparaged and even dismissed, because there seem to be so many cases where they do not apply. In fact, it seems to be the exception rather than the rule when a consumer can be said to be buying because he has been 'converted' in this way. However, before moving on to look at a more comprehensive theory of advertising, it is worth seeing how these old 'hierarchy' models can still provide useful insights into the development of advertising strategy in certain, rather specific, situations.

Consider the decision of a wealthy, retired man making his investments. Suppose an investment company is keen to persuade him to swop from his traditional savings accounts to a newer type of investment, say unit trusts, offered by the investment company. Depth interviews might establish a decision process that looked rather like Figure 3.3.

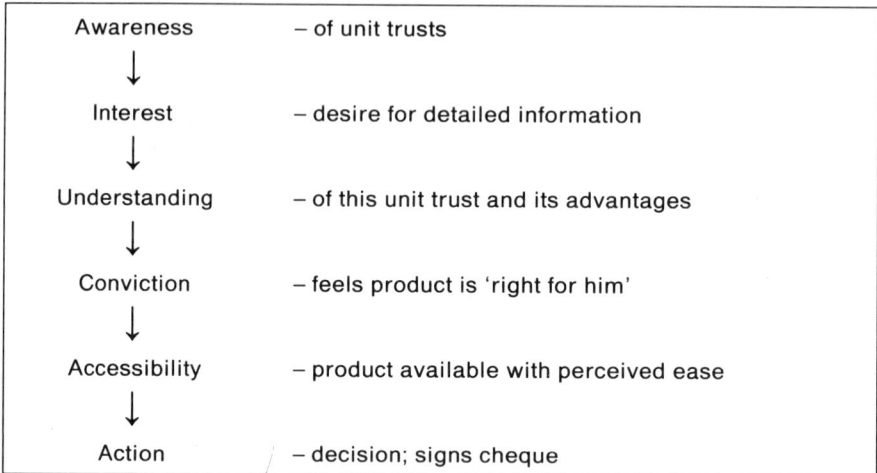

Figure 3.3   *The decision process of a first-time investor in unit trusts*

The flow chart shown in Figure 3.3 can be applied to the development of advertising strategy by working through it and asking, for each stage, first: Does this step pose a stumbling block for a significant number of consumers?

- Are large numbers of them unaware?
- Are they aware but uninterested?
- Are they already seeking detailed information?
- Do they understand but lack conviction?
- Do they know how to inscribe?

and then: Can advertising be of help in easing this stage? For example:

- Should advertising concentrate on creating interest and leave provision of detailed data to direct mail?
- Could advertising itself provide accessibility in the form of direct response?

When there does seem to be a logical linear sequence towards purchase, decomposing the purchase decision into a hierarchy format can, in fact, be a very useful tool.

However, there is that notable drawback – those many purchase decisions which simply do not follow a rational, stepwise path.

Expanding the range of decision models

Where does 'Awareness-Comprehension-Conviction-Action'* get you in developing advertising for potato crisps or encouraging repeat purchase of a TV dinner? Finding examples of consumer decisions which contradicted the 'hierarchy' models, led adherents to postulate conditions in which the hierarchy models *were* applicable. These were that:

1   The consumer is highly *involved.*
2   The consumer is making a *rational* decision.

People tend to be involved in purchases which are infrequent, which involve large amounts of money or where a mistake poses a high risk. High-involvement products are typically durables such as cars and washing machines, but also 'high visibility' products, such as sportswear or brandy and new products tried for the first time. Conversely, less-involved decisions include frequent, low-cost and low-visibility purchases – most grocery products and personal treats such as confectionery.

A decision is 'rational' if it is made primarily on the perceived functioning of the product – perhaps washing powders or computers. 'Subjective' or 'irrational' products are those chosen purely on taste and feeling – which chocolate bar?, Louis Vuiton or Cartier luggage?

In situations where the consumer thinks very little before making a decision (uninvolved) or makes decisions on emotional, irrational criteria, the hierarchy models break down. Consumers may buy a new potato crisp while being unaware of the product up to purchase, or may choose a perfume while knowing nothing about its composition and showing no interest in such details.

In 1980, Richard Vaughn of Foote, Cone and Belding[4] helped bring this chaos into order and save a useful theory from disrepute. He proposed the use of the criteria 'involvement' and 'rationality' to categorize the types of decision followed for different purchases. He put the two dimensions together into a matrix which he called the 'FCB planning square' (Figure 3.4(a) and (b)).

The exciting thing about this theory was that it hypothesized six distinct and different types of consumer decision, corresponding to different zones of this matrix (see Figure 3.5).

* Russell Colley's version from his famous book *Defining Advertising Goals for Measured Advertising Results* ('DAGMAR').[3]

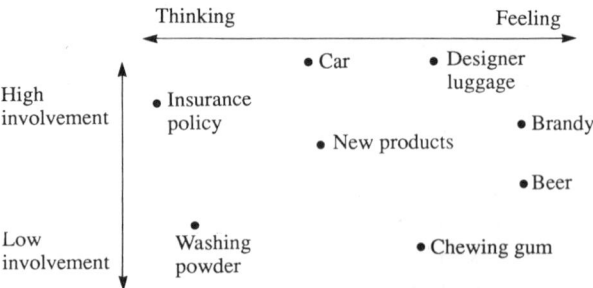

Figure 3.4(a)   *FCB's 'planning square'. Products are placed in the matrix according to the degree of involvement and rationality normal in their purchase decision*

Informed decisions

The top left zone of the matrix shown in Figure 3.5, labelled 'informed', corresponds to the classic models where the hierarchy theories hold. Consumers 'learn' i.e. take in information about the product which makes them 'feel' positively towards it. They then, thoughtfully, decide to buy or 'do'. The investment decision discussed above would belong to this category.

Convinced decisions

Moving down to the box labelled 'convinced', the consumer is *not sufficiently involved* to seek detailed information on the products. However, his basically *rational* attitude predisposes him to notice simple advertising claims or promises. If the simple claim appeals he acts on the information that he picks up – 'kills all known germs' or 'keeps baby dry even when he's wet'.

Habitual decisions

'I buy this one because it's the one I've always bought' is a frustrating response to get in research, but totally honest. The motives for this behaviour (inertia, saving effort, avoiding risk) are easy to understand. The interesting question for the advertiser is: What mechanism is needed for breaking such a habit? . . . read on.

Impulse decisions

On the emotional side of the matrix, the lowest involvement category is labelled 'impulse'. Typically, with such markets, (e.g. snacks) trial is easy to gain but loyalty hard to hold. The first contact with the brand may be

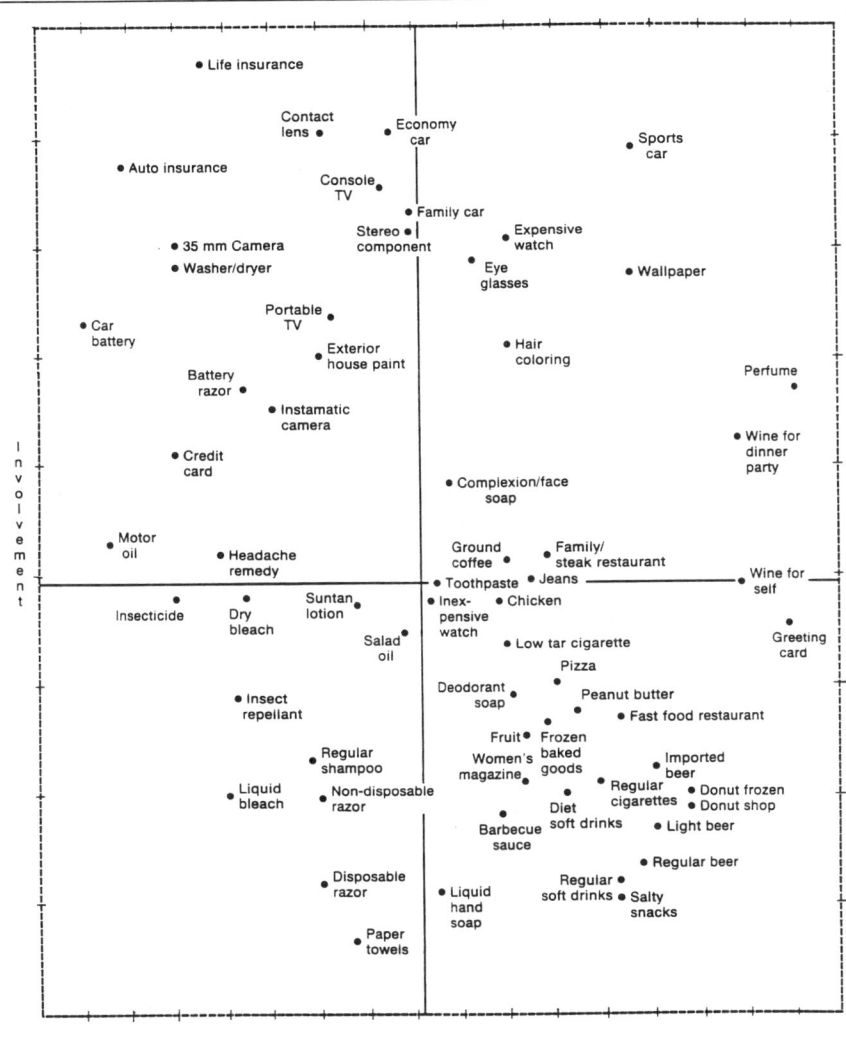

Figure 3.4(b)   *FCB's 'planning square', showing the results of an empirical study designed to map sixty common products onto the dimensions of involvement and think-feel* (Journal of Advertising Research, *Aug/Sep 1987*)[5]

purchase itself and satisfaction with the product does not guarantee repurchase. Distribution tends to be a key marketing variable – soft drinks, chewing gum, even beer are bought largely because they are there.

Image and sensual decisions

These decisions are made on feelings, not on rational assessment of the product's functions. The decision varies according to the consumer's level of

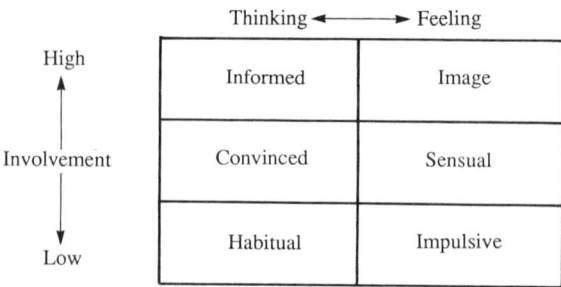

Figure 3.5   *Relating the dimensions of involvement and rationality to six different types of purchasing decision.*

involvement. High involvement here usually implies that the product indicates something about the person (the watch I wear, the car I drive). Less involvement usually means that only personal enjoyment and self-image are taken into account in making the decision (bath additives, frozen gourmet dinners).

Implications for advertising strategy

Instinctively, advertisers tend to avoid obvious mistakes such as: 'In tests, 8 out of 10 men who stated a preference, preferred Chanel No 5', 'Nothing acts faster than Johnny Walker' or 'A woman is an island, Persil is her washing powder'.

However, being conscious of these different types of consumer decision, can help to avoid more marginal errors. For example, it might warn a frustrated advertiser with a habit product such as a tetra-brick of orange juice, not to try an image-based, moody ad. It can save searching for rational arguments, when a personality or image campaign is more appropriate. It can reduce the temptation to overice the cake – if a straightforward, rational message is required, it may be an error to wrap it up in subtle, creative advertising.

The theory (and of course it is only a theory) suggests the following approaches to finding an advertising strategy, in each of the six cases.

Informed

Rationally-based research among potential and recent purchasers can be used to establish the needs and priorities of the target audience. The advertising should then be based on arguments promoting the functional delivery of the product. The advertising should recognize its audience's willingness to study information. The result will often be factual advertising, probably long copy, often demanding press. (See, for example, Plate 3.2).

COULD YOUR HOUSE PROFIT FROM THE PROFIT YOU'VE MADE ON YOUR HOUSE?

Converting a loft. Building a conservatory. Installing a new kitchen.

We all have our dreams.

But not everyone has the money to turn them into reality. That's why we've introduced Equity Release.

A scheme that allows you to get at the profit you've made on your house since you bought it.

How you use this money to improve your home is up to you.

You needn't worry about paying lofty interest rates either. (Withdraw your money as a lump sum and we'll let you have it for 15.4% APR*)

Anyone can apply for Equity Release.

Simply call into any of our branches, give us a ring free on 0800 300 323 or fill in the coupon.

We'll send you all the details straight away, so hopefully it won't be long before you and your house are better off.

TO: THE ROYAL BANK OF SCOTLAND PLC
FREEPOST PO BOX 43 RUGBY WARWICKSHIRE CV22 7BR
PLEASE SEND ME MORE
INFORMATION ABOUT EQUITY RELEASE

NAME

ADDRESS

POSTCODE

The Royal Bank of Scotland

A MEMBER OF IMRO & AFBD

Applicants must be over 18. Security, life assurance and a current account are required. Equity Release is not normally suitable for retired people.
Typical APR calculation is based on mortgage rate which is variable. The Royal Bank of Scotland plc. Registered office 36 St. Andrew Square, Edinburgh EH2 2YB. Registered in Scotland No. 90312.

Plate 3.2   *Royal Bank of Scotland – an informative ad such as this one will do the best job of flagging down genuine prospects in a high involvement area such as secured loans*

Plate 3.3   *Kia-Ora (soft drinks, UK) – this is not the case for a soft drink. The strategists should be as specific as possible in the definition of the target audience, but nothing avoids that essential creative leap*

Convinced

The 'convinced' box corresponds to the USP (unique selling proposition) theory of advertising, as proposed originally by Rosser Reeves. The key is to distil the advertising message down to one, simple, motivating, proposition. If the proposition is too complicated or subtle it is unlikely to be decoded or remembered. If the proposition appeals, the consumer will follow a rational behaviour pattern and try or repurchase the brand.

Strong feelings of commitment or liking are not necessary, and advertising which sets out to create this emotional link may fall on stony ground. In the long run, assuming a certain level of satisfaction, use and familiarity will create some positive feelings of 'for-me-ness', but creating these feelings is probably not going to be the goal of advertising.

Habitual

Advertisers tend to operate on the belief that subjected to sufficient evidence or seduction (i.e. information or emotional appeal) a buyer will reject his current brand and switch to the advertised brand. The hypothesis put forward in Vaughn's theory, is that this does not happen in habit markets. The theory claims that the best way to *change* habit buying is actually *to force new behaviour.*

This hypothesis gains support from the 'cognitive dissonance' theory, established by Festinger. Festinger showed that people try to bring their perceptions into line with their behaviour, in order to avoid unpleasant feelings of 'dissonance'. This implies that doing something (choosing brand X) encourages one to accept consonant beliefs (that brand X is a good choice). Thus, being 'forced' to try a brand, e.g. through free sampling or an irresistible two-for-one offer, encourages favourable 'consonant' attitudes towards the brand.

Conversely, buyers are inclined to ignore or reject information which brings into question their current behaviour. This implies selecting against advertising for brands that are not used, and favouring ads which support current behaviour. Such selectivity makes it even more difficult to use argument or seduction to break habits. The implication is indeed that forcing 'doing' might be the most effective way to break and change habit buying.

An example of this effect working twice over, is the story of the mustard Amora, which dominates the French mustard market. (It should be noted that mustard is simple to manufacture and differences in quality tend to be marginal.)

A tale of two mustards

Amora originally achieved leadership when it started packing its mustard in drinking glasses sealed with a slightly elastic cap. Desire for the free glasses created action and habit and consumers then stuck with the brand, despite little advertising support and pricing sometimes 50 to 100 per cent above unbranded competition.

Attracted by Amora's profitable position, a respected spice manufacturer, Ducros, decided to attack. High ad spends behind a memorable and relevant campaign ('ça demange' or 'it demolishes') established strength, the central attribute of good yellow mustard. However, Ducros made minimal impact in terms of sales. The consumer reaction appeared to be: 'Yes, Ducros probably produce a good mustard, but personally I tend to buy Amora (out of habit!).'

Meanwhile Amora were demonstrating their mastery of their market by launching a trendy fast-food 1950s-style plastic container. This 'moutardier', as it was called, never really created a repeat buying market for itself, but it generated a stream of impulse purchases (doing), some of it from own label, other brand or new mustard buyers (young people). These buyers, bringing their beliefs into line with their behaviour, ended up feeling more positive towards the whole Amora brand, and some of them thus continued to buy Amora.

Suppose Ducros had launched the moutardier, instead of Amora, and had featured the new packaging in their advertising, instead of the quality of their mustard. The decision to buy the moutardier would have been in a higher involvement or interest zone because it would have concerned a new product – the snazzy, practical dispenser. As such, rational or emotional advertising for the moutardier would have motivated some consumers. If the packaging had won purchases from Amora buyers, it is likely, according to the theory, that some of them would have stuck with Ducros long term. The brand manager might have said of his promotion: 'It is a far, far better thing that I do now, than image advertising ever was; it got a far, far better rate of sale, than I have ever known.'

In 1982 when I started working on tea brands, I asked my dear (now late) granny why she always bought Brooke Bond 'D'. 'I just buy the one with the divi (dividend stamps),' she said. 'But, Gran,' said I, bursting with newly acquired facts on the tea market, 'they stopped that in the late 1960s.' 'That's true,' said Granny as if she'd just noticed, 'they don't do the stamps any more.' My mother (Granny's daughter) swopped when the stamps stopped, to another Brooke Bond brand – the one that offered collecting cards.

A survey quoted in *Business Week*[6] found that of the twenty-three leading (US) grocery brands in 1923, nineteen had survived into the 1980s in their leading positions. The four others were still in the top five!

None of this amounts to proof, but the stability of major grocery brands and the low advertising sensitivities found in these low-interest, frequently-purchased areas, certainly give pause for thought. If this theory is valid it has interesting implications for advertising and promotion in these habit-led areas.

Disruptions in a competitor's distribution such as those caused by a strike, offer a wonderful opportunity to exploit, as do disruptions of a whole market. England suffered a dramatic potato shortage in the early 1970s, which tripled potato prices and forced widespread trial of spaghetti and rice. After the shortage the potato recovered its pre-eminent position in British cuisine, but the pasta and rice markets were permanently increased. The implication for marketing is that an event, such as an Italian week in a supermarket, may get through to consumers who are fairly immune to less intense, more repetitive efforts.

It underlines the potential for price cuts and other promotions. As long as they manage to touch a target beyond the current regular purchasers, they can do a lot more than simply bringing sales forward.

It also follows that promotions need to be signalled to non-users, say by advertising or special point-of-sale fixtures, to be most effective. This is one way that advertising can be important for habit-led purchases – mineral water advertises its new watertight screw top, motor oil its easy-pour container, coffee its attractive storage jars, milk, the tetra-brick that opens without scissors; a range of new flavours for a mayonnaise, the opportunity to win a holiday when you buy a certain brand of suntan lotion or charitable donations by the sponsor in proportion to sales (Save The Children have run cooperative operations with a number of major grocery brands in the UK).

All of these novelties are easily (and invariably) copied, but the point is that the brand who does it first (and advertises the fact!) attracts extra use not just in the short run. The benefit of this extra use or trial lasts past the adoption of the trick by the competition. 'Forced' buying will have a positive effect on future buying probabilities.

Remember that all this applies to non-users. Bolstering the habitual decisions of users against the tricks thought up by the competition is as often the priority of advertising in habit markets. The typical advertising strategy for reinforcing users' commitment is repetition with strong branding playing on the familiar characteristics of the brand (the Bisto Kids and Homepride Flour Men were brought back for this reason), strong visual links to product, reinforcing a likable, familiar presence.

Impulse

The classic advertising strategy is creating top-of-mindness, i.e. putting more emphasis on impact than a convincing product story. This is very demanding creatively, and even with a strong creative idea, it inevitably demands a fairly continuous (read expensive) media schedule. Beer brands and soft drinks are classic examples of this problem – many do manage to find excellent creative ideas (Follow the (Hofmeister) bear, Heineken, of course, We all adora Kia-Ora, Bet he drinks Carling Black Label, etc.) but they have to keep spending or the brands quickly die.

In some cases it is possible to shift the type of decision the consumer makes. Just as habit products can shift their decision to a more involved area by selling their packaging, it is possible to make decisions less impulsive. Escaping from the impulse zone is attractive because the classic strategy of creating top-of-mind is prohibitively expensive for all but brand leaders.

Chewing gum can go rational (convinced) by adding fluoride and taking out sugar. Hair colourants, such as 'Loving Care', sold as antidotes to greyness (belief/functional claim) generate a higher loyalty rate than those, such as 'Glints', sold on a young 'impulse' strategy.

However, if impulse buying does dominate purchasing, there is often no alternative to impactful, creative, advertising, spending money and making sure your product is available when the customer goes to buy (see Plate 3.4).

This does not mean that the strategists are completely off the hook, and can simply lean on the creative people. It does often mean though, that ad strategies are likely to be more arbitrary, and are suggestive rather than absolute in terms of determining the creative solution.

Plate 3.4   *John Smiths – the classic advertising strategy in impulse markets is creating top-of-mindness. The emphasis is on impact rather than a convincing product story. This decision zone is inevitably very demanding creatively*

Plate 3.5 *J Sainsbury – many ads want to convince their audiences that their product tastes better than the competition. Arguing via the ingredients is one popular route*

Sensual

This is the 'problem of pleasure', with a vengeance. The problem is recurrent because this decision area covers so many advertised brands, particularly foods – biscuits, desserts, drinks, condiments, complete meals, frozen dishes etc.

There are three classic approaches to communicating pleasure. Through users – their expressions, exclamations or behaviour, or their particular determination to get hold of the loved product. Through the ingredients – pouring chocolate, tumbling fruit, sizzling hamburgers, melting cheese, hopefully not all in one ad (see Plate 3.5). Finally, through analogy – the pleasure created by the ad itself, beautiful women or children, sunshine, having fun. This last category includes fantasies. Suburban woman (Wendy Craig) gets in from the supermarket, draws all the curtains and gets out her 'Velvet' chocolate pudding. In bursts a jewel-bedecked man on horseback and sweeps her away. Well ... pleasure *is* a problem in advertising, and the fantasy approach worked for Milk Tray (see Plate 3.6).

The chocolate manufacturers are on the sharp end of the problem. Mars prefers to bow out from the start, if they can, and shift to functional positionings. This means they can use belief or claim advertising – Milky Way (UK) is light enough not to spoil a child's appetite, Snickers (US) gives you energy, a Mars helps you work rest and play, and is usually larger than ever before. Rowntrees' biggest success, KitKat, is ideal for a break with a drink. Cadbury's bravely stick to the high stakes game, using every technique

You don't have to read the carton to find out what's in a Knorr sauce. Just taste it.

Knorr Recipe Sauces. Fresh ways to make classic casseroles

Plate 3.6　*Pleasure – Knorr (TM Regd) uses analogy. The sophisticated illustration is an analogy for sophisticated and subtle taste*

invented. The pleasures, obvious and ambiguous, of the Flake girl, in sunlit woods and with gipsies (my mother said I never should go and eat chocolate in the wood?). The mouthwatering melting chocolate in Cadbury's Dairy Milk*, Eastern Promise (more analogy) from Turkish Delight. And the returns *are* high – ounce for ounce Cadbury's sell their chocolate at about 50 per cent premium to Mars. Of course, you can't always get it right ... did Elton John communicate much pleasure?

There is some strategic scope in offering rationalizations for pleasure (the natural bar, the less-fattening centre) but it is no good talking rationally to a customer who is 'only there for the pleasure'. This again implies that the advertising idea has to lean more heavily on creative, than on strategic, inspiration. This means that the strategist's role becomes finding the germ of an advertising idea, an insight which begins to suggest the personality and feeling of the final ad, rather than a straight strategic solution. In the end the successful campaigns (say, Tony the Tiger and his 'Taste Grrreat' Frosties, or even (Mars *can* do it) Bounty's South Sea Island escapism) tend to succeed out of sheer creative punch, which lifts the ad above the 'mmm ... really tastes *good!*' sludge.

Image

Here the emotional significance of the brand, its image and associations are

*Two earlier campaigns for CDM focused on functional benefits – the milk content (one and a half full glasses), and the reward role of chocolate ('Award yourself the CDM').

Helena Rubinstein

Tomorrow's hydration today:
Performance H₂O:
Made to measure hydration.

A fundamental discovery has been made: your skin's moisture level is defined at birth, at a level specific to you, and does not vary with age even though it may sometimes vary with the environment.

So a moisturising cream can't be the same for everyone. That's why Helena Rubinstein have invented the Index System of hydration.

- Cream Index 4: for slightly dehydrated skin.
- Cream Index 7: for very dehydrated skin.
- Total Hydration Gel: a special treatment for periods of exceptional dehydration.

Performance H₂O. Never has hydration been so precise.

NEW:
Hydration indices.

HR

Helena Rubinstein (H₂O cosmetics)

Plate 3.7 *Nowhere is the difference between emotional and rational decisions more clear than with cosmetics and perfumes. Often the same companies are talking to the same target women, but skin care ads always strain to offer rational arguments, while perfume ads, like this one from Ô de Lancôme (overleaf), offer pure glossy image*

the keys to its purchase. This is an area where strategy can offer more inspiration, because the effectiveness of the advertising depends on finding the right associations for the target audience. The McClan example, using the values 'maturity' and 'culturally aware', fits in this category.

The key is to identify the image, and then to find a subtle way of putting

Ô de Lancôme
Plate 3.7 (*continued*)

it across. For example, brandy advertising may talk about its origins or manufacture to create the *feeling* of quality or authenticity.

In the case of, say, an exotic holiday, the purchaser will also require some practical information, but the decision is not rational, and too much argument is as likely as not to put the audience off.

The result is often emotional, glossy advertising creating glamorous associations. Advertising environment is particularly important. Whereas cost-per-thousand contacts might lead to putting a washing powder's slogan on the back of supermarket receipts, such logic cannot be applied to a cigar.

These 'feeling' categories are those usually associated with the Ogilvy School of Advertising, that of the brand personality. In fact, in his books Ogilvy stresses his excellent press work mostly based on the 'informed' zone, but he successfully christened 'values' advertising (see Plate 3.7).

The validity of the matrix

One can debate the accuracy and completeness of the six decision types. It is possible to find decisions not covered by this framework (recommendations from an authority, or whimsical variety-seeking on the part of a capricious consumer). The matrix ignores the issue of price, which evidently interacts with each type of decision in different ways. These problems do not, however, negate the value of the framework as a stimulus to thought. A framework which offers six plausible mechanisms for effective advertising is certainly an improvement on traditional theories such as AIDA, USP or brand personality, which offer just one.

The framework provides an explanation as to why different types of advertising can be equally valid. It is not a matter of slice of life works, yes or no? P & G are right to run side by sides but they would not work for Cinzano against Martini.

It also sheds light on the 'strategy vs creativity' controversy in advertising. There are some situations where strategy, understanding of the product and the consumers needs are key, and some where the advertising task is essentially one creative leap. It is not fashionable to say it, but there are product categories where out and out creativity is not required, and there are others where the only contribution an agency can make is a stunning creative idea.

Applying the matrix in practice

The dimensions of involvement and rational content are not easy to measure. They also change over time and vary from person to person. This means that it is not always clear which type of decision applies in a particular case. Indeed different consumers often feel differently about the same purchase. One woman may feel that perfume is a large investment and that her friends will judge her from her choice. Perfume is, therefore, an 'image' decision. Another will see it as a more trivial, 'sensual' or even 'impulse' buy.

These variations complicate the choice of the appropriate type of advertising, but in themselves can lead to viable segmentations and the chance to be different from the competition – targeting women who buy perfume on impulse or women who make a 'sensual' decision about their washing powder (is this what Persil are doing with their colourful posters? see Plate 3.8 which, unfortunately, is reproduced in black and white). This trick often means

Plate 3.8   *Persil, Lever, UK – detergents most commonly make their pitch by trying to 'convince' on functional benefits. By approaching its target on an emotional, feeling level, Persil creates a distinct image and appeal*

shifting to a more emotional zone – Cajoline fabric softener moves its appeal into the emotions, with its Teddy Bear campaign. Konica moved their cameras and camera advertising in the same direction when they introduced appealing, coloured 'fashion' cameras. Renault positioned and promoted their Renault 5 as an emotional, feeling purchase. This contrasted notably with more rational car advertising and had a strong impact on a certain target who were ready to decide about their car on 'feeling'.

So in this unifying theory, David Ogilvy, Rosser Reeves and even Russell Colley (Mr Dagmar) are all shown to be correct, and not conflicting with each other. In fact, Ogilvy and Reeves managed to segment the advertising market by offering differentiated products, i.e. types of advertising, which satisfied the genuinely different needs of different groups of clients. Their respective agencies, Ogilvy and Mather and Ted Bates benefited very justly from the resulting (agency) marketing strategies. (As far as I know, Russell Colley limited himself to writing a book, rather than exploiting his insight. He probably made much less money than the other two. I must reflect further on this point.)

Finding an advertising strategy

The marketing strategy and an analysis of the consumer decision should together begin to mould the advertising strategy. Beyond these aids, however, lurks a task which demands imagination and innovation.

My first boss was very aware of the need for imagination and innovation, and his responsibility to obtain it from his juniors. Whenever I said 'Goodness!

I can't see what on earth we can say' he used to reply 'Well start thinking, this is what we pay you for'. If this information is not inspiration enough for you, here are seven tried and tested prompts, designed to stimulate (or at least simulate) thought.

1 Approaches used to position products

Often the task of advertising is to nail the product into its frame of reference. The following list categorizes the most frequently used hammers.

Focusing on one specific attribute

- 'Kills all known germs', Domestos Bleach, UK.
- 'Engineered like no other car in the world', Mercedes cars, US.
- 'Nothing acts faster than Anadin'. Analgesic, UK

Arguably, the same singleminded approach is used in an emotional register by Impulse perfumed deodorant. If one attribute of a perfume is getting you noticed by the opposite sex, Unilever certainly focused on it.

Staking out a point on the price/quality relationship

- 'Good food costs less at Sainsbury's', Food store, UK.
- 'Pile it high, sell it cheap' (long dropped), Tesco, food store, UK.
- 'It costs more but I'm worth it', L'Oreal shampoo, US.

Perhaps more could be done to justify Stella's ridiculous price.

Aaah the exquisite Stella taste.

Aargh the excruciating Stella price. Sadly, there's very little we can do about it.

Even offering small incentives like the one on the left is beyond our means.

Making Stella properly just costs far too much money.

We could, you might suppose, adulterate our premium barley with a few bags of a more questionable grain.

Substitute ordinary hops for the rare Czech Saaz variety.

Or hoist Stella out of the vat before the customary six weeks maturation.

While these expedients might produce a price that's not ridiculous, we're afraid the same could not be said of the beer.

Stella Artois. Reassuringly expensive.

Plate 3.9   *Stella Artois positions itself at the high end of the price/quality continuum*

- 'If we don't have the lowest fare, we probably don't fly there', Continental Airlines, US.
- 'You only fit double glazing once, so fit the best', Everest double glazing, UK.
- 'Stella Artois. Reassuringly expensive' (see Plate 3.9).

Associating the brand with some particular usage (occasion or type)

- 'Have a break, have a KitKat' (Chocolate bar, see Plate 3.10).
- 'When it absolutely, positively, has to be there overnight', Federal Express.

Plate 3.10   *KitKat is an outstandingly delicious chocolate bar, but Rowntrees promote it not on pleasure but on a functional usage position. This choice of decision zone eases the pressure for continual media presence and creative innovation*

Suggesting new uses is a favourite advertising ploy for increasing the weight of use of established products. Both soup (Campbell's Beef Broth) and Sherry (Harveys Bristol Cream) have had their turn at being promoted as refreshing summer drinks 'on the rocks'. The ads make them look disconcertingly similar.

Product class

By adopting the codes of a product class a brand can position itself, and perhaps establish its difference. The brief for the alcohol-free lager Tourtel (France) was simply to look like every other beer ad ever made.

7 Up, 'The uncola', (US) used this route very directly to position itself as an alternative to cola for similar usage occasions, and similar people.

Back in the UK, Qualcast lawnmowers positioned themselves against the negatives of a competitive product class, hover mowers. Qualcast mowers did not leave rotting grass clippings behind them but did leave classic stripes. The 'product class' claim of hovers was that they were less effort. Qualcast turned this upside down with the memorable endline 'Much less bovver than a hover' (see Plate 3.11).

Plate 3.11 *Qualcast (lawnmowers, UK) – positioning with respect to a competitive product class, hover mowers*

A competitor

In the US the genre is commonly used aggressively. For example, Peugeot has recently been suggesting you calm down after test-driving its 505 Turbo by test-driving a BMW 325. Since the BMW 325 is well-known among the target audience, this positions the Peugeot precisely.

Over the counter analgesics (Tylanol, Anacin etc.) each manage to find arguments which imply that they are more effective than their competitors, thereby setting up a modern paradox worthy of Zeno.

In Europe even the use of a competitor's logo can be taken as breach of copyright, which leads to various coy references to 'another leading brand' etc. Even these watered-down versions of competitive ads are typically only used by American advertisers. European companies are still loathe to give

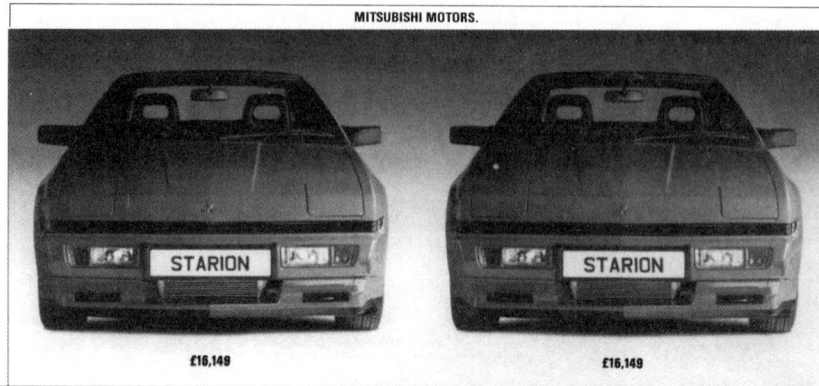

Plate 3.12   *The Mitsubishi Starion positions itself with respect to a competitor, and establishes a functional benefit (saves you money) at the same time*

free publicity of any type to competitors, or to risk negative consumer reaction to an aggressive stance. Some advertisers claim that this approach can only ever be used tactically, and can never work as brand building tool. Look at Plate 3.12 and see what you think.

The projected user, the type of person for whom the brand is supposedly designed

Some brands follow this approach by using ordinary-looking people rather than known role-models ('Real friends, real people want real taste' Winston cigarettes, US; 'People like you are switching to Player's No 6', UK) but only rarely is the characterization pointed enough to make it fly. Classic examples are Marlboro and Charlie, where a certain type of character but not a particular person, becomes the reference point for the brand.

Brand personality – the character of the brand itself

- 'The drier lager, Sats', Satzenbrau Pils (see Plate 3.13).

It is not always easy to make that personality truly particular:

- 'The world's most civilized aperitif', La Ina by Domeco.
- 'The world's most civilized spirit', Hennessy cognac.
- 'Simply years ahead', Philips.
- 'In touch with tomorrow', Toshiba.
- 'Just slightly ahead of our time', Panasonic.

Plate 3.13   *Satzenbrau Pils – attaching a personality to the brand itself is a particular form of positioning*

Symbol objects – associating the brand with objects which have the connotations desired for the brand

- 'Du pain, du vin, du Boursin' associates this industrially produced, flavoured cream cheese with the most basic and best-loved elements on a French table.
- 'Baseball, hot dogs, apple pie and Chevrolet', does a similar trick for Americans.

In many countries cigarette advertising is becoming restricted to this technique by legislation, so that developing a new campaign reduces to 'what set of inanimate objects shall we associate with this pack?'

Clearly these approaches are not mutually exclusive, in fact defining a positioning using one route usually dictates the corresponding positioning in terms of usage, type of user, brand personality etc. The use of two or three approaches coincidentally can be mutually reinforcing.

For example, Hellman's mayonnaise (UK) repositioned from being a 'high-class salad dressing' to being a 'versatile sauce to liven up everyday meals'. The advertising concentrated on usage but also redefined the user stereotype from 'posh people' to 'ordinary people who eat snack food'.

2   The generative possibilities of the classification of needs

Advertising is, by definition, intended to motivate its audience in some way. In the chapter on marketing strategy it was argued that there are only six basic motivations which can be exploited by advertising. This syllogism implies that any advertisement must latch on to one or other of those six basic human motivations. This provides one systematic way of approaching the generation of advertising strategies.

To illustrate the use of this tool consider the task of generating candidate advertising strategies for a serious newspaper. The newspaper contains mostly information – broadly speaking people who read the paper will be well-informed on current affairs.

Strategy 1: Functional benefit

There are straightforward functional benefits in being well informed – you will be better at your job, make decisions more easily, avoid mistakes. This is the approach the *Economist* often uses in its publicity (see Plate 3.14).

Strategy 2: Pleasure

Reading a quality newspaper is an effort. A strategy based on the assimilability of the articles or the lighter elements in the paper – fashion, sport, woman's page – would strike a chord with some potential readers. This strategy might

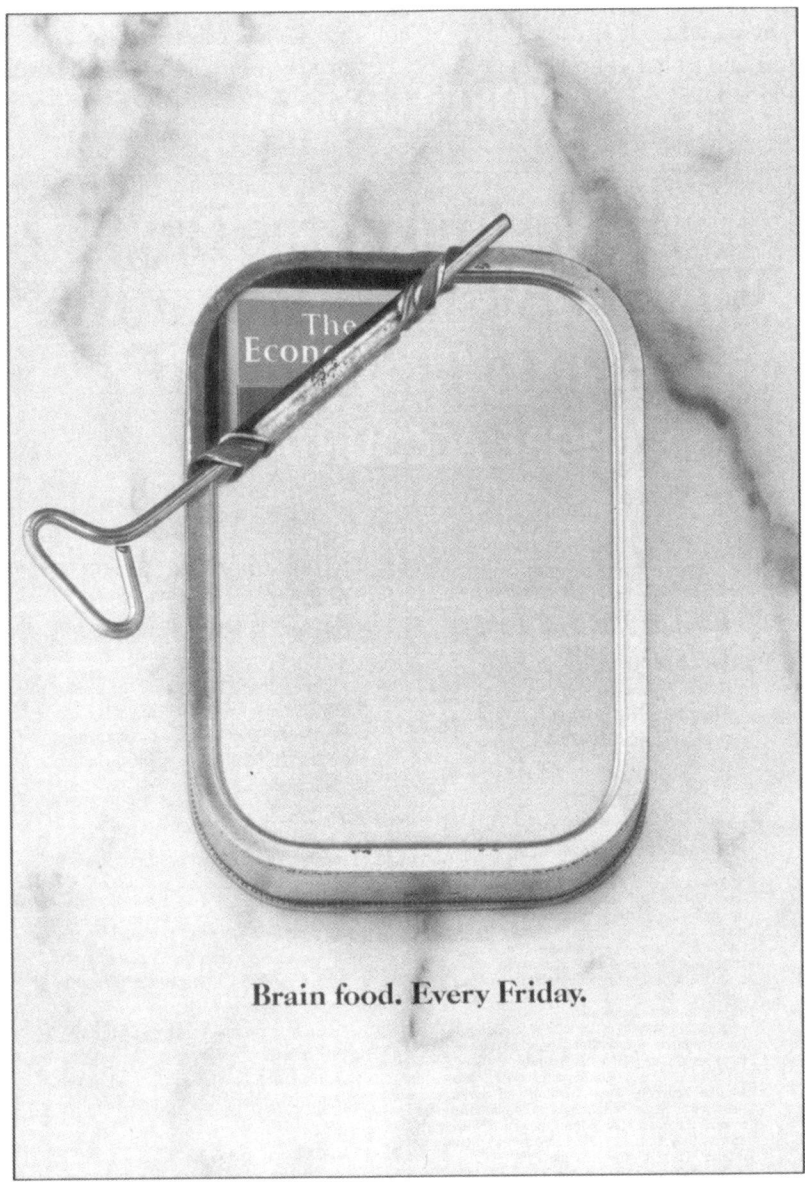

Plate 3.14   The Economist *promotes their product on its direct, functional attributes. It is stimulating, intelligent reading material*

seem particularly appropriate for attracting non-readers who have been discouraged by a perception of stodginess. Perhaps the *Wall Street Journal* thought so when it featured 'page 1 column 4' in its advertising and used the (fun and frolicky) line 'Never simply required reading. It is desired reading' (see Plate 3.15).

At the End of the Day, Why Do Business Executives Turn to The Journal?

◆

*　*　*　　　　*　*　*

Fat Cats of Venice Find the Good Life In Sleep and Soup

* * *

Mice Are No Longer a Thrill
For City's 300,000 Felines
Too Lazy to Chase Them

By Laura Colby
Staff Reporter of The Wall Street Journal
VENICE – They are everywhere in Venice.

They gather in gangs in the alleys behind the Piazza San Marco and rummage through the garbage of the city's best restaurants. They snuggle together in the folds of Vittorio Emmanuele II's bronze statue on the Riva degli Schiavoni. They scale the walls of patrician palazzi, padding deftly around the shards of glass embedded on top to keep them away.

And they sprawl in the winter sunlight on the Strada Nuova, within a paw's reach of Roberto Guadagnin's fish stand.

"Cats!" Mr. Guadagnin cries, his weather-scarred face turning an even brighter shade of red as he waves his hand toward the contented-looking bunch. "Nowadays, they wouldn't even bat an eye at a mouse. Their bellies are too full."

He shakes his head in mock disgust. "Do you know that I have customers who buy fish and take it home and cook it," he says,

After a morning session, many readers choose to peruse it later at leisure.

Barbie dolls. The Swiss Navy. The Dutch manure glut. The fat cats of Venice.

In the world of international business reporting, The Wall Street Journal/Europe has a reputation for leaving no stone unturned.

And when we uncover stories as colourful and unusual as these, there's only one place for them.

Page 1, column 4.

Of course the tales of the unexpected you'll find here rarely have much to do with the price of oil in Kuwait or the value of the yen in London.

Which is precisely why you'll enjoy them so much.

And which is why, at the end of the day, The Journal is never simply required reading.

It is desired reading.

THE WALL STREET JOURNAL.
——— EUROPE ———

Plate 3.15　The Wall Street Journal (Europe) – *are non-readers intimidated by* The Wall Street Journal? *This ad promotes the paper as also being a pleasure*

Plate 3.16 The Independent – *do you like to see yourself as a domino or a pea? Support your self-identity as an unbiased individual by buying* The Independent

Strategy 3: Identity

One likes to feel that one is a well-informed person. This desire was effectively exploited by the *Financial Times*'s famous 'No Comment' campaign. The ads showed groups of businessmen in slightly informal situations, in a lift or

Plate 3.17   The Guardian – *are you a liberal, open minded, original and trendy person?*
Tell the world about it by tucking The Guardian *under your arm*

walking to lunch, talking enthusiastically. All except one, the one who was
not carrying a copy of the *FT*. The voice over was kept very topical – 'Last
week the *Financial Times* explained the reasons behind the dollar's latest fall,
investigated the new fight for the microcomputer market . . . ' and ended with
the line 'No *FT* No comment' Ambitious young executives squirmed in front
of their televisions as they were forced to see themselves as unable to comment
on these undoubtedly important topics. *The Independent* ads shown in Plate
3.16 use the same type of approach.

Strategy 4: Image

Newspapers are quite public accessories. You carry them on the train, you
leave them on your desk, you quote from them at dinner parties, so it is easy
to imagine a strategy based on 'me→them' communication. This seems to be
the approach of the *Guardian* with lines such as 'Many *Guardian* readers are
just like their newspaper. Eloquent, incisive and successful.' (See Plate 3.17.)

> # Guardian readers like buying something with a bit of individuality. (After all, they do it every morning.)
>
> **THE GUARDIAN**

Plate 3.17 *(continued)*

Strategy 5: Admiration

Why would one admire a newspaper? Perhaps because of its historical import-ance, age and experience. Perhaps because its writers and photographers win awards. *The Times* (UK) created a very well-known campaign using the idea and line 'Top people read *The Times*'. At first glance this might seem to be an image strategy, but in fact it seems more likely that it touched a different nerve. The readers attracted by this campaign were not trying to establish themselves as 'top people', but simply to share something with top people. They wanted to associate themselves in a modest way with the power and prestige of the paper. They liked the idea that what they read each morning was also read by the Prime Minister, industry chiefs and high court judges (see Plates 3.18(a) and (b)).

Strategy 6: Altruism

It would overstretch this illustration to suggest strategies based on the eco-logical soundness of recycled newsprint, or the fact that the paper was the

Plate 3.18(a)   The Times *has long cultivated the admiration which one can have for a newspaper. You may never become a high court judge or MP, but you can read the same newspaper*

profit-making organ of a desirable cause or party. Rather, the lack of a plausible strategy based on altruism signals a warning – not all motivations are appropriate to all products.

Figure 3.6 summarizes examples of the strategies generated.

Functional	Me→me	Admiration
You'll make better decisions if you read X	You will feel able to comment intelligently if you read X	You can read the same paper as the Prime Minister
Pleasure	Me→them	Altruism (??)
X is interesting and entertaining as well	People will think you trendy and intellectual if you read X	We don't cut down trees for our newsprint

Figure 3.6   *Five possible and one rather dubious ad strategy generated for a quality newspaper*

THE ✥ TIMES

We resolutely speak our mind too.
Yet The Times continues to be the most popular daily in the house.†

THE ✥ PLACE

† *It's a fact. Call us.*

Plate 3.18(a) (*continued*)

Bearing in mind the caution about the irrelevance of certain needs to certain product fields, the exciting thing about the list of needs is that it can be used to generate alternative strategies which might otherwise not have been considered.

3 The 'sales increasing tautology'

Sometimes this banal construction can suggest an idea, either for the target, or for a 'how'. The tautology first observes that to increase sales either current buyers must buy more or non-buyers must start purchasing. The obvious tautologies are then applied over and over again to give the diagram shown as Figure 3.7.

Figure 3.7 is used by taking each final box in turn and asking how such a target could be touched, and what potential it would represent. These 'potential' targets can also form the objective of qualitative research. The 'new to

Plate 3.18(b) (*continued*)

product field/new uses' box (bottom right) is the most challenging, but can also be the most rewarding. This is where breakthroughs such as running shoes for everyday wear (Reebok), computers for individuals (Apple) or Post-Its (3M) as office stationery belong.

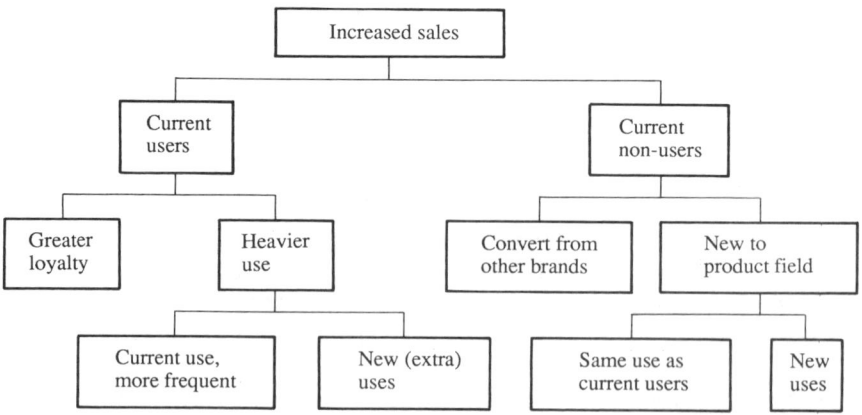

Figure 3.7   *The sales-increasing tautology. To use it review each of the final six boxes and ask what could be done to increase sales in this manner*

4 *Value chains, difference analysis*

The idea is to examine any little differences between the product and its competitors. The value chain refers to the process which converts basic raw materials into something of value to the consumer. By focusing separately on each of the stages at which the competitors *add value* to the raw materials, it is possible to consider each of the elements which could differentiate the offer to the consumer. Clearly the chains will vary from industry to industry, but a general example is given in Figure 3.8.

By far the best way of drawing up this chain is to trace its path physically – go to the factory, talk to the people who buy the raw materials, who control the manufacturing process, design the packaging. Inspect the distribution outlets, visit them with a salesman, talk to the retailer, compare the products, their prices. Watch the competitive communication and, last but not least, use the product and its competitors.

Burgerking (hamburger restaurants) promote as their point of difference 'Broiled, not fried' – a difference in their manufacturing process; Wendy, one of their competitors, focus on a difference in raw materials with their famous 'Where's the Beef' campaign.

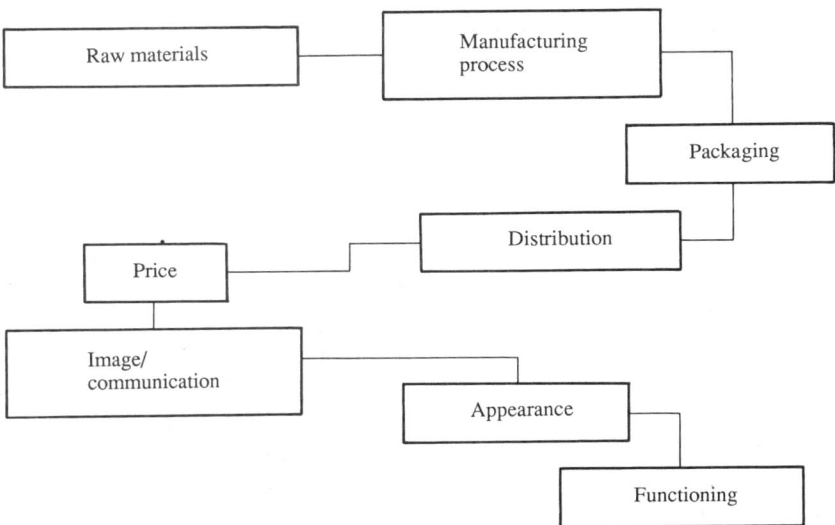

Figure 3.8 *A value chain used for comparing the different elements of 'value' added by competitors*

5   *Qualitative research*

The target for advertising is essentially a qualitative idea, a question of understanding the consumer's feelings. Getting from the quantitative definition of target in the marketing strategy to the qualitative advertising target is often helped by qualitative research.

The marketing strategy, the research carried out in the development of that strategy or one of the four suggestions given so far for finding an advertising strategy should generate:

1   A quantitative description of the likely target audience(s), from which to recruit some qualitative respondents.
2   A list of candidate 'hows' which can be presented verbally, on concept boards or using pictures, competitive advertising or advertising from other product fields.

The objective of this research is not to test the concepts. The concepts are simply stimulus material presented with the objective of exploring the sensitivity of the target audience to different approaches and appeals. This is why competitive advertising (or relevant styles of advertising used in other product fields) may be a very useful source of stimulus material.

Qualitative research investigates human feelings. In producing good advertising it is human understanding (whoever the humans – company chairmen, doctors, employees, housewives or children) that provides the inspiration.

Here are some examples of snippets of 'human understanding' that have been helpful in producing advertising in the past:

- Tea drinkers like to believe they're 'addicted': 'I'm not nice to know 'til I've had my first cup in the morning!' etc.
- Parents like to peek on their children playing with their toys, unaware of the parents' presence: 'They're in a world of their own.'
- Mothers see through the eyes of their children: 'When I see an ad that I think my children would like, I know they'll be after the product.'
- Women who dye their hair are afraid it might change colour: 'I often think I'd like to try it, but I'm afraid other people might notice.'
- Children like to believe their breakfast cereal will make them big and strong.
- Buyers of expensive watches like to believe that they need to know the time to the exact minute.

6　*Consumer experience*

Similar to the value chain approach, and a technique often requiring qualitative research, the idea is to follow the experience of the consumer with the
product:

- What is the process of buying? A revealing, but labour-intensive experience
  is to accompany consumers to the point of purchase, and ask them about
  the decisions they are making, as they are made.
- What is the effect of owning? The convenience, the pride, the security?
- What is the process of consumption, how, when, in what company, with
  what feelings? Maxwell House in France have long underlined their quality
  with the promise that just one spoonful makes a perfect cup. The advertising touches a chord through its acute observation – everybody adds just
  a little touch more to guarantee the flavour.
- What is the effect of consumption? or the effect of not having the product
  available?
- Recast the product benefit in terms of the consumer need or problem. For
  example, the proposition of a savings product might be: good returns for
  capital tied up for a fixed period. This proposition can be recast in the
  consumer form: 'Are you one of those people who has accumulated a tidy
  sum for your long-term future and now doesn't know the best way to hold
  it?' Contac 400 was a remarkable drug which dried up the symptoms of a
  cold. They recast their benefit into the memorable line: 'Hey, you with the
  runny nose.' (See also the ads for Radio Rentals and Midland Bank, Plate
  3.19.)

Another way of coming closer to the consumer view is to work out how you
would sell the product personally to a (relevant) friend or acquaintance,
preferably by trying it out in practice.

7　*Life cycle*

The life cycle concept suggests that sales of a product follow a somewhat
predictable pattern from launch to grave, often represented as in Figure 3.9.
　Some products, particularly in technology-led markets such as systems
razors (Gillette's Techmatic, Wilkinson Sword's Bonded, Gillette's GII, Wilkinson's WII, Gillette's Contour and Wilkinson's Profile) do follow this pattern,
but many do not. Well-managed brands such as the mega-washing powders
Tide in the US or Persil in the UK enjoy a seemingly indefinite maturity phase.
　However, the concept that there are identifiable phases in a product's life,
and that products have a tendency to follow the cycle unless they are

Radio Rentals (TV and video hire, UK)

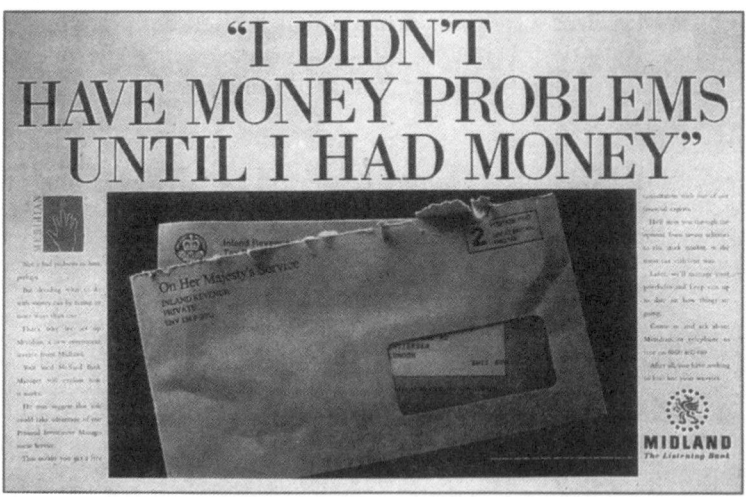

Midland Bank, UK

Plate 3.19   *These ads both found their propositions by looking at their services through the eyes of their consumers. By recasting their differential advantages (marketing strategies) from a consumer perspective they found more original, and probably more arresting, advertising propositions*

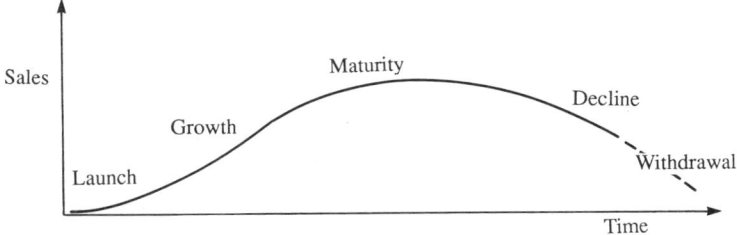

Figure 3.9   *A typical product life cycle*

continually rejuvenated, can be useful for planning marketing and advertising strategies.

Overall sales trends only provide a vague indicator to life stage. More telling are the ratios brand aware/non aware, tried/aware, new users/all users, lapsed users/all users, light users/heavy users and how these ratios move over time or compare to the competition. Other indicators are trends in average weight of use, trends in average age of users and technological strength of product compared to competitors.

Each phase suggests typical advertising approaches:

Launch

The key objective is to establish the brand as quickly as possible in a position which a me-too will find difficult to pre-empt. This usually implies a clear and singleminded communication of the differential advantage defined in the marketing strategy. Launch advertising is often relatively easy to create as the idea of the product is news in itself. However, branding or name registration may be a tough nut to crack.

Growth

The advertising campaign for growth will usually be a development of the launch campaign. Post-testing the launch campaign, analysing who has been attracted and why, whether they stayed with the product and why, provides the input for evolving the next stage of the advertising. This will either be a continuation of the launch idea, or a shift in response to the reactions of the trialists and repeaters interviewed.

Maturity

The product has a steady group of regular buyers. The first priority is to reinforce and subtly update the image that is appreciated by this group. Any advertising produced has to be pre-tested among users for consonance and appeal and major changes in advertising should be treated with the greatest of caution.

The basic positioning of the product is well understood and secondary benefits can thus be featured to ward off upstart competition or gain some new users e.g. Fairy Liquid's main differential advantage is 'gentle on the hands'. In their mature phase they also run 'value for money' ads showing how their superior product can even beat cheap brands on economy.

A low-fat spread launched as an economic alternative to butter, extended its usage successively by attracting slimmers and then health-conscious users. Such broadening out of the product's benefits can build resistance to competitors – any competitor has to pick off one of the segments, which in itself may not be large enough to justify the investment. Ideas which promote extra usage or new types of use to established users are also appropriate at this stage.

Decline

The key implication to take out of indicators showing decline is that something in the basic product/marketing mix is running out of steam.

It is essential to understand what is causing the decline. Is the fundamental consumer need reducing (as is the case for porridge oats – consumers with centrally heated houses do not need a hot breakfast) or are customers buying something else instead (cars instead of railway tickets, though they still need travel).

A decision then has to be taken. Either the decline is accepted and the product managed for profit, probably with minimal advertising investments, or the problem has to be redressed.

If the objective is to recover sales, it is pointless blindly pushing the strategy of previous stages, a story the consumer already knows and is in the process of rejecting.

To redress the problem, whether for a functional or image product, it is essential to go right back to the marketing strategy. It may be necessary to modify the product and packaging, find new sources of users (a notable achievement of Brylcreem, the outdated hair oil, which jumped at the opportunity posed by new wet-look and sculptured hairstyles among the young) or to spin-off new products (Ajax cream from Ajax powder, Robin spray starch from soak-in starch). In the case of image products, where advertising is used to create the differential advantage, the task is to evolve towards the new positioning and segment, without alienating remaining loyal users.

Handling alternative advertising strategies

Applying the ideas described above should generate two or three plausible strategies. A question then poses itself – should these concepts be tested competitively and only the best be progressed to creative work, or should each concept be briefed for creative work and the resulting campaigns tested comparatively?

Logically, it would seem systematic and efficient to run evaluative concept tests on the 'hows' and chose one optimal concept for the creative briefing. In most cases it is, in fact, better to progress *each of the alternative solutions to creative work*. Surprising, but true for the following pragmatic reasons:

1   The inherent unpredictability of creative solutions means it is good practice to produce alternative creative solutions. A famous academic paper[7] argues that agencies should make more effort than they do, to produce multiple creative solutions. Many experienced clients demand that their agencies present them with more than one creative option. This means that agencies either have to produce several creative solutions to one, identical, brief or they can brief several different concepts and produce one creative solution for each of them (compare the two diagrams in Figure 3.10). Creative teams find it hard to generate more than one treatment of a particular concept. They tend to home in on one preferred solution and reject all others. Besides, it is simple human nature to resist repeating a task which one feels one has already fulfilled satisfactorily. Second or third concepts, on the other hand, renew their inspiration and thus help them to generate a range of alternative creative solutions.

2   Testing the concepts before they are translated into creative treatments is often not workable. The usual research approach to such a question is to formulate the concepts as explanatory paragraphs and present them to respondents on cards ('concept boards'). The respondents are then asked questions about the 'appeal' of the concepts. Unfortunately, consumers do not react to concepts in the same way as they do to the resulting creative executions. Recall, for example, the two concepts for McClan Whisky which would have to be shown on boards, for testing:

How 1:   McClan is the whisky for people with the maturity to discern the true values in life. The brand for those who choose the authentic and true over the ephemeral and gaudy, those who value 'being' over 'having', who make their choice according to their own tastes and not to impress other people.

How 2:   McClan embodies the spirit of France today, that of the new adventurers. Although dynamic and aspirational, ambition is

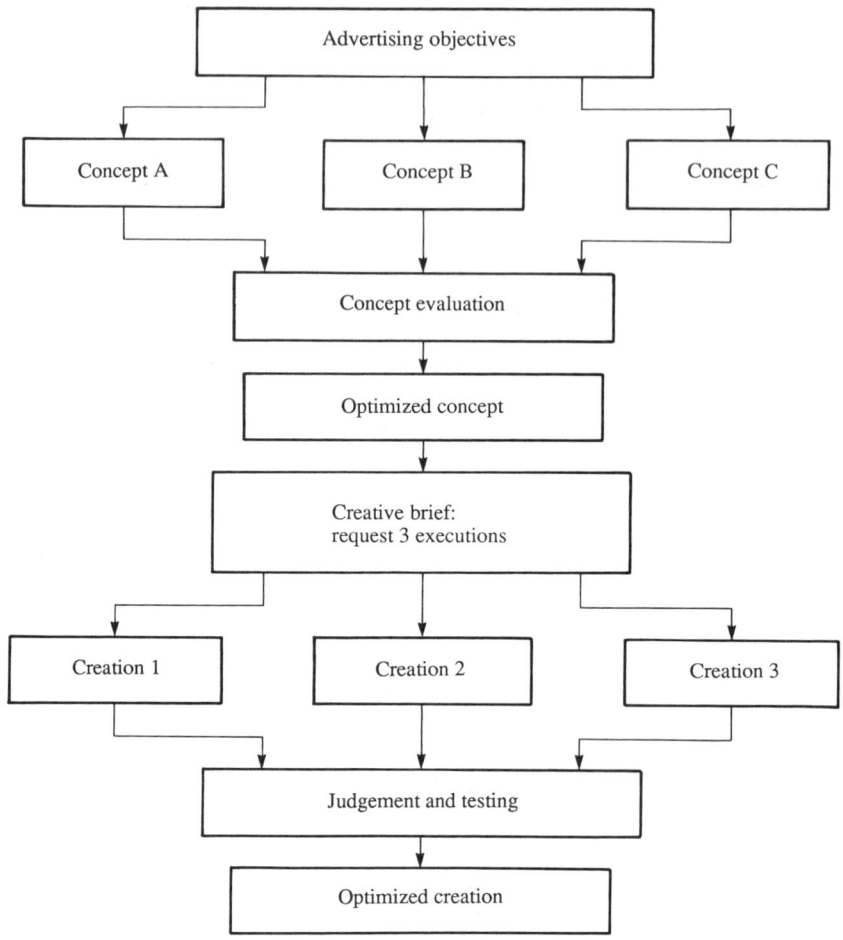

Figure 3.10(a)   *A logical procedure for dealing with alternative 'hows' or advertising concepts*

directed to self-expression and appreciation of culture and not social standing or political power.

3   The last reason is the most interesting – the differences in effectiveness of the selling concepts may be smaller than the differences found between the appeal of the creative approaches that they generate. Thus, even if it was possible to measure the difference in appeal of two concepts, this difference might be turned around by the creative solutions. In practice, the value of alternative strategic concepts is often less in getting the advertising strategy 'absolutely right' than in terms of inspiring the creative process.

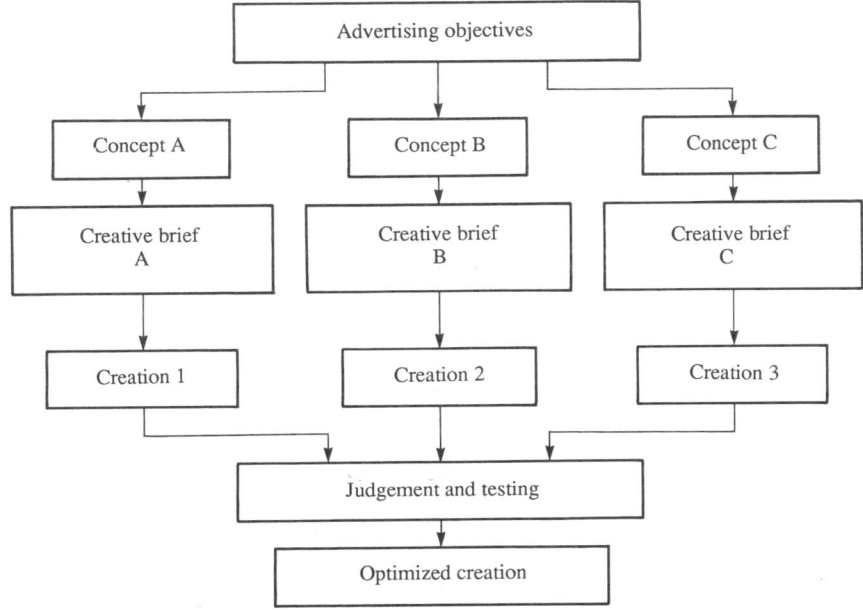

Figure 3.10(b)   *A pragmatic approach for benefiting from alternative advertising concepts*

Figures 3.10(a) and 3.10(b) visualize the alternative development processes.

Following the process described in Figure 3.10(b) implies generating two or three sets of answers to the questions What?, Who? How? and Media? which will each be presented to the creative team as alternative creative briefs.

Armed with this precise definition of the ad, or rather ads, required, the next task is to translate this definition into a helpful brief for the creative team.

Notes and references

1   Book, Albert and Cary Norman, *The Television Commercial*, Crain, 1970.

2   Lavidge, Robert C. and Steiner, Gary A. 'A Model for Predictive Measurements of Advertising Effectiveness', *Journal of Marketing*, 25 October 1961.

3   Colley, Russell, *Defining Advertising Goals for Measured Advertising Results*, Association of National Advertisers, New York, 1961.

4   Vaughn, Richard, 'How Advertising Works: A Planning Model', *Journal of Advertising Research*, vol. 20, no. 5, pp. 27–33, 1980 and 'How Advertising Works: A Planning Model Revisited', *Journal of Advertising Research*, vol. 26, no. 1, pp. 57–66, 1986.

5   Ratchford, Brian T., 'New Insights about the FCB grid', reproduced from the *Journal of Advertising Research*, August/September 1987, pp. 24–38, Copyright (1987) by the Advertising Research Foundation.
6   *Business Week*, 21 October 1985, 'Cover Story'. Survey quoted was carried out by Booz, Allen & Hamilton Inc, New York.
7   Gross, 'The Creative Aspects of Advertising', *Sloan Management Review*, Fall 1972.

4 Creative briefing

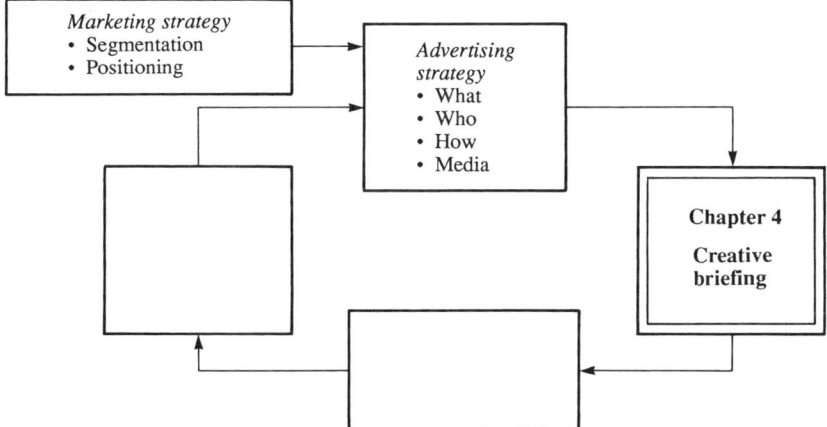

The creative brief is the culmination of the strategic work. It is the distillation of weeks of thought and discussion. It is the bridge (or bottleneck) between all the knowledge accumulated and the thinking done by the 'strategy' people, and the creative people who are meant to be converting that knowledge and strategy into a real advertisement. It is the springboard for the creative idea (see Figure 4.1).

It is not easy to provide a good creative brief, and good briefing requires a number of skills. The first is having genuine ideas to give to the creative team, rather than simply processing and summarizing relevant data. The second is being able to express and communicate those ideas to the creative team. The third is knowing what to throw away. It takes real willpower to leave out all the fascinating background and analysis of which the strategy team is so proud, but which will not help the creative team.

In practice, creative briefing is always verbal as well as written, and contact between briefers and creative team does not end with the delivery of the

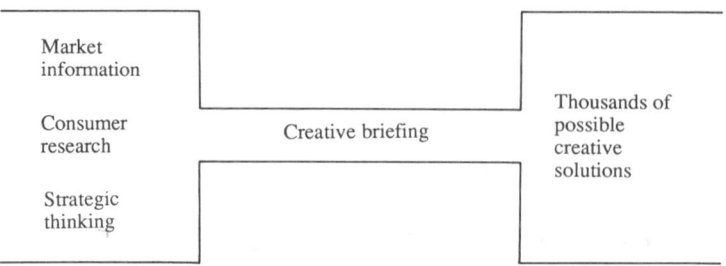

Figure 4.1   *The creative brief is the bridge or bottleneck between strategy and creation*

written brief. This direct and continuing communication obviously deepens the understanding given to the creative team. However, this chapter concentrates on the theory of the briefing and the written brief, for if these are inadequate, long verbal talk-abouts and chummy daily chats are unlikely to compensate.

What is a creative brief?

A creative brief should be a complete definition of the ad. It should be possible for anyone reading the brief to imagine the ad that is required and to see the idea that is in the brief, even if they cannot themselves satisfy the brief in terms of the creativity expected.

Writing a creative brief cannot be treated as a discrete task which can be described or taught, comparable to instructions for baking a cake or ironing a shirt. This book could fairly be entitled *How to Write a Creative Brief* for the starting point must always be the marketing strategy followed by the various stages of advertising strategy development.

In fact, the hardest part of creative briefing is usually knowing exactly what you are asking for. This critical question is answered by the advertising strategy, and was covered in the last chapter. By the time you sit down to write the creative brief you must already have clear in your mind what you want the ad to do and how you think it is going to do it. The ad's objectives, the key motivations to be touched within the target audience, alternative means for doing this and the choice of media should already have been specified in the advertising strategy and agreed between agency and client.

At this point the challenge is to translate the *advertising strategy* into a clear and simple *brief for the creative team*, in consumer language, and without marketing preoccupations (such as brand share or business objectives) clouding the issues.

Remember – if on reading the brief it is not possible to visualize a plausible, if uninspired, advertisement there is something muddled or missing in the brief. Re-read the brief and ask yourself: If I came to this brief afresh, would I know what was being asked for? If the answer is not a clear 'yes', ask 'Did I even start with a clear idea of the ad that was required? Then you know whether it is back to the strategy drawing-board, or just a question of rewriting the brief.

The need for a written brief

The original reason for demanding a written brief was to formalize the act of briefing and establish it in agency procedure. The briefing created a clear division between the task of strategic thinking and that of creative inspiration. Years ago the processes were frequently lumped together – advertising development was a matter of hitting on one complete 'advertising' idea. Dividing the task into a rational, data based, 'message' problem and an irrational, creative leap, 'vehicle' problem, was a massive evolution in agency thinking.

These days most agencies automatically produce a written brief for all, and any, creative work. There are two good reasons for this: First, clarity. If creative briefs are not captured on paper it is too easy to be vague. Writing is a good discipline. In some ways a written brief acts as a legal document might – agreed with the client it confirms what is being requested from the agency, and it is proof of what was transmitted at the briefing to the creative team. Second, the creative brief presents the most obvious and convenient juncture for management to control. The most efficient way to monitor whether an account team is coming up with creatively fecund, well-reasoned advertising strategies is to monitor the creative briefs they produce. To enable management to control the quality of briefings, without having to sit in on all briefing meetings, it is essential to have the brief summarized on paper.

The insidious evil of creative briefing forms

Given that a written brief should be produced, many advertising companies and agency managements feel that it is a logical next step to introduce a fixed format for briefing.

Forms simplify and control business, indeed, business would grind to a halt without them – purchase orders, holiday request forms and so on. To managerially-trained minds the advantages seem obvious – briefs written to a pre-determined form are easier for management to scan and control. They remind scatterbrained or inexperienced staff of the vital elements to include. They are easily translatable to help harmonize international accounts.

Before looking at the dangers of creative briefing forms, it is worth having in mind an archetypal creative briefing form, or creative work plan as it is often called, following the nomenclature of its originator, Young & Rubicam (Figure 4.2).

The original CWP emerged from Y & R's New York office in 1970. It clearly answered a crying need in large international advertising agencies because it, or close plagiarisms, were adopted over time, by Ted Bates, Ogilvy & Mather, Grey Advertising, McCann Erickson and Doyle Dane Bernbach to name but a few. Via these international agencies and their clients (who also appreciated the systematization brought about by one universal form) this simple little form was eventually modified and adopted by many local national agencies worldwide.

Creative Work Plan

Client..................   Brand..................

1   Key fact

2   Problem the advertising must solve

3   Advertising objective

4   Creative strategy:

    (a)   Prospect definition

    (b)   Principal competition

    (c)   Promise

    (d)   Reason why

5   Mandatories and limitations (if necessary)

....
   Account   Date   Copy supervisor

Figure 4.2   *A typical creative work plan*

Despite this impressive vote in favour, such briefing forms have enormous disadvantages.

The problems with forms

An inherent weakness of such forms is the risk of the imposing one catch-all form of advertising. Forms tend to adopt an implicit model of how advertising works. This then encourages anybody using the form to adopt the same model of how an ad functions, and force their problem into that type of solution.

For example, the CWP imagines that the advertising will 'solve a problem' by making a 'promise' which it justifies with a 'reason why'. This is similar to a USP-type advertising model as described in the previous chapter. This model is appropriate to products where the decision depends on the consumer being 'convinced' of some simple proposition. There are certainly products where this type of model applies. In the late 1960s when the CWP was being developed that approach dominated marketing. Nowadays, where near-identical products are often competing in saturated markets, the roles of advertising have been extended and developed, and this approach has severely limited applications. Concentrating on only one type of advertising would place an impossible restriction on an agency operating in the current competitive climate.

Focusing on the brand's problems is also a strangely negative way of looking at the world – what is the problem facing an excellent new product waiting to be launched? Advertising is, at least as often, a question of opportunities.

However, these weaknesses could probably be remedied with perhaps a range of forms, and more subtle titles. These are not the key problems with forms.

The critical problem with forms is that they trivialize the importance of creative briefing. They put creative briefing on the same level as purchase orders and holiday request forms.

Forms exist to be filled in. Any normal person handed a form has an almost irresistible urge to fill it in and expects to be able to do so without too much thought. Given a creative briefing form it is too easy to complete it as if it were an application for a provisional driving licence. Forms act as a trellis up which grows a bindweed of idealess, empty words.

A creative brief should be the summary and distillation of weeks of work, thought and discussion. Forms belittle this effort by providing the wrong titles and spaces for the manager who has developed an original creative brief with thought and care. Meanwhile, they lead less diligent managers down well-trodden thought paths, rather than helping to generate anything new.

In the example briefs presented at the end of this chapter there is an illustration of the sorry type of creative brief that is all too frequently encouraged by a rigidly formatted brief.

The blank piece of paper

The opposite extreme to a form is a blank sheet of paper. If you know what you want to say (and respect the 'golden rules' explained below) you are probably best off creating your own structure on a blank piece of paper. Purists might also say that if you do not know what you are going to say you are also best off with a blank piece of paper. This will at least bring home the fact!

Simply think of the brief as a letter from yourself to the creative team. Think of their reactions as they read it. Think of the questions they will ask. Think of the mistakes or blind alleys they must avoid. Test the brief by asking the question mentioned earlier: If I came to this brief afresh, would I know what was being asked for?

A compromise

The blank-sheet approach is basically very sound, but it does demand a certain level of experience, discipline and effort. It is useful and possible to develop a briefing system which guides and supports the briefer, without trivializing the task or restricting the output.

The secret of such systems is to generalize the requirements which a good brief must satisfy. (J. Walter Thompson's 'T-square planning system', based on asking open-ended questions such as 'Where are we?' 'Where could we be?' is an example of this type of approach.) The system must define the issues which the brief must tackle, without dictating its precise form, and without imposing a particular type of advertising.

The key component structure

The aim of a structure for creative briefing is to be 'tight' enough to offer real guidance or discipline to the authors of the brief, and yet 'loose' enough to allow them to develop whatever type of advertising is appropriate. One way of getting to such a tight–loose control, is to formulate the brief in terms of the key issues it must resolve.

These requirements help to structure the brief, and afterwards to test its sense and completeness. The six essential components of a creative brief are:

1   The key facts behind the brand's current position.
2   A statement of what the advertising can genuinely be expected to achieve.
3   A caricature of the person who is to be affected by the advertising:
   - His key beliefs and attitudes now, that will be exploited, reinforced or changed.
   - What he is doing now.
   - Qualitative feeling, developing a human image.

4 A statement of what the advertising must communicate to change the target's beliefs, attitudes or behaviour.
5 Guidance as to the tone of the ad (e.g. 'aspirational' or 'avoid humour').
6 An explanation of the choice of media.

Rather than labour through these 'key components' describing in the abstract what good answers should be like and the pitfalls that exist, let us consider an illustration.

Good and bad briefs – an illustration

The 'goodness' or 'badness' of a brief has to be a subjective measure. The only objective measure is the quality of the resulting advertising and reluctantly, one has to admit that this is not a reliable indicator. Good briefs do not automatically lead to great creative work and good creative teams are not held back forever by lousy briefs. The illustration uses an analogy which both simplifies and exaggerates the commonest errors, to highlight the dimensions where a 'good' brief scores over a 'bad' one.

An analogous situation to 'brand meets consumer' is boy (Jacques) meets girl (Jill). The (business) objective in both cases is to 'win her hand'. Jaques' situation is, however, clearer and simpler than that of the typical brand. He knows both himself and Jill reasonably well (i.e. good data on product and consumer), he has a clear overall objective and a clear target.

The two 'briefs' produced by Jacques 'le fataliste' and Jacques 'le stratégiste' are shown in Figure 4.3. In each case the 'creative work' required is a script for his first, hopefully of many, evenings with Jill.

Le fataliste has chosen to use the Creative Work Plan format, while le stratégiste follows the key component structure.

The example is humorous, but it serves to illustrate some very typical differences between good and bad creative briefs which are less clear in more complex real life, where good and bad tend to be merged together.

First, consider the two treatments of the key facts behind the brand's position, the context explained to the creative team:

Key facts, background

Good briefs explain both the reasons behind the situation described (my clothes, past advertising) and information that will be built on in the creative strategy (well-informed, engaging talker). Bad briefs typically report in detail all the current problems without stressing the elements that could provide leads to a solution.

The context should concentrate on issues material to the briefing. The fact that other men of thirty-nine are happily married or the reason why Jacques was dropped by his last user represent all the waffle about business issues that often creeps into briefs ('this brand accounts for 50 per cent of Smith's revenue' etc.). However, comments which close off blind alleys (he cannot change his wardrobe/packaging) are often worthwhile.

What can the ad genuinely achieve (or problem and objectives)

An ad cannot 'sell more product'. Nor can it convince people that black is white. The aim of the ad has to be some simple task the creative team can immediately understand and believe in.

A good brief concentrates on consumer perceptions and the changes that could benefit the brand (bring into question current perceptions, excite her curiosity). Bad briefs tend to concentrate on the product itself and its problems (I'm lonely, want a girlfriend, qualities not appreciated). Often good briefs are more forward-looking and positive, because their writers already have a solution in mind.

Characterize the target audience

Typically, this is the area of creative briefing which is most drastically under-exploited.

A good brief must give insights into the target's beliefs and motivations which will allow the creative work to hook on to some motivating quirk in the consumer's mind. What is the point of all the qualitative research and hype about understanding the consumer if in the key document in the ad development process, the consumer is reduced to a 'heavy buyer, middle-income household, with children'?

The Jacques example illustrates the point beautifully because the target is so precisely defined – it is Jill. One individual, known and measurable on every statistic.

Typically, the bad brief believes that a quantitative definition, in this case 100 per cent precise, is what is required. The good brief gets under the target's skin and indicates how she can be touched. In this case three vital pieces of information:

- She is not really seeking hyper-modishness, she would feel upstaged by such a man.
- It is not really for herself that Jacques' image is a problem, it is for her friends (hence give her a rationale for her choice).
- She knows and likes Jacques already (so telling her he is loyal and faithful would be flogging a dead horse).

Jacques 'le fataliste'

Key fact

I'm thirty-nine (an age when most men are married and sharing the joys of a happy family with a loving wife) not very good looking or well-dressed. My last user dropped me for a younger brand because I'm perceived, not very fairly, as old-fashioned.

Problem the evening must resolve

I'm very lonely and I'd like a girlfriend, but women tend to dismiss me as old-fashioned without seeming to appreciate my positive qualities of loyalty, fidelity, intelligence, a certain wit and humour.

Evening's objective

Make Jill realize that loyalty and fidelity and other qualities of personality are really more important, long term, than charm, good looks and a flashy image.

Creative strategy

Target: Jill
Principal competition: All other, and particularly younger, men
Promise: She'll be happier with me in the long run
Support: Because I have the traditional qualities of loyalty and fidelity

Jacques 'le stratégiste'

Explain the key facts behind your current position:

I'm perceived as old-fashioned, partly because of my clothes (which I cannot change in the short term) also because of past advertising which stressed my loyalty and fidelity which (though valued) are perceived to be dated as an approach. On the positive side, I am well-informed and can talk engagingly on many contemporary topics.

What do you genuinely believe the evening can achieve?

Bring into question Jill's perception of me as old-fashioned and excite her curiosity to know more.

Characterize the target

She sees herself as being fairly with it, though far from hyper-modern. She cares intensely what other people (her friends) think about her escort. She already has a reasonably accurate impression of me and my character, and is kindly disposed towards me.

State what you will communicate to her to modify her attitudes

Demonstrate in my conversation my wide range of interests and experience. It is less important to stick to subjects that interest her than to give the overall impression that I am well-informed and a 'fascinating person to be with' thus justifying her choice of escort.

Tone

Lighthearted, even humorous. Direct claims on specific attributes should be strenuously avoided.

Media choice

Dinner in a little-known restaurant in a fashionable part of town.

Figure 4.3   *Two briefs for a first date with Jill*

Communication (promise/support)

The key characteristic of a good brief is that it has *already done part of the creative work*. It may as a result offer two or three alternative creative strategies or 'hows' (as recommended in the last chapter). Each one will contain an idea. These ideas will all be strategically based but angled differently and probably based on different snippets of data.

Le stratégiste's 'how' made use of his real attributes 'well-informed, able to make engaging conversation'. The idea is that repositioning as 'fascinating to be with' would make the attribute 'with it' less critical (see 'positionings' in Chapter 2). An alternative 'how' would have been to attempt directly to establish the belief that being interesting is more prestigious than being fashionable. Another possibility would have been to make it seem smart for fashionable women to attach themselves to conservative men (c/f Lady Di and Prince Charles).

A more aggressive, comparative approach could have been tried – e.g. that all fashion-conscious men are insecure.

A weak brief, on the other hand, offers no help beyond the bare bones of what has to be done. Often this is apparent when reading a brief because the so-called creative strategy introduces no more than has been implied in the background and objective. In the case of le fataliste the promise and support are exactly, and no more than one would have anticipated from the problem and objective given.

It is typical also, that the bad brief deals with the most crucial parts of the brief (target and message) in only nineteen words. While verbosity is undesirable and a short summary thought (such as 'fascinating to be with') is useful, this degree of terseness is invariably a bad sign.

Ironically, the tighter the brief, the easier it is to have creative ideas. The French say: 'L'Art vit de contraintes et meurt de liberté', but this is, of course, no proof of validity. Rather, convince yourself by trying this simple test. Consider these three instructions: draw me a picture; draw me a picture showing happiness; draw me a picture showing the happiness of finding something that was lost. Which conjures up ideas the most readily?

Tone

Qualitative research covering competitive advertising often suggests what sort of advertising seems right. Consideration of the type of consumer decision also gives information as to type of tone most appropriate. Much current advertising works simply by creating images and associations – 'the *tone* is the message'.

Tone is often an important strategic decision and should not be left to the creative team to resolve. Often the creative team will have a natural sensibility to this aspect but the nuances are sometimes subtle – zany humour may work well for a vodka, but not for a whisky. Guidance saves wasting time.

Choice of media

It is amazing how often this topic is left untouched in the creative brief. Media is a critical part of the advertising strategy, and the creative team need to understand it. Clearly, they have to produce the right material physically, but apart from this the reasoning behind the choice of media often adds to their comprehension of the message or tone being aimed at. The idea of dinner in this little-known restaurant in a fashionable part of town is richly evocative. . . .

Naturally, a brief must also include practical details such as timing, legal constraints and mandatory inclusions. If the budget is strictly limited there is no point in keeping the bad news a secret until the creative team come back with an idea that costs thirty-six times too much.

This, then, gives some idea of how to write a creative brief. Here to round up are five golden rules.

Five golden rules

1 Strenuously sift out 'non-ideas'

An ability to recognize a non-idea at a distance of three printed pages, is a quality that will be of inestimable value to you in all creative briefing, and possibly in many other important areas of your life.

A non-idea is a concoction of words which sound something like an idea, but in actual fact contain nothing useful at all. The brief informs no less if the phrase is omitted completely.

They can often be spotted by trying out the negated thought, e.g. 'the ad must be impactful, memorable and original' negated gives 'the ad must lack impact, be instantly forgettable and unoriginal'. Another way of smoking them out is by looking for indefinite descriptions which avoid an explicit notion, and asking 'What x?'. Common examples are 'for the way you want to be' or 'for the life you lead'. Ask 'what way?', 'what life?'.

An overlong 'brief' full of non-ideas which do not affect the creative team's thinking is illustrated in Example 4 below.

2 Recognize when you don't have an idea

One of the reasons that people fall into the arms of non-ideas, is the lack of a real idea. An ad, as we have seen, consists of two ideas, one strategic and the other creative. Creative people sometimes don't come up with an idea on time, and sometimes strategic people don't. It is best to be honest. Don't go and hide in a pile of platitudes such as 'this chocolate bar really is delicious' or 'make the choice of car tyre seem more important than it actually is' and fool yourself that you've solved the problem. Talk to the people you're keeping waiting, tell them how far you've got and where you've been looking. The discussion itself may unlock something. At the very least you are not undermining your credibility by handing out mudpies that look like biscuits.

3   Be singleminded

The extraction of the essential idea from among all the interesting but peripheral ones, is one of the most important skills of the advertising strategist. As with marriage and writing books, *much has to be given up to create anything worthwhile.* Offering ten ideas is no better than giving none – the best idea will not shine out from the other nine, it will get lost. It is essential for you to choose.

Similarly, the fact that you could write a thesis on your product and its market must forever remain concealed from your creative team. The sole contribution of a hugely expensive research survey may have been to invalidate your favourite strategy. So be it, the survey is history and gets no memorial in the brief.

4   Avoid business and 'businessese'

The advertising strategy should start to move from business preoccupations and jargon towards consumer language and priorities. The transition should be complete by the time the creative brief is written. Creative people should be, and need to stay, as close as possible to the consumer. It is up to the strategic people to move nearer to that world, and not to try and teach the creatives to understand the world of production lines and distribution channels.

The brief should contain only words which could be used directly to, or by, the consumer. Consumers do not eat countlines or other portable snacks, nor do they shop for fmcgs (fast moving consumer goods). If you don't want or expect to see words such as 'ubiquitous' or 'inscrutable' in your ads, don't put them in your brief (even if you know what they mean).

Similarly, the brief should contain only information which can be turned into a meaningful consumer benefit. For example 'from their new factory in Essex' is almost certainly worthless businessese, as is the chemical content of the product being sold. Consumers tend to care much more about what they get than how, or by whom, it was made (in the largest factory in Europe, by the lowest-cost producer). It is not just manufacturers who fall into this trap. I noticed an ad for the London Business School the other day, whose headline and 'selling story' was based on the fact that they had doubled the number of places available on their 'Senior Programme'.

5 Give examples

Examples of other advertising (from competitors, from other product fields, from the past or from abroad), an 'account man's uncreative ad' or references to films, television programmes etc. can all help to communicate the type of ad that is being sought. These are often found useful by creative teams, who are used to thinking in these terms.

Examples of creative briefs

Creative briefs are often felt to be rather private and are rarely published. Given the practical nature of this book, however, such coyness would be unacceptable. This last section is given over to real examples of good and bad briefs.

Based on the criteria for good and bad briefs presented above the following four examples (two good, two bad) have been adapted from real briefs produced recently, in earnest, by major, international advertising agencies. The briefs have been chosen from product fields that are generally known to be difficult i.e. where clear product benefits are not available and advertising plays an important role in promoting the products.

Clues to the brand's actual identity have been disguised to preserve confidentiality and, in the latter two cases, to save embarrassment.

Briefs 1 and 2 are presented as model briefs (though no brief is above criticism or improvement) while Briefs 3 and 4 represent how not to do it and are accompanied by a sarcastic commentary. The briefs were chosen as examples of briefing – in each case the underlying strategy (where it exists) may or may not be valid.

Brief 1: Skanda breakfast cereal

Skanda was a small brand that had been around for years with virtually no advertising support. For the previous four or five years it had been growing steadily of its own accord so that eventually the client decided it merited a small ad budget.

Its Scandinavian positioning from the launch in the 1960s was felt to be of no further use and its healthy/slimming image was, technically, not supported by the real product attributes.

Creative brief for Skanda

Background
Skanda is a really good product, adored by its users. Its users tend to be relatively loyal and heavy compared to other cereals. When non-users are given free samples to try many are converted to regular use. There is enormous potential if we can only get people to try it. Although users like to believe the product is healthy (slimming/fibre), no real claims can be made in this area. The product and packaging suggest healthiness and our policy is simply to let people go on believing it.

Role of advertising
Generate curiosity and hence trial among people who don't know the product.

Target
Fairly well-off, older (thirty-five to fifty) women, because of the high price and the preference among older women for 'healthy/high fibre' cereals. They will be buying this cereal more for themselves than for their family and children.

Qualitative target
She is intelligent, wily, ingenious. She is self-assured, confident in her choices and enjoys discovering things for herself that are a bit different, original, unusual, away from the 'mainstream'.

Message
It is always very difficult to attract the non-users of a brand. They tend to look at an ad, see that it is not for a product they use and move on. We have to find an idea which catches their attention for a few seconds and makes them notice the product Skanda. Naturally we want to imply that the product is enjoyable, but the message is simply 'here is something interesting, different, rather special, rather select'.

Tone
Following the description of the target, we suggest that humour, or rather wit, is the best way to create the intrigue that we want. For example this is the type of woman who watches Lexicon, the intelligent, more intellectual quiz show on television. Hence some series of puzzles, or slightly clever ads which she will feel clever to have 'got' would be a good way to attract attention to the product. This would also suggest that it is a somewhat 'esoteric' cereal, for more discerning women. The approach used in the scripts for Swansong Milk seem to us to be just right here! (*Swansong was another agency client. The campaign involved a series of slightly bizarre situations in which the milk was surreptitiously pilfered by characters who then tried to deny what they had done. It created both intrigue and a zany humour around a rather dull product, while also suggesting that it was delicious.*)

Requirement
A campaign of two or three executions for press or posters. The ads should work on just one viewing, though, as the schedule is light, so a woman may only get to see one execution.

Brief 2:   Cara washing powder

The agency had been asked to produce launch advertising for Cara, a washing powder, for a country where it had never been distributed before. It was not as effective (or chemically active) as the out-out-damn-spot brand leaders (Ariel etc.) but its price was at parity. The positioning was 'neutrality to the skin' and the market segment was people who wanted to provide security for their skin, and particularly mothers.

Creative brief for 'Cara'

Background
By far the largest part of the market is for all-usage, heavy-duty, low-suds washing machine powders such as Ariel, Persil, Dash and this is where Cara will be competing. The most important characteristic of these powders is that they are effective, the second consideration is that they are not too damaging to the clothes. Several powders deliver these benefits already, either by promising effectiveness at low temperatures or by adding a fabric softener. Cara offers a new benefit – while some detergents are corrosive and chemically violent (they can even cause mild skin irritations) Cara is made from ingredients chosen for their mildness and non-violence.

Advertising objective
To establish Cara as a mainstream washing powder in competition with those mentioned above, but with the additional benefit of neutrality to the skin.

Target
The target is not women who have a genuine allergy to powerful detergents – our prospects do not perceive a problem with their current powders. The ad has to touch satisfied users of heavy duty powders and attract them to the idea of a less aggressive, safer powder. We are looking for women who demand a reasonable degree of effectiveness, but who have a psychographic tendency towards caring for themselves and their family, protecting and playing safe. They are the women who avoid food products with colouring or preservatives or who drink decafeinated coffee. This tendency to 'softer' and 'lighter' products is growing in other markets (beer, cigarettes, cheese and dairy products) and it seems likely that a detergent positioned on this 'more natural – less aggressive' axis will discover a growing need.

Message
The best way to express the idea of a detergent made from ingredients kind to the skin is to present it as suitable for families with babies and small children (c/f Johnson's Baby Shampoo). The message is: Its effective but safe formula makes Cara ideal for the family, suitable even for laundry that will go next to baby's senstive skin.

Tone
The ad should latch on to the growing enthusiasm for naturalness, health and caring for the body, but it is also vital to adopt washing powder values –

bright, white clothes, lively washday – which will position the product along-side other machine powders. It must not be 'medical'.

Requirements
We are going on television in order to be alongside the mainstream washing powders. At this stage we need ideas for two or three thirty-second films.

Brief 3:   *Occasion ready-to-eat dessert*

This brief concerned the launch of a ready-to-eat dessert, sold in a little plastic pot from the chiller cabinet of the supermarket. It is included here because it is a classic example of a 'form filling' brief and one can well imagine the content of this brief being thought up as the author read the titles off his Creative Work Plan. It resembles the old joke:

Parachutist to passer-by: 'Excuse me, can you tell me where I am?'
Passer-by: 'Certainly sir, you're hanging from a tree.'

. . . it is technically correct but gets the creative team precisely nowhere. Comments are provided paragraph by paragraph.

Creative brief for Occasion

Key fact
The quality of Occasion, its elaborate construction (sponge, mousse and topping of real fruit pieces) elegance and classiness, puts this dessert in a class of its own in the chiller cabinet, by far the most luxurious of currently available desserts.

(Comment: This background concentrates solely on the product and the manufacturer's point of view. Elegant and classy in a plastic pot?)

Problem the advertising must resolve
There is a risk that the consumer will perceive Occasion as just another chilled dessert.

(Comment: A moment ago it was in a class of its own. This pertinent problem indicates precisely why marketing and advertising strategies would be useful.)

Objective of the advertising
Make sure that Occasion is positioned well apart from other chilled desserts by suggesting its use in rather more prestigious circumstances, which haven't already been used by other chilled desserts.

(Comment: Is this realistic when the product will be found among the other chilled, plastic-potted competition on the supermarket shelf?)

Creative strategy.
Target: All consumers of chilled desserts.

(*Comment: Does this help visualize the ad? 'Hey you chilled dessert consumer, want to add some real pazzaz to your dinner parties?'*)

Key competition: All other chilled desserts.

(*Comment: Another utter non-idea.*)

Promise:
- A unique dessert, really different from the others.
- A dessert that you serve for occasions that are rather special

(*Comment: Positionings have to respect reality; these promises do not. Beyond this they are too vague to inspire the creative team. The shame of it is that this brand had a real product difference.*)

Support: Elaborate, sophisticated – the presence of sponge, real pieces of fruit.

(*Comment: Non-idea – it adds nothing to what is already assumed.*)

Mandatories (if necessary):
- Appetite appeal.
- Type of scenario – after dinner, special sophisticated occasions ... to make use of name.

(*Comment: Not actually necessary but there was an empty space on the form.*)

This brief is really saying: 'We've got another premium-priced food product to launch. Have you got any ideas as to how we could make it seem different, or at least how we could lodge it in people's memories?' A good creative team might come up with the goods, but at least have the grace to give them all the credit and don't claim to have written a brief.

Brief 4: *Yummy, a chocolate countline*

This is one of those awful, long-winded and well-written briefs that take twenty minutes to read and afterwards you're not sure that it really told you anything that you didn't already assume.

Despite its length the brief manages to give no specific indication of target, message or ad objectives. The author appears to have limited his study of advertising to learning the jargon, which is used fluently throughout.

Creative brief for Yummy

Introduction
The launch campaign for Yummy has been extremely successful in creating trial and acceptance of the brand.

(Comment: Non-thought. What is interesting is why people tried and accepted. What in the launch campaign caused this?)

Our task is now to develop advertising which communicates a long-term and sustainable brand positioning in order that Yummy may maintain its position as a major volume brand in the chocolate confectionery market

(Comment: Non-idea – how about a short-term, unsustainable positioning ... in the baked bean market?)

Background to the brief
We know from research that Yummy is a complex brand that has succeeded in breaking the standard marketing conventions.

(Comment: This knowledge is, however, not to be shared with the creative team.)

It has very broad usage and perceptions and future development should not aim to narrow this position by dictating a strict role for the product. However, we must create a positioning and personality that allows the brand to stand out from the crowded market and guarantee it a regular and primary niche in the consumer purchasing repertoire.

(Comment: This helps one visualize the author walking round in circles and wringing his hands. It certainly doesn't help one visualize the required ad.)

In order to achieve this the positioning must be:

● Individual
● Discriminatory
● Motivational

Research has revealed that the strength of the brand stems, currently, solely from the product and, most specifically, from the eating experience ... we should take this strength and communicate it in a way. ...

(Comment: this is the crux, what way?)

... that gives the brand character because by doing this we will ensure that our communication is unique to Yummy.

Three alternative positionings
After lengthy discussion and deliberation ... we now go through these alternative positionings in detail:

1   Light but satisfying. The positioning is based on the light texture of Yummy which allows the product to deliver satisfaction in several ways. First, the product melts in the mouth as soon as you bite into it so you get an *immediate chocolate taste which is satisfying*[1].

(Comment: Try launching a chocolate bar that doesn't melt in the mouth with an immediate chocolate taste that is satisfying.)

Second, the texture and ease of eating allow the product to fill a gap or meet a chocolate need *without being too heavy or 'claggy' an eat*[2]. This leaves you feeling *satisfied without being weighed down*[3] and has the additional benefit of *alleviating the guilt*[4] usually caused by indulging in a chocolate bar ... light you can *eat it anytime, anywhere*[5] ... *don't need to need it*[6] ... *on the move*[7] ... *food and taste satisfaction immediately but feel less full*[8] and guilty ... lightness may be communicated physically or mentally, but satisfaction must stem from the specific nature and delivery of the product.

(Comment: Giving too many ideas is as bad as giving none. If a single benefit of lightness was isolated, and related to a need of the target audience we might get somewhere. The above paragraph offers no less than eight possibilities (indicated by italics and raised suffix).)

2   Absorbing eating experience ... it is the actual sensation of eating the product that produces the pleasure ... the important thing is it can happen anytime and anywhere because it lasts only as long as the product lasts – it is transient.

(Comment: This is the old 'problem of pleasure' once again – how can advertisers continually find new ways of expressing ever-more delirious levels of delight? This paragraph certainly doesn't offer the solution – say it's over quickly?)

3   Contradictions ... it looks like a solid chunky bar of chocolate but when you bite into it you have the surprise of the soft, light centre. That surprise, even when previously experienced, is an important part of the pleasure of eating Yummy. It never ceases to satisfy and provide enjoyment. The thought is that there is more ...

(Comment: more? Explain this 'more'. This is what we need to create some advertising.)

... to Yummy than meets the eye and because of this ...

(Comment: Of what?)

... it will surprise and intrigue you every time you eat it.

Brand personality and executional guidelines
Yummy must develop a brand personality ... remind ourselves that Yummy is competing in the countline market ... convenient, accessible, modern and contemporary way of eating chocolate ... must communicate that the product can be eaten anytime and anywhere ... further guidelines below. The final requirement ... the advertising should be highly distinctive and different.

(Comment: This last line is not only a non-idea (should advertising ever lack distinctiveness?) but an insult to the creative team who suffer permanently from the eternal pressure to be distinctive and different.)

Perhaps examples of bad briefs do not seem very instructive. The point of these two examples is that they are so typical of briefs currently produced – on the one hand, neat tautological platitudes filling spaces on a form, on the other a marketing treatise on what needs to be done which never comes down to saying *how* it proposes to do it. Reviewing these two rather extreme examples may help to make the simple achievements of the 'good' briefs clearer.

If you have the time and the nerve you might find it interesting to try to produce creative work for each of the four briefs!

5 Creative development (pre-testing)

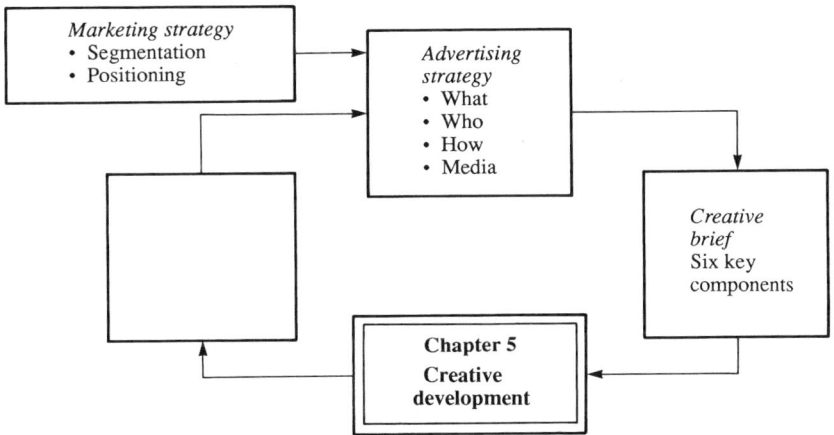

This chapter is about the period between the creative team coming up with their first response to a brief, and the final go-ahead for major investment behind the chosen creative work.

The decision to run with a certain creative idea is one of the most crucial that an advertising manager has to make and one on which the agency tends to feel strongly. Pre-testing is a controversial issue and in general the creative development period is characterized by tension – tension between client and agency and between account group and creative team, by time pressures, budgetary pressures, risk, bluff and doubt.

'Expert opinion' vs 'objective tests'

Expert opinion

One of the most thrilling moments in the client–agency relationship must be the presentation of new creative work. Until then all the discussion is somewhat theoretical, but at that point marketing jargon and hope give way to plain words and pictures. This is the climax of agency life, when agency and client come together to see the culmination of months of their combined efforts. Exciting though it is, this is a tricky situation, and potentially counterproductive.

A 'client-led philosophy' (see Chapter 1) implies that the agency's clients are asked to *assess* the creative work presented to them. They are expected to accept the work, or to ask for modifications, or to reject the work out of hand.

An 'agency-led philosophy' emphasizes the role of the agency as 'the advertising experts' – clients are expected to respect the agency's 'creative judgement'. Agency directors say with pride: 'We fought for six months to get this outstanding piece of work approved.'

But the shocking truth is that even the best advertising professionals are unable to assess the effectiveness of proposed creative work presented to them in limbo, with any degree of confidence.

This may sound controversial – advertising managers, marketing men and certainly directors of advertising agencies, are assumed to be employed partly for their ability to judge advertising. They are expected to be able to examine advertising presented to them and, on the basis of their 'experience', estimate whether or not the advertising would have the desired effect in the marketplace. They are expected either to approve the ad or be able to say why it would not be effective and suggest ways in which it could be improved.

In fact, most ad professionals feel very uncomfortable when asked to perform this task, recognizing intuitively its impossibility.

And it is impossible, simply because estimating the effectiveness of advertising implies *guessing how a typical member of the target audience would react to it* when he came across it in its advertising medium. There are five simple reasons why advertising professionals are unable to do this:

1 The 'expert' is rarely in the target audience and (with the possible exceptions of Filofaxes and Porsches) he will not have a direct, personal and typical relationship with the product. (Typical here really means 'representative'). He may be typical of one customer, but he cannot be representative of the whole target.
2 He views the advertising knowing the brand and the product in advance. Similarly, he has prior knowledge of the advertising strategy – there is no chance that the ad tells him something new, or that he fails to understand the message. Ironically, it may be that the longer one works in advertising the less possible it is to react naturally and normally to advertising, and the more tainted one's judgement becomes.
3 Not only is the advertising professional trying to double guess the consumer, he is also conscious of the effect of his comments on his

colleagues. The agency representative is tied up in mental convolutions as he tries to guess how his colleagues and client are going to react. For his part, the client is sensitive to the feelings of the people who have faith in the ad, enough to present it to him. He doesn't want to upset and demotivate his suppliers with harsh criticism. This further erodes his ability to react spontaneously or naturally to creative work.

4   Past experience provides scant guidance in the area of advertising. Past data on the effectiveness of other campaigns is hard to come by anyway, but the problem is actually more subtle than this. If the best ads are the freshest, the most innovative, the most unexpected, then the scripts or scamps that originally represent them are going to be the hardest to compare to previous advertising, or previous advertising experience. As with genius and madness there is a fine line between the best advertising and the biggest flops. The scripts and scamps which *might* spawn the best ads are also those which run the greatest risk of being misunderstood or rejected by the consumer. If an ad is predictable for the professional it is also predictable for the consumer, and as such, probably suboptimal.

5   The experts are not financially or emotionally disinterested. The systems of remuneration used by most clients to compensate their agencies give the agencies a vested interest in 'selling' the creative work. It is difficult to estimate a precise value to the agency, but any creative work can be assumed to represent a significant investment. The agency's representatives cannot ignore the agency's business interests and so are bound to lose some objectivity and with it any residual ability to judge the advertising. The client thus finds his chosen advertising adviser giving him biased advice (though he doesn't know how biased – if he overreacts he might distrust something genuinely good!). Beyond this he has a time schedule to preserve and an eye to the effect his decision will have on his own image (creatively enlightened? off his rocker?). These aspects are a further hindrance to his ability to 'judge' the advertising presented.

The inability of experts to judge effectiveness is implicitly recognized by the industry in the way it gives itself prizes. The advertising industry awards 'creativity' which it never tries to justify on the basis of market effectiveness. The prizes are awarded by a panel of judges, usually from within the advertising industry, who do not consider a campaign's effects, but simply give a subjective opinion on its appeal in their eyes.

Separate award schemes are run for case histories which try to prove how effective advertising has been. These case histories invariably use research and statistics and never rely on a critique of the creative input!

In the UK, where both reward systems are fairly well established, unkind observers have pointed out that there is no systematic relationship between the two types of award – as often as not the two types of award are won by different agencies and for different campaigns. Advertising 'experts' claim to judge 'creativity' – imagination, originality, entertainment value, beauty even ... but not sales effectiveness.

Faced with new creative work it is simply not possible for advertising professionals, client or agency, to say with confidence whether an ad will be effective in the marketplace. Meetings which set people up to do this, and people who claim to be able to do this, are mistaken.

Objective tests

Perhaps it is no great surprise to be told that it is unsafe to rely on the subjective opinion of the professionals involved in an ad's production. What is more interesting is news of a research technique that can be applied to proposed advertising to give some *objective* estimate of its likely effectiveness. Unfortunately the truth here is equally grim.

Prediction, in any sphere, involves two tasks. A doctor predicting the fate of his patient, a farmer predicting his next harvest or the weatherman predicting tomorrow's rainfall, all go through the same two-stage process. The first stage is to identify the current situation with similar situations encountered in the past (diagnosis), the second is to retrieve the results, the outcomes, of the similar past situations, from which a prediction can be made (prognosis).

Similarly, being able to test advertising confidently, implies being able to:

1   Identify or classify the ad so that it can be compared or matched to other, past advertising.
2   Use past results, the measured success or failure of previous similar advertising, to project the expected success of the new ad.

For example, if one could classify an ad as being easily recalled and could also say that previous ads with good recall had worked well, one could infer that the ad in question would probably be effective. (For a generally applicable rule one would also need the information that ads which were not recalled well were not generally found to be effective. Without this information there would be a risk of rejecting good ads, at the cost of missed opportunities and an acrimonious relationship with the people who produce the advertising.)

Matching a new ad with past advertising

A key aim of any advertising is to get noticed among the clutter with which it will appear. For this to happen, it seems reasonable to assume that the advertising must be fresh and original, different from the competition and from ads which have been seen before. Good ads will therefore not usually physically resemble other advertising. Hence there has to be some 'measure' for matching ads.

Many measures have been suggested for matching ads – recall of ad, recall of message or brand, memorability over time, comprehension, credibility, attitude change, measures of persuasiveness, interest, identification, involvement, emotional response, liking ... and a case can be made for the validity of each of these measures in particular circumstances. Our first concern is the straightforward reliability of these measures.

A measure is said to be reliable if the same measure applied to the same entity on different occasions always gives the same result.

Response to advertising has been shown to be significantly influenced by:

- The environment in which the ad is viewed.
- Position in reel/magazine.
- Elapsed time since viewing.
- Research company and the rules used for classifying responses.
- Respondent (e.g. user/non-user, old/young, intelligence).
- The type of prompts used (e.g. verbal vs visual, product field vs brand name).
- Product category.
- Previous level of media spend of brand.
- New campaign vs established campaign.
- New vs established product.

These influences imply that the same creative work tested in several separate, seemingly valid tests, would probably give a considerable range of results. They also mean that creative work of theoretically the same quality, but applied to different products or different brands would generate different results.

It is theoretically possible to control or compensate for the *testing* variables, though the number of influences makes this difficult. Even if such a method is devised, the existing data banks of past research will usually not be comparable to the new information gathered.

However, compensating for the influences of *product*, previous media spend, new campaign etc., is even more difficult. Building up a data base for each brand is a sensible solution, but implies severely limited amounts of data.

It is fair to say that the lack of directly-comparable measurements is usually a severe limitation when trying to match new ads with past advertising.

The validity of the measures

Validity asks whether a measure is a good predictor of effectiveness. Those measures which in the past have shown themselves to be most closely associated with effectiveness, are the most valid for pre-testing an ad.

To establish validity, measures need to be related to the desired action. How does attitude change affect brand switching? What is the meaning in sales terms of emotional arousal, as monitored by reduced electrical resistance of the respondent's skin? Can 'Intention to purchase' measures or 'persuasion' scores be treated as equivalent to sales? What relative value should one attribute to one measure compared to another? For example, recall is good, so 45 per cent is better than 40 per cent, but how do those extra five points of recall compare to an extra three points on the persuasion score?

The industry is notorious for its inability to evaluate its past successes or failures. This endearing foible is celebrated in advertising's most famous quotation: 'I know only half of my advertising works, but I don't know which half.'[1] This, compounded by the variety of measurements and the difficulty in comparing measures (see above) means that it is extremely difficult to obtain sufficient past data to validate any measures convincingly. The quest for validation is thus somewhat hampered from the start.

Here are three other issues about validity, which you might like to ponder briefly, before we tackle the question of how best to pre-test advertising:

1   *Type of product* – in practice no two ads are going to score identically on all measures, but if by chance an ad for a brand of jeans and an ad for a brand of cheese did score identically, would the ads be equally effective? The discussion of advertising strategy underlined how different advertising approaches are appropriate to different types of product. The evidence available[2] suggests that while, for example, a factor such as recall may make a critical contribution to effectiveness in some circumstances, it is not even a necessary condition in others. In other words, a measure which is valid in one set of situations, might not be valid in others, say for different products.

2   *Legs v stockings* – do you want the man you fancy to say to his friend: 'She's got a stunning pair of legs' or to say: 'She was wearing very glamorous stockings last Tuesday'? A subtle but important difference. Most advertisements are meant to be creating value for their sponsors and not for themselves, in the way that a frame should show off a picture. Are reactions to the ad itself (e.g. recall, liking, understanding or recognition) relevant if the right feelings, prestige or information are not associated with the product?

3   *Types of advertising* – how can one devise a test which is equally sensitive to the strengths of both thinking and feeling ads? Research has shown

that 'verbalized' tests, such as asking for recall, penalize visual and feeling ads, which may do much better in recognition and emotional/physiological measures. Who can afford to use a test which threatens to cut out either one or other range of powerful advertising tools?

Research companies would love to establish a standard measure and a fixed methodology and develop norms applicable to a variety of product fields and brands of varying familiarity and penetration. The chance of producing an accurate, validated system of this type is currently completely remote.

Given the basic shortage of data, the complexity and multidimensionality of advertising and the wide range of different types of consumer decision, it is impossible to derive simple relationships between the many possible measures and their effects or their relative worth.

However, this does not mean that the measures referred to above are meaningless and uninteresting. It simply means that using any one test or measure as a universal yardstick of effectiveness would be myopic.

The constructive approach

Given that expert judgement turns out to be a mirage and objective testing systems a holy grail, how should the effectiveness of an ad be measured before vast investment is spent on production?

The answer is in fact that there is no answer – it is unrealistic to expect to rate an ad precisely on some index of effectiveness.

Giving the go-ahead to produce a new advertisement will always involve uncertainty and risk. Even with exhaustive pre-testing, there is no such thing as a 'safe' ad. Every ad produced balances on a tightrope between being suboptimal through being tedious and being a disaster through being misconstrued.

The challenge is to design pre-testing research which provides the most meaningful information on the advertising, from which to form a judgemental decision. The final decision will always rest partly on knowledge and partly on judgement and the outcome partly on luck.

The 'constructive' approach tries to analyse the ad through pre-testing chosen according to the way the ad is expected to work. The constructive approach adopts the modest objectives of:

1 Trying to weed out advertising that would not be effective.
2 Moving seemingly acceptable ads further in the right direction, towards greater (though still unknown) efficiency.

This approach is described as constructive because it does not try to prove that the ad is effective. It sets out to generate information which will help the decision makers estimate whether the ad achieves certain minimum requirements and further, whether the advertising can be improved in some way.

The ABC of good advertising

The minimum requirements which any ad must satisfy fit neatly into the mnemonic ABC. Specifically they are:

Good levels of attention and branding

This is axiomatic – if the ad fails to attract attention, so that it is not read or viewed, it cannot affect the consumer. If the consumer fails to associate the advertising with the right brand, the advertising cannot benefit that brand particularly.

American Express recently had to withdraw a television ad in France which featured Luciano Benetton. Viewers only recalled Mr Benetton (and a field of coloured sheep). This sort of error should be picked up in advance.

Measuring attention (or 'impact') is not a simple matter and creates a certain amount of controversy. For example, measures may penalize visual ads or be easily influenced by the type of test. However, the criticisms concern a failure to estimate impact accurately, and do not bring into question the importance of impact itself. Similarly, *measuring* branding is a controversial issue (e.g. which is more meaningful – spontaneous or prompted identification. Is it sufficient for the ad to be recalled when the product is seen?), but the fundamental need for the ad to be associated with the correct sponsor is never questioned.

The ad must communicate what it set out to communicate, as defined in the advertising strategy

The advertising strategy summarizes the best estimate of what the ad should communicate to be effective. Thus it forms the best available guide against which to assess the ad.

It can happen that while testing creative work, a better, alternative advertising strategy is discovered or that the original advertising strategy is found to be wrong. The criteria for an acceptable ad will then change. This is rather like a little boat in a big sea steering by the only star that is visible. If some recognized landmark comes into view, it switches to this new and better frame of reference. One has to be pragmatic. When tackling a pre-test, the best guide available initially is the advertising strategy which summarizes the thinking that has gone into the ad's development up to that point.

Alternatives to ABC

Other criteria (such as *credibility*, *recall* and *liking*), have sometimes been suggested as essential, but the evidence supporting them is pocked with counterexamples. These criteria are not fundamental, comparable to *A, B and C*, but simply *measures* for getting at those three. Credibility is sometimes part of the communication objective, recall may be useful in estimating attention or branding. Liking can be an indicator of attention or again a communication objective.

Since most advertising sets out to persuade, direct measures of *persuasion* or *'effect'* are sometimes proposed as requirements. The argument against such global criteria are that they are at too high a level.

Advertising objectives should be set on the lower level, that of communication (not that the ad 'should persuade people to buy more', but *what it should say* in order to achieve that). Ideally, research on strategy should be done before the ad is written. If this is not possible, pre-testing which verifies the strategy may be useful. Checking persuasion usually means harking back to the strategy level, and is less likely to provide diagnostic information on the working (or non-working) of the actual creative product.

A further requirement sometimes suggested is *'campaignability'*. In most situations, advertising is not expected to be a one-off. Just as it would be folly to change strategy with each ad, it is equally undesirable to change creative approach. Even in situations where the message will vary (e.g. a political campaign) from ad to ad, visual, tonal or thematic links are needed to help the viewer pull the different ads into one coherent whole. However, there are one-off ads which are worth making. For this reason it is best to recognize that the branding in an ad is often dependent to a large degree on campaignability, and to consider the campaignability factor when assessing 'branding'.

The 'palate' of pre-testing research

The idea is to use research, often of several different types, in order to develop a 'portrait' of the ad under examination. As the portrait becomes more complete, it becomes more possible to make an informed judgement. The aim of the research is to understand how the ad is working, what is working, what isn't and whether the ad can be improved in some way.

Carrying on the analogy, this section discusses the paints that are available to colour the portrait.

Recall

Description
The oldest and most frequently applied test. It has the winning advantages of intuitively plausible meaning and being easy to carry out. Respondents are shown the ad among some other material and subsequently asked to recall it, its main message, the brand, product field etc. The measure is quantifiable and thus suggests comparability across ads.

Uses
The measure is used first as an indicator of attention or impact. It is also used for branding – if the correct brand name is recalled, and communication – if the correct message is recited.

Discussion
Measurement is *sensitive to many extraneous factors.* Those related to product (familiarity, interest), to the method of the test (content of surrounding material, order in showing, elapsed time before questioning), and to the definition of recall (any recall of any element of the ad, specifically the brand name, spontaneous or prompted etc.).

The variety of methods and the influence of the product and type of ad make it *difficult to compare results.* A recall level for a washing powder ad will not be directly comparable to that of a car or perfume ad; is it comparable to that for an air freshener, whose penetration is half that of the washing powder?

Ads which have a simple jingle or catchphrase are favoured by verbalized recall tests, visual ads do less well – is it consistent to demand the same levels from both while believing that ads can work in different ways?

Even the assumption that if the ad is impactful the ad itself will then, inevitably, be well-recalled has been brought under question. It may be possible to attach strong associations to a product with an ad which itself is not easy to describe or bring to mind. Alternatively an ad may work very strongly against a very small proportion of viewers. This may be sufficient in the marketplace, but such an ad could look pretty sick in a recall test.

Recall is only ever claimed to be a necessary factor (not sufficient in itself to make an ad effective). How important is every extra point of recall? Is recall among people outside of the target audience of any value? Recall seems to be unrelated to persuasion[3] i.e. recall and persuasion measure independent phenomena, one concerning the ad and the other the ad's subject. If persuasion is good but recall seems low, is there a critical level of recall below which the ad cannot be accepted? How should one be traded off against the other?

Conclusions
Recall gives a precise, quantified score but is usually meaningful only if the test is identical in methodology to others involving the same or similar products and type of advertising. In many cases it is extremely difficult to assess whether the level of recall is good or bad.

Recall is tantalizing for advertising professionals because they sense that it is meaningful data which tells them something, but its actual usability often seems to fall short of their expectations. Even for the simplified task of comparing alternative executions it is not evident how to trade off recall against other (probably independent) strengths such as persuasiveness.

Persuasion

Description
Persuasion is more difficult to quantify. It is a subtler, more qualitative concept than recall. Different indicators of persuasion can be employed – changing intention to purchase or changes in brand preference, self-assessment of persuasion, added value in blind vs named tests or even actual behaviour.

Since persuasion is a matter of change, its measurement implies collecting and comparing two sets of data. In quantitative research this means either taking pre- and post-measures with a reasonable chunk of intervening time, or using a matched (control) sample not exposed to the advertising. Both solutions are cumbersome and expensive, especially when two or three alternative advertisements are being compared.

Qualitative research is reasonably good at capturing the change, especially where it is conscious so that respondents can talk directly about how persuasive they find an ad. Qualitative research is essential to understanding how an ad persuades and how it can be made more persuasive, even though it fails to measure the persuasive power in any precise way.

Uses
In a sense, persuasion is at a higher level than communication – it doesn't matter what has been communicated (or if each respondent takes out the same thing) as long as the ad persuades.

Persuasion measures often vindicate the advertising strategy (if this has not been assessable beforehand), rather than the creative approach. To diagnose and improve an ad it is essential to understand why it is or isn't persuasive. This usually means finding out what the ad is communicating, and how.

Discussion

Measures of persuasion generally have a good record for correlating with sales effectiveness. (See the McCollom Spielman results[4] for one data-rich example, though that research is not without its critics.) Persuasion is, therefore, easier than, say, recall to evaluate in the absolute. However, it is less clear how it should be traded off against impact, involvement or recall.

Measures of persuasion taken in a pre-test seldom depend on the ability of the ad to gain attention and brand. These two factors will evidently modify the persuasive power of the advertising in the real world.

Conclusions

If an ad persuades it is probably effective, but persuasion is often difficult to measure directly. As often as not it has to be deduced from successful communication or from attitude change, relying on the logic which originally dictated the message. Attention and branding often need to be assessed in addition.

Communication

Description

Functional factual communication is the easiest to measure. Communication of emotional and value associations pose significant problems. Communication is essentially a qualitative phenomenon and finding out what an ad communicates is often best investigated by qualitative methods. Quantitative research techniques can be used but in this area they tend to replicate the result which can just as easily be obtained qualitatively, while being less rich.

Worse, quantitative results can be misleading, as it is often difficult to formulate questions which really get across to consumers what information is being sought. For example 'Do you think this is a moving ad?' can be interpreted to mean 'Was it meant to be moving?' or 'Did you personally find it moving?'.

Uses

It is a fundamental prerequisite for an ad to communicate what it set out to according to the advertising strategy.

Discussion

Questions direct consumers' minds, perhaps away from the aspects which were really most important. For example, consumers realize that advertisers are trying to get over a message and the question 'what did this ad tell you' will get them trying to work out and play back what that selling message was. In fact the first and strongest impression from the ad may have been something quite different, for example their *personal reaction* to the message. It is essential to allow respondents to add those important little qualifiers such as: 'But I thought What rubbish!'

Research companies have tried to develop more sensitive techniques such as cognitive response or 'thought listing' – list all the thoughts that went through your mind when you first saw this ad. The problem here is that the responses become so numerous that it becomes difficult to process the data in a quantitative way. The data is rich but unmanageable.

Conclusions
Pre-testing research has to find out what the ad communicates. The research has to be designed and executed sensitively to avoid misleading simplifications.

Attitude (perceptual) change

Description
This measure has the advantage of being close to what many ads set out to do, but in addition the data is often easy to record quantitatively. Attitudes are most frequently recorded as ratings on 'semantic' scales (e.g. rating brands on a five-point scale of effectiveness, 1 being ineffective and 5 being highly effective). Alternatively, attitudes can be recorded as levels of agreement with given statements. As with persuasion, pre and post-measures or matched samples have to be compared.

Uses
The measure is one step on from communication and one step back from persuasion. Its main value is for checking communication, but also that the communication is indeed pushing the respondents in the right direction towards persuasion.

Discussion
Attitudes are very complex – it is easy to collect mountains of overlapping data. No single statistic can represent attitude change, so it is less easy to process than, say, recall. Some way has to be found to cope with the multidimensionality of the measure – are all the attitudes monitored equally important or are some critical to the purchase decision and others incidental?

Measuring attitude change can have the advantage of focusing on the effect of the ad rather than reactions to the ad itself. For example, where respondents are asked to rate the product on some key dimensions before and after viewing the ad rather than being asking directly what the ad told them.

It is usually not clear whether the changed attitudes will affect sales. However, following the belief that the advertising strategy is the best 'theory' of how the ad will work, measuring attitude change usually provides meaningful data for developing the ad along the lines chosen.

Conclusions
If the ad has objectives stated in terms of attitude change, then attitude measurement makes good sense. Even when this is not the case, attitude change may be a subtle way of investigating communication.

Attitude change is not, however, a universal answer in pre-testing. For example, in impulse markets where distribution is often the key marketing variable, and advertising's role may be simply to make the brand salient, more and more favourable attitudes would not be significant.

Attitudes towards the ad (liking)

Description
Liking is easily measured by both quantitative or qualitative methods. In fact it is difficult to *avoid* taking this measure because everybody wants to say whether they like an ad or not. It has intuitive meaning and forms a direct comparison between ads because respondents rate an ad against their own idea of a norm.

Uses
The main argument for using 'liking' is the idea of communication by association – if the ad is liked the positive feelings will rub off on product and advertiser.

An alternative defence of 'the need to be liked' is that 'liking' is an indicator of impact – the viewer will watch rather than zap. However, since irritating ads have been known to have good impact, liking is probably not the best available indicator.

Discussion
Putting a value on the measure is very difficult. Well-researched surveys[5] have found no direct and systematic relationship i.e. consumers do not generally say: 'I liked (disliked) the ad for that brand, so I will (won't) take that one.'

However, there are some types of advertising where liking for the ad contributes to the positive feelings which are generated to the benefit of the product. In those cases liking may be a legitimate part of the ad's communication objectives.

Problems arise when this mechanism is assumed without justification. My all-time favourite consumer quote concerns this point: 'It's a shame Ariel has such awful advertising because it's certainly the best washing powder.'

Conclusion
Given that most advertisers would prefer to be associated with pleasant things rather than tasteless, patronizing and irritating things, liking is usually considered to be a desirable attribute for an ad. The risk is the temptation to exaggerate the importance of this easily-collected information, which often coincides with the professional's own emotional response. This is particularly true where alternatives are tested qualitatively, as respondents usually insist on 'choosing' the one they like best. In such cases qualitative researchers have to be very disciplined to analyse the data objectively in terms of the ad's objectives.

Physical response/emotional response

Description
Easy to collect, given the right equipment. Physical response seems precise and scientific. Methods of collection include monitoring physiological indicators of emotional excitement such as skin resistance, brain waves or pupil dilation. Less intimate physical measures include cameras which follow the eye movements of a respondent studying an ad, or tachistoscopes which record the time lapse between seeing an ad and responding to a question such as brand identification.

Uses
Emotional response may be an indicator of impact and attention.[6] In qualitative research the emotional response is automatically communicated to the researcher and certainly contributes to his overall impression of the impact of the advertising.

Discussion
The results are always fascinating and sometimes unexpected. The difficulty is naturally in the interpretation and evaluation. It is intriguing to see the path taken by a man's eyes over the face and body of the girl in the ad. It is difficult to deduce from this information his thoughts about the car she was lying on.
    Quantified data of this nature is often difficult to aggregate and process.

Conclusions
Interpreting this data meaningfully is the big challenge – it usually needs to be interpreted subjectively in a way similar to qualitative research. As such it is likely to make most sense to a researcher who has been closely involved with the respondents, and talked to them about their experience as well as seeing the physiological measures.

Sales

Description
Currently there are three methods involving actual or simulated market response. These are area tests, split copy (or, for television, split-cable) and laboratory tests. All are expensive, and area and split copy tests require the production of finished material, so these methods are rarely used as genuine pre-tests. For this reason, we look at the details in the next chapter, which deals with evaluating advertising once it has run.

Uses
Sales tests are another higher level test, assessing overall effects of marketing strategy, advertising strategy and creative strategy, combined. As such they tend to give rather poor information on the intermediate steps which are the direct goal of the advertising.

Conclusions
Pre-tests which actually aim to measure sales effects are in fact quite rare. Perhaps, given the opportunities arising from information technology, this is about to change. However, the value of pre-tests depends on providing results before too much money is invested in production, and in suggesting the path forward to effective advertising. Currently sales-based methods score badly on both these criteria.

This list covers most of the popular measures used for pre-testing advertising. The fact that there are many different types of ad, means that different measures are needed to capture the different effects. Each of the above measures can be useful in certain circumstances. The aim in planning the pre-testing is to select the measures which will help most first, in estimating whether an ad satisfies the basic requirements of attention, branding and communication, and then how to develop its strengths.

The brushes

Deciding what measures will be the most useful is only the first part of the question. If the measures are the paints, we now come to the question of how the paints should be applied, the brushes. The way the research is set up and carried out is crucial to its validity.

Pre-testing means organizing experiments involving the target audience in order to find out about an ad's effect before investments are made in production and media. This definition makes the task sound pretty straightforward – in fact the process is beset with difficulties. Being aware of the difficulties helps somewhat in designing the research – and also in assessing the validity of the results. Here is a list of the 'traps for the unwary', which still remain, unfortunately, for the fully wary. For the latter some helpful, partial solutions are suggested.

Purity of the respondents – the blank slate principle

How is it possible that the consumer (usually characterized as 'six housewives from Wapping') has better advertising judgement than advertising professionals?

The idea of pre-testing is to design experiments, involving consumers, which shed light on important aspects of the advertising. The consumers chosen can be likened to laboratory rats (or, if they prefer, a wind tunnel). Their role is not to judge the advertising, indeed, asking consumers to *judge* advertising is an elementary mistake often made by qualitative researchers. Their role is simply to provide *experimental data* which is representative of the universe from which they were picked (e.g. suburban housewives). This data is processed by the advertising professionals, who then form their judgements. The essential characteristics of the housewife from Wappng, which enable her to fulfil this role, are her purity and her representativity.

Purity means respondents should feel and react as naturally as possible; their minds should be a blank slate with respect to the research project. If the consumer knows, for example, the name of the brand sponsoring the experiment, or that he must remember the brand names for subsequent questioning, the experiment is biassed and the results worthless. The ideal of a completely virgin respondent naturally becomes less attainable as market research develops in a country, but it is important to preserve some of the mystery. A respondent who has occasionally participated in research before will usually be acceptable, but a respondent who is, for example, pretending to be something he is not, to serve the researcher's wishes, is too sophisticated, in the old sense of the word – corrupt and worthless.

The blank slate principle is well illustrated by the example of a pre-test for a Fisher-Price (UK) ad called 'Baby'. The ad opens on an empty, sunfilled room with net curtains billowing in from high windows and a polished wood floor. A dramatic chord heralds the magical appearance of a perfect little boy on a white blanket. An enthusiastic but gentle voice-over suggests the baby's thoughts: 'Where am I? How d'I get here?' Another chord and the baby is surrounded by Fisher-Price toys: 'What's this box?, What if I push?, What if I pull ... etc.' The ad closes with the thought: 'Fisher-Price, for the most enquiring minds in the world.'

The agency loved the ad and it researched well among focus groups of women talking about babies, toys and toy manufacturers. However, when the ad was presented, without introduction, in a reel of general advertising (in fact to test impact) many mothers said they had been terrified by the opening sequence. The billowing curtains and dramatic chord had suggested Alfred Hitchcock rather than creation. When the baby arrived the mothers expected a harrowing public warning film (500 babies die each year through being left alone ... etc.) and not some plastic toys.

This information was reviewed by the agency – perhaps it increased impact? In the end it was judged to be a negative association for Fisher-Price and the beginning of the ad was changed. The point is that anyone viewing the ad knowing it was for toys missed the decidedly sinister overtones at the start.

Representativity of the respondents – the target audience principle

Pre-testing research must be carried out among members of the precise target audience chosen for the ad.

Just suppose, for the sake of example, that you had been asked to research one of those Telecom ads, run during the tourist season, which say 'It's not expensive to phone back home' in one of the gobbledegook languages spoken by tourists. Just suppose you set up a hall test in Wapping and discovered that 99 per cent of respondents found it incomprehensible. Could anybody be that stupid? In effect, yes.

If the marketing logic was valid enough to dictate the development of the advertising, it is certainly valid enough to dictate the design of pre-testing research. Criteria such as usership, or intention to purchase in the near future have a major influence on reactions to advertising, not least the initial decision of whether to pay attention.

The target audience principle was key in the pre-test of a low-budget television ad for a chain of English caravan parks. The creative vehicle was a cartoon, featuring an animated signpost whose role was, inevitably, to guide holidaymakers around the attractions and activities to be found in the parks.

The style of animation lent a certain classiness to what was actually rather a down-market product. Agency and client were very pleased with the effect. However, shown to cynical groups of hard-bitten holiday camp users, the ads generated nothing but suspicion: 'If they haven't the guts to show a real photo of the camps they must be that bad! Old caravans in the shadow of a gasworks and a stoney beach the other side of a railway line!'

Difficulties arise when the definition is psychographic (for example the 'Cara' target described in the last chapter – 'caring, protective women') or narrow, say under 5 per cent of the population, especially if they spend less than an average proportion of their lives loitering in shopping precincts. Psychographic or narrow targets (even down to 0.1 per cent of the population) work as advertising targets because the target will self-select from a broader-based media plan. This may imply that the normal methods for finding a sample are impractical.

One solution is to use computerized data banks holding profiles of people (this is more advanced in the US), or lists developed by the advertising company (e.g. of people who took one of their adventure holidays last year) and telephone recruitment/interviews.

Type of material

Advertising in an unfinished form will seem peculiar to respondents. Worse, this effect is stronger for some ads than others. Ads which depend on visual effects (the charm of babies, succulent foody shots) rather than words and argument will suffer particularly badly. More finished rough material may actually increase the problem as respondents become inclined to confuse the rough with finished material.

One solution would be to test after production, but the expense involved often negates the value of the research as the decision to change elements, or junk the whole ad, becomes untakable. Testing two or three alternatives after production is usually unthinkably costly.

The arguments for pre-testing ads again after production and before media spending are in fact good – test results on finished material are likely to be more accurate though the (measurable) cost of failure or change is higher. Many large companies (such as Mars Ltd) are hard-headed enough to make post-production pre-testing automatic. However, the political, emotional and sunk costs are high at this stage and for many companies outweigh the benefits of more accurate results.

A more viable solution is to make sure that the respondents understand how the roughs differ from the finished versions. In qualitative research, respondents can often be steered clear of presentation-related misconceptions and helped to imagine the finished advertisement by timely explanations from the researcher. In quantitative research, respondents may be helped if they are shown familiar advertising or editorial material brought back to the same rough form, alongside the ads being tested.

Observing the respondents during the research helps to reveal misconceptions which are directly related to the rough presentation.

Once a campaign is established, this problem is substantially reduced. The past executions can then be used to introduce, or illustrate, the new work (bearing in mind the need to respect the blank slate principle). This point is touched on again under the heading 'post-testing' in the next chapter, but it is worth just noting here that post-research on previous executions can contribute very usefully to the next pre-stage of development.

Artificial viewing conditions

People are not usually paid to watch ads and then asked questions on them. This artificiality is bound to affect the response to some degree, for example, by increasing concentration or rationality. Again, the bias may not be systematic. An ad with poor impact but a simple rational message may be favoured in a test, compared with an ad which would get watched, but which works in a more subtle way, say, by building up associations around a brand.

One partial solution is to create a more normal viewing environment by presenting the work among other similar material. This is expensive on a one-off basis (e.g. constructing a mock magazine filled with 'rough' ads and similar editorial, is expensive in relation to testing one press ad) but can be amortized quickly by a busy agency.

Another helpful technique is to avoid questions directly analysing the advertising in favour of questions which probe the before and after attitudes towards the product. Projective techniques ('What effect do you think this ad would have on most people watching it?' etc.) can also be useful to reduce the respondent's focus on the fact of being questioned.

Lack of effects over time

Most advertising is expected to have a cumulative effect over time (this is why media plans usually aim to touch each prospect more than once). This is difficult to replicate in a test.

The advertising itself can change the consumer's frame of reference. Lines which become catchphrases, characters which develop a life of their own, advertising ideas which are adopted into the national culture (no less) may seem quirky, strange, nonsensical at first sight. Again, this is a greater problem for some ads than others – arguably an ad which has long-run usefulness will be rejected in favour of a simple ad which 'wears out' quickly.

The implication is that rough material should be shown a number of times during a pre-test, and a range of executions may be useful to build up the feeling of a campaign and simulate longer-term familiarity. This is easier to do in qualitative research than quantitative, and indeed the quality of longevity, an idea with 'legs', is more likely to be picked up by qualitative techniques (see below).

The influence of research on research results

Taking a pre-measure in a test, to get a view on change of attitudes or a measure of persuasion, usually implies violating the blank-slate principle.

Asking respondents questions alters those respondents from other consumers. Questions suggest a certain way of looking at things, which might lead respondents to feel differently. Being encouraged to think and talk about something which is normally subconscious or at least unverbalized, changes the mental set.

There is always an order effect in research with earlier stages affecting the response later on. For example, if respondents feel they have been highly critical of the first ad shown they may try to compensate by exaggerating their liking for the second one.

The qualitative researcher can minimize the influence of questioning by encouraging respondents to lead with the issues that they think are important, or the thoughts that strike them. Pilot research before a large quantitative survey is often worthwhile in order to understand how the questions are being interpreted. Observing a proportion of the interviews once the survey is in progress also helps guard against effects of the research process.

Research has to be designed with this thought in mind, and rotations and fresh respondents used as appropriate. Loading more and more questions onto the discussion guide for a focus group or onto a questionnaire, is a recipe for generating misleading results.

These six problems are always present to some degree and inevitably bring into question the validity of the findings. All one can do is try to minimize the effects in the ways suggested, and be duly cautious when interpreting the results.

The difference between qualitative and quantitative research

Ideal data would have two characteristics. First it would capture and communicate all the information required without loss or ambiguity, second it would be easy to handle, store, compare and process.

Numbers are easy to handle, store, compare and process. Once entities are translated into numbers, or quantified, they can be processed mathematically bringing order and simplicity to any amount of data. Quantitative measures come in four varieties:

1   *Ratio scales* – these are the easiest data to handle, as they can be subjected to the full range of statistical or mathematical tools. They are ordered, numerical scales which have a natural zero. Money is a good example – £4 is a completely unambiguous entity and is twice as much as £2.
2   *Interval scales* – these are the next easiest to process. These concern things which can be easily related to a quantified scale, though the data does not allow all the mathematical manipulation that works with ratio scales. Temperature is a nice example – you can compare temperatures and even average them, but you can't add them or halve them.
3   *Ordinal scales* – these are less manageable. They are used for entities that

can be compared on a dimension, but are not readily quantified. An example would be the attractiveness of entrants to the Miss World competition. An ordering is given, but no attempt is made to estimate the winning margins. The data allows little mathematical processing, and at the same time information on the entity (beauty in this case) seems to have been lost. The data has become less rich.

4   *Nominal scales* – these are the least tractable. They are used when direct comparisons are meaningless, but it is still possible to group similar members of a population. Colour is an example. Snooker balls can be classified as red, blue, pink etc. Colours cannot be added, averaged or even ordered, but the relative size of each category can be summarized as a proportion (i.e. a number) for comparing between populations or over time.

These four types of scale encompass all the ways of converting information into numerical data. To use quantitative methods, and benefit from their simplifying and summarizing powers, it is necessary to reduce information to one of these four forms.

In normal conversation people use scales when they are the most effective way to communicate, for example: 'I earn £25,000 per year (ratio scale), I have an IQ of 102 (interval scale), I am slightly overweight (implied ordinal) and I am divorced (nominal scale).'

However, people also communicate successfully without scales, ordinal, nominal, ratio or interval: 'We feel very well off these days', 'I really fancy that new guy in accounts', 'Funny? We laughed till we cried' are the sort of terms used, and communication involves tone of voice, facial expression and gesture as well as colourful words.

Numbers and scales are not used in these latter cases because wealth, fancying and funniness are all essentially *qualitative* entities – they concern feelings and human experience. Conversion to numerical scales would involve an unacceptable loss of information. Though real and commonly recognized, they cannot be *scaled* reliably and unambiguously.

Now, researchers investigating a market prefer to handle quantified, scaled data, but they also want to capture the full richness of the information they seek. It makes good sense to get data into the form that can be handled most efficiently, within the constraint that the data must still contain all the information required.

In some cases this raises no problems – number of packs of butter bought each week clearly forms a ratio scale, so the information can be scaled with no ambiguity or loss in richness.

Other dimensions are less easy to capture. The funniness of a television commercial could be related to a five-point (interval) scale ('Please tell me on a scale of 1 to 5 how funny you found this commercial'), but it is questionable how meaningful the data is. After it has been processed will it really communicate to the user of the data exactly how amusing the ad was thought to be?

'Which of these products do you prefer?' maps overall preference on to an ordinal scale, but the information loses richness in the process, and ordinal scales are not that wonderful for processing anyway.

Differences in a population which have an on/off quality can be gathered and summarized on a nominal scale. The differences between an advertising executive who has read this book and one who has not, would be qualitative and difficult to scale (assuming it is not zero!). However, the simple fact of his having read it or not could easily be recorded on the nominal scale (read/partially read/not read). Similarly people can be grouped into categories (liked the ad/indifferent/disliked the ad).

Clearly the information is partial, quantifying the categories but not attempting to capture the qualitative differences between them. As noted above, nominal data is not very manageable anyway.

These attempts to convert essentially qualitative entities into scaled data all involve a loss of quality in the data and the use of scales which are artificial, in the sense that they are not used in real life. This is because they are not the most efficient ways to communicate such information.

Conversely, as quantitative research is made more sensitive it becomes less quantified, and so swops one set of advantages for another. For example, it is quite common to ask respondents to identify brands on a series of adjectives (Would you say that brand X was: good quality, effective, prestigious, for young people and so on). The richer these data become the more complicated it is to process and summarize them in a meaningful way.

The solution that researchers use is to employ a totally different approach for measuring essentially qualitative entities.

Qualitative research carefully creates a human contact between researcher and respondent, and uses all the tools evolved for normal human communication – words, voice, expression, gesture, anecdotes, analogies, even drawings, fantasies and imagination. The aim is to collect information of a qualitative nature i.e. that cannot be described using numbers. The data is processed and interpreted by the human who collects it, not as numbers, but as words and impressions. The same human processor then communicates his findings to the users of the data. He uses words, voice, facial expression, anecdotes, analogies, even drawings etc., to pass on the human reactions he noted.

Advertising consists of words and images designed to motivate human beings. Though some of the reactions to advertising may be satisfactorily quantifiable, many responses are of an essentially qualitative nature. The reactions which are absolutely qualitative can only be captured and processed by a human being talking to the respondents who have had the experience of seeing the advertisement, and thus require qualitative research techniques.

The implication is that advertising professionals have to use both qualitative and quantitative techniques if they wish to obtain the best possible understanding of the consumer's reaction to their advertising. No pre-testing exercise is complete without qualitative research.

Sample size in advertising research

Both quantitative and qualitative research can be carried out on a small or large scale, from a sample of one to thousands. (The most frequently used sample size is one – that used when people speak from their own case.) The technical difficulties both in collecting and processing qualitative data, mean that sample sizes for qualitative research exercises are often smaller than those used for quantitative surveys.

Fieldwork is expensive, so it is desirable to use the smallest sample possible, within the constraint that it is necessary to minimize the risk that the sample is 'quirky', i.e. unrepresentative of the population under investigation.

Statistical confidence is the measure used to describe a sample's reliability. Statisticians give their estimates in the form 'There is an x per cent chance that the answer lies between a and b', for example, 'There is a 90 per cent chance that the true proportion of people with blue eyes lies between 18 per cent and 22 per cent'.

This means that in a survey exactly 20 per cent were found to have blue eyes. Since that one sample may not have been exactly representative of the whole population, projecting the result obtained from the sample would not necessarily be accurate.

Statisticians cope with this possibility by saying that the result will be pretty near 20 per cent (plus or minus 2 per cent) but that there is a 10 per cent chance that it isn't even that near.

This measure of reliability works like a see-saw – you can also say: 'there is a 95 per cent chance that the proportion lies within 16 per cent and 24 per cent.' The chance side (the x per cent, called the level of confidence) goes up as the possible range (a and b, called the confidence limits) gets larger.

If research is very reliable, the confidence level is high and the confidence limits narrow. As reliability slips the confidence level drops, or the range of estimates can be widened, and for any given level of reliability you can swop one for the other.

The reliability of research findings depends entirely on how accurately the sample mirrors or represents the whole, parent population, on the dimensions under investigation. This representativity, in turn, depends on three things:

1 *How the sample is chosen* – the most useful type of sample is a random sample as then the results obey certain statistical laws. (The definition of 'random' is that every member of the population has an equal chance of being picked for the survey.) It is cheapest to stand in a shopping centre and take whoever comes along, so a compromise usually has to be made somewhere between the two extremes.

2 *The homogeneity or variation in the parent population* – the more homogeneous the population, the less likely that the sample will be quirky. At the extreme, if every member of a population is identical, a sample of one will suffice to give accurate data on the whole population (this is the assumption we quietly make when we speak from our own case). If there are good reasons to believe that, for example, a group of experts such as stockbrokers all use similar criteria for say, judging a company i.e. are extremely homogeneous in this respect, research with half a dozen of them might be sufficient to elicit the main criteria and their relative importance. This homogeneity/representativity relationship is the reason why it is so important to get the recruitment for focus groups exactly right – they must be representative of the precise 'population' under investigation, so that the group's attitudes are likely to be a true reflection of those of the parent population.

3 *Sample size* – the chance of picking a quirky sample reduces as the size of the sample increases. Other things being equal, a larger sample will have a better chance of being representative of its parent population than a smaller one.

Knowledge of the way the sample was taken, the homogeneity of the population and the size of the sample allow statisticians to work out the reliability of the results which is then given in terms of a confidence level and confidence limits.

Since the randomness of a sample is limited, and the homogeneity of the population is given, sample size is the only one of these three variables that can be varied significantly by the researcher. Increasing the sample size increases the reliability but increases the cost. Choosing the most efficient sample size is clearly important.

The amount of reliability required depends on how high each of the sides of the see-saw need to be:

The precision of the answer being sought

Suppose an advertiser says his advertisement should be understood by everybody in his target audience and he will not run the ad if it is understood by less than 90 per cent of them. Suppose that of a quota sample (not as good as a random sample) of 100 people taken from the target audience, only fifty understood it. The advertiser can then be sure, at the 95 per cent level, that not more than 70 per cent understood the ad. The confidence limits are horrendous, in fact they are + or − 20 per cent, but in this case greater precision would be unnecessary.

In the same way, if a qualitative research exercise picks up that 'quite a number' of people found the ad hard to understand, off-putting or stupid, the issue is 'how can this problem be resolved?' and not 'precisely how many consumers react this way?'.

(Note though, that focus groups cannot be thought of as samples equal to the number of participants. Group effects, such as respondents explaining things to each other and willingness to come to a consensus, mean that the 'sample size' in focus group research is actually somewhere between the number of groups and the number of participants.)

The level of confidence that the decision makers demand

In certain circumstances, for example sending a man to jail, one wants to be very certain of one's facts. When imposing a custodial sentence, a probabilistic answer would not be acceptable, even say at a level of 95 per cent confidence. In other cases and most particularly where one is being forced to make a guess, it makes sense to go with the best estimate available, even if it is not very reliable. In fact, any improvement on a pure guess will be accepted in certain circumstances. Weather forecasts are a case in point.

The issue then becomes one of balancing the value. Is the cost of getting the somewhat unreliable data worthwhile in terms of the average improvement that it will give over a complete guess? Is the cost of making that data more accurate worthwhile in terms of the incremental, expected improvement?

Statisticians often refer to results which fall below their usual levels of confidence as 'directional'. A manager who follows these 'directional' clues will be right more frequently than if he makes pure guesses.

In advertising pre-testing research both these factors are constantly in play. Ballpark type results are often usable, quite sufficient to avoid the big mistakes not uncommon in such an originality-orientated endeavour as advertising. The uncertain nature of the pre-test decision often makes chancy results acceptable, and accurate results unaccessibly costly. Thus there are often situations in the area of advertising pre-testing, where small sample sizes can provide cost-efficient opportunities for guiding what must remain, rather risky decisions.

Reasons for not wanting to pre-test

You do not have to work in advertising for very long before you hear somebody say 'pre-testing kills good creative ideas'. This is perfectly true, and one must add that, at least as often, research offers its wholehearted support to a complete dodo. If this were not true then the research being done would be inefficient. Advertising research gives probabilistic answers, like the weather forecast, and not scientific truths. Maybe one finding in ten is wrong. In some cases this means losing a good idea, and in other cases it means making a bad investment. The point is that you don't know which finding is wrong beforehand, and the balance of probability is that the research finding is true. You cannot usually persuade a client to invest £1m on the basis that there is a one-in-ten chance that it is not a waste of money.

The reasons for not wanting to pre-test are more often less honourable, ranging from shortage of time and overconfidence, to incompetence and fear. The current agency remuneration system often gives an agency every incentive to push work through and start spending the media budget.

The evidence available does not suggest that using pre-testing research reduces creativity. In fact comparing the output of the relatively small number of (UK) agencies who claim to mandatorily pre-test with the majority that do not suggests, if anything, the opposite.

This is not altogether surprising, as one of the major reasons that an ad will fail with the consumer is that it is boring, patronizing or stupid. Conversely, one of the major reasons that clients reject ads is that they are too avant garde, controversial or innovative. The consumer is usually more open to new ideas and 'creativity' than the risk-averse client decision maker. Decision makers are apt to become more daring once they have seen their target audience respond positively in a pre-test.

Reacting to the pre-testing results

So far this chapter has outlined the objectives of constructive pre-testing, the available measures and the pitfalls in the testing. Now we tackle the issue of how to get from this as-good-as-we-can-get data, to the judgemental decision.

In pre-testing research the facts very rarely speak for themselves. The constructive approach is the most efficient way to allocate resources to produce information which is most likely to help produce effective advertising. It involves experiments which throw some light on the possible reactions of the target audience. It is not a foolproof system, but simply the best hope for a manager aiming to optimize his overall hit rate. There always has to be an interpretive stage between the research findings, and the decisions about changing, accepting or rejecting the creative work.

The design and execution of the research requires technical knowledge, but a thorough understanding of the advertising, its objectives and intended way of working is equally important in the interpretation. These two expertises have to be brought together for the pre-testing phase to be successful. The pre-testing task has to be seen as an integral part of the advertising development process, involving the advertising team, and not something that can be delegated to a professional researcher.

The interpretation of research results is often more meaningful when it is combined with observation of the respondents during the research process. Understanding of the circumstances, and recall of incidental comments adds a further dimension to the recorded responses. For this reason, some agencies insist that the most sensitive and revealing pre-testing research arrives when the research is designed and carried out by somebody who is part of the team involved in the development of that advertising.

At the minimum it implies that the research fieldwork should be attended by one or more of the advertising strategists. This is a heavy responsibility, but given the critical importance of the decisions to be made and the potential value of resulting suggestions, not a disproportionate effort.

Pre-testing as described above, will rarely give completely unambiguous answers. It can be twisted by partisan players. The information provided can only ever make judgement more reliable if the decision makers are committed to an honest assessment of the ad. However, given a genuine commitment to effective advertising, constructive research can provide definite and actionable data.

First, let's be specific about what the research should provide:

Debriefing pre-testing research

Pre-testing research does not have the responsibility to 'kill' ads which are substandard. Its responsibility is to provide the clearest possible information to the decision makers on the strengths and weaknesses of the ad, plus information likely to form a usable basis for improvements or, ultimately, for a new brief or even new advertising strategy.

A debrief should explain (in this order):

1   How the target audience reacted to the ad

First, and in detail, the good points. The basic good points are easy to forget – if it's okay it isn't news. This is important because it is more likely that the ad will be enhanced by expanding, or sharpening up the positive aspects, than by eliminating those which failed.

For future ad development it is also more useful to know what to retain and what to build on, rather than to know what to avoid. This 'ad appreciation' feedback probably forms the account group's main source of knowledge and understanding of how consumers react to their advertising and as such has a wider importance than simply evaluating the one execution.

Second, the ways in which the ad was not working, with just sufficient emphasis to be unambiguous. If something does not work it probably fails in a dozen different ways: 'The car would not start, it could not be made to move, it was useless for the purpose for which it was designed, it caused me to be late, my confidence in it has been reduced, a bicycle would have been quicker, it wouldn't even go backwards.' The root of the failure must be isolated and stated in its simplest form (the battery was flat).

2   What caused the reactions described

Every reaction noted needs to be related either to the aspects of the ad, or to the characteristics or mental set brought to the ad by the target audience, which caused those reactions. Research which is unable to do this is simply inadequate.

So, for example, it is not enough to say people did not find it amusing, this has to be explained – they identified too strongly with the victim, or they did not appreciate that the advertiser was laughing at himself. Conversely, if they *do* find it comical that has to be explained – the children laughed at the father, because his sense of helplessness is something they often feel themselves, and the feeling of reversal amused them. The women thought the cereal must be healthy because the country scenes suggested naturalness, which is strongly linked in their minds to ideas of healthy food.

While (hopefully) avoiding pedantry and intellectualization it is necessary to dissect the reactions, because it is this type of information that helps you know where to go next.

3   Clues from the research for developing the advertising

The researcher's personal opinion of what he would do if he had the creative responsibility is *strictly not required*. This is sometimes difficult for researchers to accept, but the two jobs of research and creation have to be kept separate.

Creativity comes from inside one individual, research depends on suppressing self and listening to others. If the researcher tries to be creative he will start to impose his personal view on to the views of his respondents, and get his delicate objectivity in a terrible mess. Even the most humble person loves his own ideas, and as a researcher it is too easy to justify your own modest creation with the (imagined) approval of the respondents you have just seen.

Creativity is not playing back to people what they already know, but getting them to jump to a truth or insight which is just ahead of where they would get on their own. (This sounds grandiose, but even a modest play on words has to achieve this, otherwise it is not punny.) Advertising ideas need to be generated away from the consumer, then tried out with the consumer. If they are lacking, the understanding gained may help inspire the next idea, but it is usually a mistake simply to bend and remould a creative idea according to the specifications consumers are only too willing to give.

What the researcher should try to do is highlight aspects of the *research results* which he feels offer fertile directions for the creatives to explore. This may be reactions which he found surprising, say a small incident in the ad which received a disproportionate amount of comment or respondents being more knowledgeable than he expected. It might be some joke or aside made by one of the respondents. It might be a framework which seems to organize the respondents' reactions, such as an analysis of how they allocate their leisure time. It might be the results of experiments that he carried out during the research, how the respondents reacted to various suggestions (What if this character had been a woman not a man? Could this advertising be used for the main competitor of this product?)

It is quite possible to carry out research without picking up such clues. The clues need to be picked up in the fieldwork even if they are only made productive by the subsequent analysis. The search for them has to be recognized as the research is being done.

Even in the case of an ad which seems to function perfectly, these points are important – any successful ad is bound to have a successor, and these pointers will help to direct the development of the overall campaign.

Setting norms or action levels

Often research comes back with various statistics – 58 per cent recall the ad shown among a reel of ten ads, 22 per cent of them said they found the ad convincing. Indicators which seemed important when planning the research have now been quantified and need to be interpreted.

Professional researchers sometimes venture comments such as 'personally, that number strikes me as high/low', but usually drift off into vagaries if pressed for significance. Levels of response vary by product field, brand, ad objectives, type of respondent and the research methodology as well as the creative work. Direct comparisons between different tests on advertisements for different products are usually invalid. Unfortunately, if you have got yourself into this situation, there is not much you can do to get yourself out of it with your professional honour intact. You simply have to guess and wave your hands about and hope thus to convince your colleagues that you know what you are doing. You should also resolve, in future, to think about this problem at the pre-test planning stage.

There are four ways to avoid this problem:

1   Perhaps the most rigorous solution is to have two or three *alternative creative approaches*, tested separately but simultaneously, and using the same methodology. If testing was the only argument for producing alternatives, it could not be justified. However, as was explained at the end of the chapter on ad strategy, there are strong arguments for producing more than one creative solution to a problem, rather than having a sufficing approach (this one is good enough, so why explore further). Comparisons between the reactions to the different ads add to the team's ability to interpret the results of tests. When norms are hard to establish, being able to test alternatives certainly provides valuable insight.

2   An alternative way to generate the same effect and develop a 'feeling' for an expected level is to use *comparable tests for successive advertisements* for the same product. This demands a certain discipline and consistency, and the benefits only start to accrue after two or three rounds. Often this policy works better when it is imposed at a company, rather than brand level.

3   A short cut with some of the same advantages is to use a *research company which offers a standardized methodology*, and is willing to provide you with relevant backdata[7]. This will not overcome all the problems of comparability, but if the research company are willing to allow you access to a range of their previous results, analysed in terms of type of product, brand penetration and target audience, it will be easier to get a feel for the significance of the scores obtained. If this method is chosen, it makes good sense to ask for the backdata in advance, and work out what reactions you would have to various results, before receiving your own results. This helps to avoid the effect of post-rationalization.

4   Lastly, you can allocate the pre-testing resources towards measures which provide their own action standards. This tends to mean diagnostic types of research such as measures of what the ad communicates. It may be that the issue of impact is left entirely up to judgement, but there is no point in spending money on information for which there will be no action standard. It might as well be spent on information which could affect the advertising being produced.

Developing, changing and rejecting advertising

The discussion of constructive pre-testing insisted that it must rely to some extent on qualitative research. It also pointed out that objective or 'normalized' action standards for quantitative tests are difficult to establish. The conclusion is that, in the end, the information has to be poured into human data processors who have to weight it up as best they can and come up with a 'best-estimate' type decision.

An absolute, objective system may be wrong half the time but at least its directives are unambiguous. The constructive approach has the practical disadvantage that its indications can be twisted or ignored by partisan players. It is an aid to judgement which is a complete waste of money if the decision makers choose not to take any notice.

This comes back to the starting point of this book which pointed out that market-led meant, more than anything else, a frame of mind.

The challenge is to cultivate an openness among the whole team towards the possibility of change or even outright abandon. The marriage of research and creation is bound to cause some tensions, and the research input has to be carefully handled if it is genuinely to affect the creative output. This is why research must always offer explanations behind its findings and new information suggesting ways forward. It should never simply put up a brick wall of rejection.

The constructive approach is not ambiguous in itself. It says that if the available information tends to suggest that the ad will fail to be noticed, will fail to become identified with the right brand or will not be understood as intended, it has to be rejected or reworked and, depending on the degree of change, re-pre-tested.

The constructive approach boils down to this – sit down in front of the facts with an open mind and say: 'Do I really believe this ad will work?'

Notes and references

1 Attributed to Lord Leverhulme, among others.
2 For a comprehensive review of research on copy testing see Stewart, David, Pechmann, Connie, Ratneshwar, Srinivasan, Stroud, Jon, and Bryant, Beverly, 'Methodological and Theoretical Foundations of Advertising' in *Current Issues and Research in Advertising*, vol. 1 1985.
3 Baumwoll, Joel P., *Recall Testing can be Dangerous to your Brand's Health*. Paper presented to the First Pan-cooperative Marketing Research Conference of General Mills inc, Alexandria Minn., 1978.
4 Klein, Peter and Tainiter, Melvin, 'Copy Research Validation: The Adver-

tiser's Perspective', *Journal of Advertising Research*, vol. 23, no. 5, October/November 1983.

5 Lutz, Richard J., MacKenzie, Scott B. and Belch, George E., 'Attitude Toward the Ad as a Mediator of Advertising Effectiveness: Determinants and Consequences', Proceedings of the Association for Consumer Research 13th Annual Conference 1983; Gresham, Larry G. and Shimp, Terence A. 'Attitude Towards the Advertisement and Brand Attitudes', *Journal of Advertising*, vol. 14, no. 1, 1985.

6 Watson, Paul and Gatchel, Robert, 'Autonomic Measures of Advertising', *Journal of Advertising Research*, vol. 19, no. 3 June 1987.

7 Millward Brown of Leamington Spa seems to have cornered this lucrative part of the research business, in the UK.

6 Feedback from the marketplace

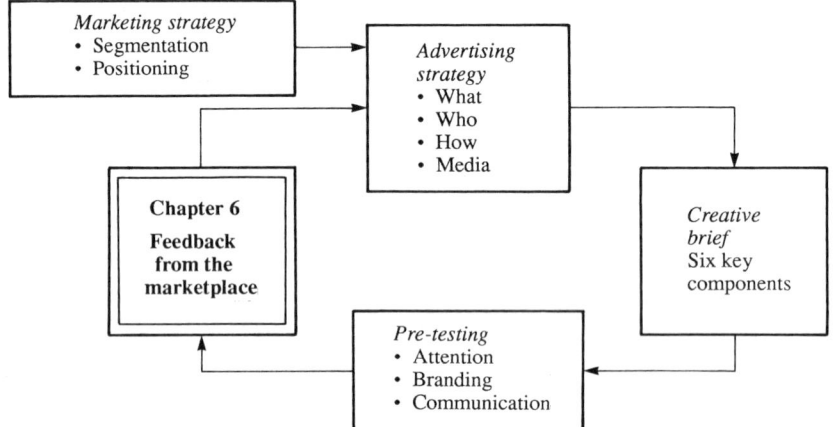

If heaven exists and advertising is permitted there, its effects will doubtless be completely measurable. Advertising will be perfectly accountable for its contribution to celestial profits. However, on Earth, outside of direct response advertising and the claims in agency house ads, well-laid plans more often result in the confusion illustrated in Figure 6.1.

This chapter reviews the most popular and esteemed methods for evaluating the sales effects of advertising. The objectives and limitations are considered pragmatically.

Feedback vs evaluation

Why bother with things that have happened, that are past? History *is* bunk, if its only purpose is to justify past action. The aim of feedback should also be to find clues as to what will happen in the future, and how it might be possible to influence what happens.

Sales area	Media test scheme	Actual media delivery (GRP)	Sales change on last year
Atlantis	100% upweight	1010	+10%
Utopia	50% upweight	750	+ 3%
El Dorado	Average weight	500	+ 8%
Erewhon	50% downweight	235	+ 7%
Gotham City	Zero weight	0	+12%

Figure 6.1 *Typically confusing results from a sensible media weight test*

Feedback is about understanding. There are many situations in which it is not possible to *quantify* (evaluate) the precise effect of advertising, but the goal of understanding the role played by the advertising can still be addressed. Feedback is always essential background for the next round of advertising development. Feedback could be seen as the first, and not the fourth step in the advertising development cycle. It is a unique chance to gain experience which is genuinely relevant and applicable to the development of future advertising.

Feedback is dynamic. If past advertising is simply rated a success or failure, one either has to repeat exactly the past success (which is, in fact, impossible in the case of advertising) or one is back to square one, making a different guess trying to avoid the past mistake. Progress under such a regime is chancy.

Feedback should aim to measure differing responses to differing levels of expenditure, or the comparative effectiveness of different copy or different media scheduling. It is this 'responsiveness' information that helps to optimize future advertising effort.

Feedback is diagnostic. An ad which is a success may yet be improved and advertising can fail or be weak for a variety of reasons. It is essential that feedback provides the information which analyses successes and identifies the causes of problems.

Feedback is contextual. Advertising response has to be assessed in terms of its contribution within the total marketing mix, and not in isolation. As an extreme (and rather trivial) example, consider the case of savings institutions. Since their interest rates change frequently they sometimes produce ads where the interest rate on offer can be changed without changing the rest of the ad. The companies in question can measure their sales very accurately and find that the same advertising can be highly effective or a complete flop depending on whether at that moment they have got their interest rate in front of the competition.

The levels of feedback

The overall objective of feedback is to get definite answers on the market's response to the advertising, and to answer the basic questions of how and why the advertising does or does not work.

To do this it is insufficient to look only at sales effects – advertising effect has to be monitored through all its intermediate phases. The intermediate effects provide indications on causality, which is usually difficult to assess simply from correlation between advertising and sales. The intermediate measures also help to pinpoint reasons for failure, or limited success, if sales do not appear to respond to ad spend.

The levels of feedback are:

1 *Media achievements* – physical delivery of the message to the target audience; number of contacts, penetration and to which people.
2 *Communication achievements* – the absorption of, and reaction to, the ad by its audience.
3 *Sales/response achievements* – the effect of that reaction on the consumer's behaviour.

Advertising has to be checked through each of these separate phases (see Figure 6.2).

Figure 6.2   *The different levels of advertising effect to be monitored*

1 *Media delivery*

'Over half our target saw our ad at least seven times during the two week period ... but they were also subjected to an average of eighteen viewings from our closest competitor. Here are the two ads ....' Not many media debriefs make this much effort to capture and present the real advertising experience of the target audience.

Media is too often treated as a subject separate and independent from the rest of advertising. As a result it has generated its own criteria of assessment which are often unrelated to the actual advertising task.

Advertising achievements are usually consumer responses of one sort or another (recall, comprehension, attitude and behaviour change) while *media achievements* are usually measured in physical and money terms e.g. cost per thousand contacts.

This is important because the choice of measure has a significance above the success of the investigation in hand – it can change the buyer's perceptions of the whole issue and dictate the factors on which subsequent decisions are made. To a large extent, what you measure is what you see.

For example, the usual measure for summarizing an 'amount' of television advertising is the Gross Rating Point (one GRP corresponds to one per cent of the viewing population viewing one spot). Now, a GRP for a forty-second ad or a thirty-second or a twenty-second ad look rather similar sketched on a media schedule, so quietly swopping to shorter lengths can preserve the total number of GRPs, while seeming to save money. Spot lengths have been steadily decreasing, over a number of years while number of spots broadcast per week is increasing, perhaps as a result. Had television bargains been measured in terms of Consumer Seconds Watched (CSW) presumably spots would have got longer and longer instead.[1]

An appreciation of the advertising experience of the target audience is essential background to understanding their response to the advertising. Good media feedback should help you get back to the frame of mind of your consumers. Ideally, media reporting should give a complete image of the target's media experience within that product field, during the period under consideration, including examples of all the creative work. Regional differences and mixed media may complicate the picture, but some meaningful summary has to be created as the basis for analysing the advertising effect.

The distribution of opportunities to see is generally more meaningful data for the interpretation of ad effect than the absolute number of viewings. Competitive activity may be important to advertising response and is as much part of media feedback as the brand's own activity. It is worth noting that despite its influence on advertising *effects*, competitive activity has only marginal effect on the *media costs*, as usually reported.

2   Message delivery

Media delivery is a necessary but not sufficient condition for getting an advertising message to its target. Monitoring its arrival with the consumer covers the next two links in the chain – the reception of the advertising and the decoding of the intended message.

The importance of continuous data

Simple pre- and post-tests are often used to assess the delivery from a burst of advertising. They consist of a benchmark study, before the advertising has started, and a follow-up survey, usually organized to capture the estimated maximum effect, around the end of the advertising period. Although this may provide some reassuring information, it falls far short of satisfying the requirements defined above for feedback.

Advertising is dynamic.   Awareness and attitudes are not bought but hired. Very little communication is for ever (enjoy these words now, gentle reader, you may have forgotten them next week) so any measure of communication has to cover the dimension of time. Awareness was not 'increased by 10 percentage points' but 'remained increased by over 5 per cent for the rest of the year'. It is essential to get a feeling for cumulative effects and decay rates to be able to plan a reasonable media strategy.

Advertising is competitive,   a tug of war. Media reporting has to cover competitive activity and it is equally important to find out what the competitors managed to communicate. Continuous data is the only sure way of capturing the effects of competitive activity on the consumer. The effects of past advertising are studied in the belief that they provide understanding of consumer response and thus guidance for the future. Much more knowledge can be gleaned if this information is also available on competitive brands. It may be possible to compare four media approaches and four strategic or creative approaches, with a corresponding four-fold increase in learning rate.

A. C. Nielsen understood the appeal of data over time when they invented their retail panels. Until then, manufacturers had got by with a fairly approximate knowledge of brand share and distribution levels. Once those statistics were available on a continuous basis, for all competing brands, they began to seem invaluable. Now many manufacturers would feel lost without them. Advertisers are beginning to appreciate that a regular check on their share of consumer preference is as essential as keeping tabs on actual consumer sales. Perhaps even more essential, as these statistics can give earlier warning and diagnosis, allowing for speedier reaction, and providing clues to the causes.

What to measure

Whereas the media report measures what was bought, consumer monitoring attempts to capture what was actually delivered. Any statistic which suggests the advertising arrived can be useful – advertising awareness, prompted recall or recognition of prompt material are all frequently used.

The primary value of these measures is not evaluative. In fact, none of these measures is proven to link to effectiveness and they are difficult to relate to any norms or standards which would allow the ad to be evaluated. What they do help to establish is a picture of how many people could have been affected by the advertising. This is important background for understanding sales effects.

If only 20 per cent of the target audience even recognize the ad in the week after the campaign has finished, advertising response can only be expected in a fifth of the target. So, for example, if the target was all current users, an increase in weight of use of 10 per cent among all who had seen the ad would only translate to an overall sales increase of 2 per cent. This is vital context for the last level of feedback, the traditional focus of evaluation, the persuasive effect of the delivered advertisement.

The 'delivery' results are unpredictable in advance, not just because of the impact of the ad itself, but because of the qualitative and unpredictable aspects of media – environment, targeting, concentration. For example, my experience suggests that child GRPs are significantly more powerful than adult GRPs. That is to say, there is a different relationship between media bought and message delivery for adult and child audiences.

The methods of media research not only ignore its 'absorption' but also use some rather theoretical measures for assessing media achievements e.g. classifying anyone who has looked at a magazine as having read the whole thing. Media statistics are often designed with the objective of setting relative prices, and do not necessarily even try to capture the reality of what people saw. Monitoring message delivery is, in fact, also valuable feedback for evaluating media.

The next step is to understand what the consumer took out of the advertising. This is essential feedback for *explaining* subsequent action or inaction. In cases where sales response to advertising is really unobtainable, such interim measures often provide the best possible estimate of whether and how the advertising is working.

Recall of the advertising message or content, changes in attitudes or perceptions and change in brand preference scores are all useful measures for getting at the communication effects of advertising. These are frequently measures which coincide with the defined advertising objectives and indeed with the way much advertising works.

Focusing on the brand rather than the advertising can avoid ambiguous, direct questions on what the ad was trying to communicate, and the problems of trying to articulate non-verbal messages. For example, an ad for denim jeans uses a pastiche of a war movie, mixed in with female sensuality and 1960s soul music. A fifteen year old may find it difficult to analyse, summarize and articulate the message he takes out (this is better investigated quali-tatively, see below). The *effects* of the communication on his *perceptions and preferences* between brands of jeans, is often more accessible.

Monitoring attitudes to chocolate bars in the UK shows one brand, Mars, completely out on its own on dimensions of 'foodiness' and 'energy giving'. Since the Mars bar is a permutation of the commonest and sweetest countline ingredients (chocolate, caramel and nougatine) these attitudes are the clearest possible measure of the communication effects of years of consistent 'work, rest and play' advertising.

The attitudes and attributes monitored need to cover all the important aspects of consumer judgement – functional, user image and brand personality and their relative importance should be collected or calculated (as described in Chapter 2). Since attitudes change slowly, comparable long-term studies are required. If all this is done, the resulting data deserves to be taken as seriously as the store panel.

One leading manufacturer of consumer paper products cancelled a well-run and thorough tracking study because in its three years of existence it had 'failed' to show any significant changes in attitudes or perceptions following their (modest) advertising bursts. An alternative would have been to drop the media spend in one or two areas and monitor the long-run effect. If the media invoices say media was bought, it is hard to believe that no effect was delivered. It is easier to shoot the messenger.

Claimed purchasing and usage can provide useful insights, particularly if monitored over time. They cannot be taken as factual reporting of behaviour, but they can provide a subtle way of monitoring attitudes. Claimed purchasing may be a more sensitive measure for low-interest products or habit purchases, where attitudes are extremely show to shift or where the advertising is reinforcing existing attitudes.

Continuous tracking is valuable for monitoring a brand's share of mind and preference over time, and the communication effects of advertising. However, such studies provide little explanation of the effects in terms of the advertising content. An in-depth analysis of consumer reaction to specific advertising executions is best dealt with separately, using qualitative techniques.

Qualitative post testing

Qualitative *pre*-testing is widely used despite its substantial drawbacks (rough material, artificial viewing situation, time compression) because it provides invaluable insight into consumer reaction to creative ideas before production money is invested. Qualitative post-testing can often provide more reliable and richer data, which can have an equally significant impact on the development of subsequent advertising.

In the case of press advertising, where the pre-testing problems are at their most extreme and where series of similar advertisements are common, post-testing has an even larger contribution to make.

Quantitative tracking of advertising has many of the limitations described with respect to quantitative pre-testing and in the same way, qualitative information on the reception of an advertising campaign can capture the qualitative reasons behind the quantitative results.

Post-testing does not duplicate the findings of pre-testing research, but complements it:

1 The objective is partly to verify that the advertising functions in the marketplace in the way predicted from the pre-testing. This means finding out how the change from rough material to finished advertising, and viewing in a real as against test situation, changed the reactions recorded in the pre-testing.
2 Markets and attitudes change over time, and in particular feelings about advertising change, often quite rapidly. Ads which initially seem rather odd become accepted through familiarity, while ads which were interesting or attractive in their novelty become boring or irritating as they 'wear-out'. Timing the change from good creative work to maximize use while avoiding wear-out is important, and qualitative post-testing is a key opportunity for estimating the need to change. Methods which imply market measurements are by definition too slow.

The post-testing sample should be selected from members of the target audience who have had the opportunity to see the advertising in question. The first part of the interview consists of probing their recollections of the advertising in question, and if appropriate, that of competitive advertising. The second stage involves showing the advertising as a prompt and continuing to talk about the respondents' reactions to the advertising, when it was seen in real life ('When you first saw that advertising, can you remember what you thought?'). Lastly the advertising can be discussed as it is perceived at that moment, and ideas can be floated for its development into the future.

This type of post-testing is of little value to a team who simply want to *evaluate* their (past) advertising. On the other hand to a team genuinely interested in developing their understanding it provides some of the richest feedback possible, whether the ad was judged to be a success or not. The wonderful thing about this sort of feedback is that it often in itself suggests directions forward and furnishes the starting point for the next round of advertising development.

3 Sales effects

Sales effects are rarely so unambiguously linked to advertising that one can clearly deduce a causal effect and quantify the increase in sales attributable to the advertising. The difficulties arise because many factors apart from its own advertising influence a product's sales. However, there are methods for zoning in on the likely effects.

Picturing advertising response

When looking for something, it is useful to have in mind an idea of what it might look like. Quantifying advertising response is discussed in detail later, but for now let's take a broad view of what an advertising response curve might look like, and the uses that could be made of it, if it could be found.

Advertising is supposed to increase sales, and more advertising is expected to achieve more. In most cases some sales could be made without advertising and sales would reach a limit that extra advertising could not surpass, if other influences were held stable. It is interesting to notice how much of your disposable income you spend on things for which you ·have never seen advertising – socks, babysitters, houseplants, dentists, pencils, bicycles, houses, slippers, Marks and Spencer. Intuitively, a response curve for one individual might look something like Figure 6.3.

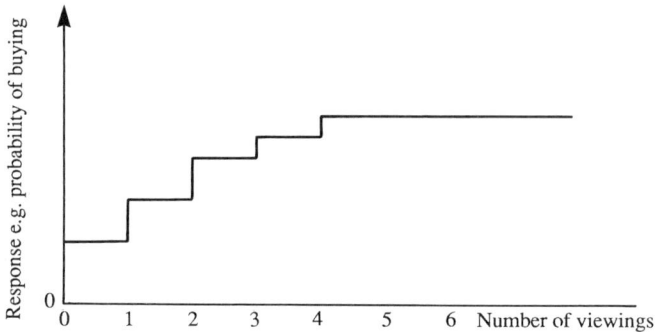

Figure 6.3   *An individual's response curve to advertising exposure*

The curve (or rather, step function) makes visible the 'rules' which advertising response is often assumed to obey:

Rule 1   Increasing exposure has a positive effect on demand, though with diminishing returns.
Rule 2   There comes a point where further exposure to advertising has no extra effect on demand.
Rule 3   If ad exposure is zero, demand still exists at a certain base level.

In some situations, particularly for new products, a new campaign or where competitors are advertising heavily, there may be a threshold effect, several exposures being needed before response is triggered. That is to say:

Rule 4   The first exposures to an ad have less effect than later exposures, up to the point where diminishing returns take over.

This would alter the shape of the response curve. People who were taught to read from medieval manuscripts call the result an S-curve (Figure 6.4).

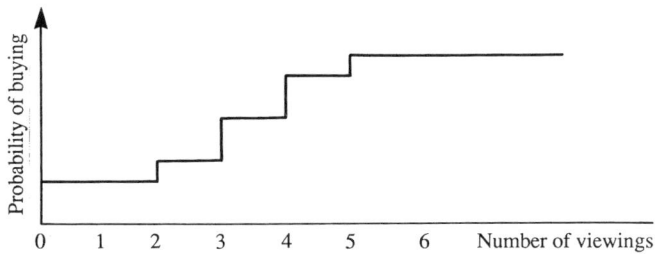

Figure 6.4   *An individual's response to advertising, showing a threshold effect*

Since a response curve found in one situation is unlikely to be generally applicable, it is not possible to say whether response curves are generally of one shape or the other.

Advertising response curves are more usually modelled for whole populations (not individuals) against a summary of the exposure level – often money. Adding together all the individual graphs would give a smooth curve, something like that shown in Figure 6.5

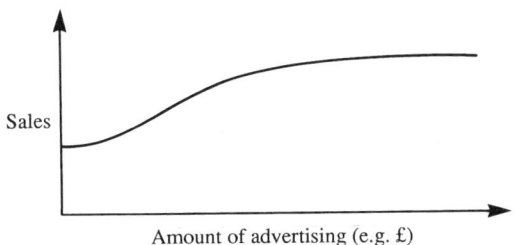

Figure 6.5   *A plausible advertising response curve*

Having some such curve in mind is immediately useful. This simple concept gets rid of the non-logic which says: 'If an agency can show a good advertising response their budget will be increased, but from the agency that cannot shall be taken away even that which they hath.' Perhaps the 'good' agency is towards the right-hand end of the curve, perhaps on the top plateau, and the 'bad' agency towards the left. A more professional response to success might be: 'Can we get similar results by spending less', and to failure by: 'We should experiment with higher budgets to see if that is the problem.'

Having a response function in mind emphasizes advertising's dependence on media and the need to measure response dynamically. Frequently, advertising effectiveness studies simply show that the advertising had an effect, or at most, that the effect paid for the investment. Satisfaction with such results usually indicates that they were undertaken with the aim of justifying past advertising outlay, and not with the objective of optimizing future investments.

The advertising response function (or ARF) depicted in Figure 6.5 represents how sales respond to advertising. If it could be estimated accurately, it would solve many of the most difficult advertising questions at a stroke.

It contains the information needed to make critical advertising decisions such as:

- Whether it is worthwhile (profitable) to advertise.
- Setting the budget.
- Scheduling media across time.

and, by developing and comparing several response curves:

- When to develop new copy.
- Allocation between regions.
- Allocation between media.
- Choice between alternative copy.

In order to aid these important decisions, it is necessary to specify and quantify the curve. However, some extremely thorny questions have to be tackled if the curve is to be discovered and calibrated in practice. These thorny questions are discussed in the next section. The last three sections of this chapter examine different ways of quantifying the curve – econometrics, experiments and turbo-charged guesswork.

A quick overview of some mindboggling problems

The quest is to find a mathematical form (i.e. curve) which accurately represents the theoretical curve sketched in Figure 6.5, which relates sales effect to amount of advertising.

First, let's look at why I keep referring to this nice curve, Figure 6.5, as 'theoretical'. Without meaning to be facetious, if we really wanted to plot it, this is roughly what we would have to do: Construct half a dozen exact replicas of planet earth. Run six different-sized bursts of the same advertising (ranging from zero weight to an estimated saturation level), while making sure that in every other respect the history of the planets remains identical.

Monitor subsequent sales accurately until a stable state is regained on all six. Plot the six weights against the six cumulative sales totals on a graph and join up the dots (see Figure 6.6).

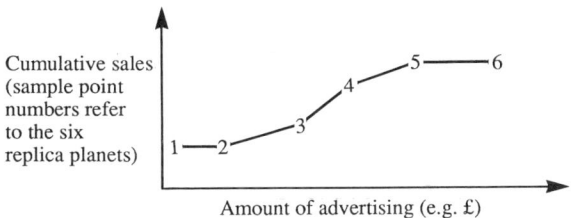

Figure 6.6   *The results of an implausible advertising experiment*

It is impossible to construct an experiment from which the advertising response curve can be plotted directly. We have to try to 'model' the curve from information that is available. The mindboggling problems referred to are those encountered when trying to use measurable information to throw light on this theoretical curve.

A 'model' in this context refers to the curve which is created to estimate the ARF. It is a model in that it is not the actual curve, but a mathematical approximation to what the ARF would look like if it could be plotted. Any model of the ARF will only ever be an approximation, but to be good enough to help with the decisions mentioned, it has to overcome the following problems:

Specifying the type of model (i.e. shape of the curve)

The shape of the curve should not contradict simple intuitive or observed rules as to how advertising works. This means the model should obey the rules 1, 2 and 3 listed on page 170.

While still obeying those rules, the curve can vary from a straight horizontal line (no advertising effect) to a close-up view of a stair carpet (Figure 6.7).

Clearly the rules define a very wide range of response functions, but if a model for an ARF does not fit within the rules it contradicts some very modest and reasonable assumptions about how advertising works. This is important because certain familiar models such as the straight line (other than horizontal), which shows no diminishing returns, or multiplicative or product form* which gives zero sales at zero advertising are not satisfactory by these criteria. Their ability to help with the critical decisions listed is seriously undermined.

---

* In the product form sales $= a \times X_1^{b1} \times X_2^{b2} \ldots \times X_n^{bn}$, where a and b_i are constants and the X_i are the independent variables (price, distribution etc.).

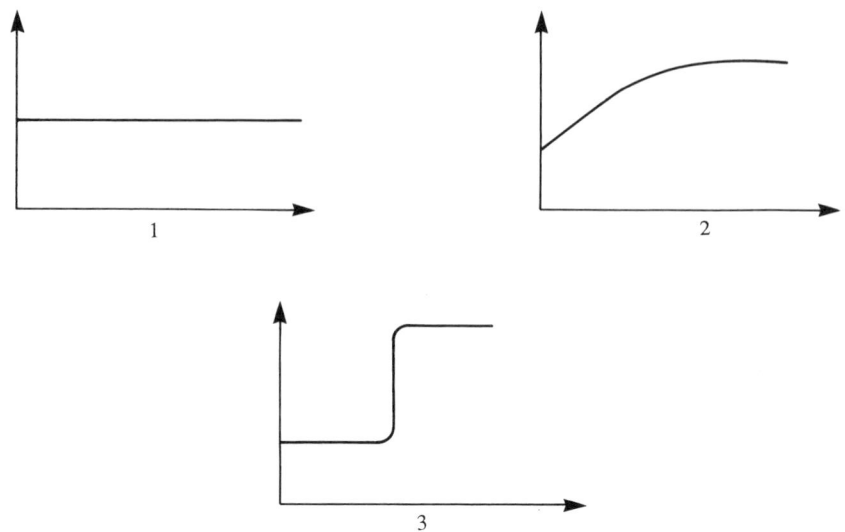

Figure 6.7   *While obeying rules 1, 2 and 3 response curves can still vary through a range of shapes from a horizontal line to a close-up of a stair carpet*

If a model is to help budget setting, media planning and scheduling, it should be allowed to take the threshold form (Rule 4). Many widely used models (including the straight line and multiplicative form) do not allow for this.

Choosing a form for the model which truly reflects reality is far from obvious, but any choice affects the answers which eventually result.

Coping with carry-over

The theoretical curve (Figure 6.5) purports to relate amounts of advertising with all the sales caused directly by that advertising, for all time. The theoretical curve transcends time, whereas measurement cannot.

It is generally assumed that advertising effect happens soon after the advertising is seen, and peaks immediately. From this initial peak, as people forget the advertising and are seduced away by competing brands, the effect is expected to diminish. The problem is that it is not known how quickly or following what pattern. Building a model of the ARF implies becoming specific about how the effect arrives and subsides.

Might some residual effect remain for years? Everyone can bring to mind advertising images stored from their childhood – the sparkling black and white tiles cleaned with Flash, the swishing Wilkinson Swords and jet setters swigging Martini Bianco. Such images, and jingles as indelible as nursery rhymes ('Guinness is good for you, but a diamond is for ever') may influence people throughout their lives. In the larder of any immigrant you will inevitably find a stock of imports with their jolly, familiar names and packaging from his country of origin. Does this extreme loyalty have its roots in some far off, half-forgotten advertising?

A related complication is the cumulative effect of much of the best advertising. Brands are envied for having long running campaigns. An established advertising vehicle is felt to be a valuable asset for a brand because consumers find it easier to assimilate, attribute and remember ads which form part of a familiar campaign.

This implies that ads which form part of a campaign are more effective because of the previous advertising. Arguably, some of the response to the later advertising should be attributed back to the advertising which established the campaign.

This is most extreme in cases where 'old' advertising is 'revived'. How should one allocate extra response created by effects of nostalgia for the revived campaign, say, for the Guinness Toucan or the Bisto Kids? The valuable nostalgia effects could not have existed the second time if the first campaign had not existed.

This 'stored' type of effect is different to the long-term carry-over effects directly associated with some specific piece of advertising. Perhaps the best way to talk about the two effects is to call the on-going effect of past advertising a long-term effect and the building of some kind of memory which can be tapped into for subsequent point-of-sale material, follow-up campaigns etc. a 'stock' effect. Stock effects are probably almost impossible to measure reliably (most particularly where they have yet to happen!).

In practice, measurement tends to concentrate on short-term effects. Decisions are based on the simplifying assumption that a campaign which is best in the short- to medium-term will tend to be best in the long-term. This rule of thumb is unprovable but it affects key decisions such as the choice between alternative campaigns.

Instability of the response – tracking a moving target

The shape of the (actual) response curve is not fixed and unchanging. Clearly the *shape* will change according to the quality of different creative work, but also as a result of competitive activity, price changes, market conditions and a multitude of other reasons.

This is a significant problem for methods which set out to separate the influence of advertising from other influences (such as price, promotions, competitive advertising, distribution). It is wrong to assume that the influences are independent of each other and that their effects can be added and subtracted as if the responsiveness to each influence was unchanging.

For example, since the same consumers choose between competing brands, the same consumers watch and process advertising from several brands at one time. Advertising response will vary according to the quality and quantity of other advertising existing at the time of the advertising input. Similarly, the effect of an advertising burst coincidental with a price reduction cannot be assumed to have the same effect as the sum of the effects of those actions carried out separately. The idea that the responses might compound or detract from each other is entirely plausible. Even weird, discontinuous interactions are intuitively plausible.

Advertising response is never stable and unchanging over time. Nobody runs the same advertising for ever because the response is expected to diminish, an effect described as 'wear-out'. This implies that if exactly the same advertising activity was repeated on several different occasions, the response curve would change (in fact, flatten). This effect is invariably observed with a series of mail-order or coupon-response ads appearing in one publication.

The solution, changing the copy, is actually designed to change advertising responsiveness, in this case, upwards.

In using data over time to explore advertising response one has to cope with the responsiveness changing, whether or not new copy is developed. The thing being modelled is moving all the time!

Measuring the amount or intensity of advertising

The theoretical description did not specify too carefully what is meant by 'amount of media'. In practice this is important – share of voice, amount of money, number of contacts could all be used. If sales improve due to a change in choice of media, while media spend is constant, has the *amount* of advertising changed?

In the individual case it was possible to imagine the number of viewings, but this is impractical for populations. Often cost is taken to be the best measure, but this ignores the appropriateness and quality of the media actually purchased. Using cost as the measure of advertising input implies, for example, that all possible divisions of the budget between press and TV would be equally effective.

The truth is that the same money can buy a greater or smaller 'amount' of media, depending on the skill and understanding brought to the task by the media planners and buyers.

The question is actually bizarrely circular – the only meaningful measure of amount of media is in terms of the effect it has!

This last section has given a brief summary of the severe technical problems involved in bringing the ARF from a cute theoretical tool to measurable reality.

The statistical tools put forward for doing this are called econometrics, and it is important to have the above issues clearly in mind while examining the techniques which claim to overcome them.

Econometrics

Few advertising professionals can resist the temptation to superimpose past advertising activity on to the sales graph to try to spot advertising effects. Few can resist cheering if the bumps coincide or blushing if they do not. Anybody who is in the habit of doing this has to be interested in methods which use computers to do the same thing but in more detail and relate many graphs (i.e. variables) instead of just the two, sales and advertising.

Econometrics is sometimes described as 'the analysis of variation' because this is exactly what it does. The computer looks at the variation in sales and matches it with variation in the explanatory variables.

Cheap computer power has brought the capacity to carry out such data analysis within the reach of even the smallest company. What does this new tool mean to advertising professionals?

The purpose of the following illustration is to outline both the method and the pitfalls of econometrics as simply as possible. It assumes no understanding of statistics.

Clueless and Cassata – an illustration

Cassata, a brand manager at a company of high quality ice-cream manufacturers, thought it would be rather smart to ask Clueless, his account manager at Huxter's ad agency, to use econometrics to assess the effect of their advertising on sales. Clueless was clueless, but he quickly read some published studies[2], borrowed a small computer from the agency's media department and equipped it with a promising looking statistics package.[3] He then casually informed his client that they could start whenever he liked.

Their first step was to collect together data on the variables which they felt might affect their sales, These were:

- Price
- Temperature
- Disposable income
- Advertising spend
- Distribution

Average temperature was available daily, the other variables were available bi-monthly for the past five years, giving thirty data points. Daily temperature was averaged over each bi-month to fit with the other variables.

The next step was to specify the 'form' of these inputs. This meant processing the inputs to make them reflect the real world more accurately. They indexed price and disposable income on the retail price index so that only real differences were considered. Advertising effect was 'lagged' so that the effects of advertising were taken to continue beyond the period, i.e. bi-month, in which they appeared.

This lagging was carried out in the most usual way. The 'accumulated' weight of advertising in a certain period was said to equal the advertising in that period plus $d \times$ advertising in the previous period plus $d^2 \times$ the advertising from two periods ago etc., where d is some number between 0 and 1. $1 - d$ is called the 'decay factor'.

Distribution had been almost unchanging throughout the five years, it showed no correlation with sales and was at this point dropped as an explanatory variable.

It is often advantageous to use sales share as the independent variable as this excludes the need for global market variables such as temperature and disposable income. In this case competitive sales were difficult to estimate, as the competition was a huge variety of snacks, fast food, confectionary and even desserts. Sales were, therefore, left as absolute volume sales.

Clueless then ran the econometrics program to explain the variation in the sales graph (the dependent variable) in terms of the variation of the other five graphs (the independent variables). Computer programs offer different ways to do this, but our heroes used straightforward multiple linear regression. In slightly simplified terms this is what the computer does: Initially it picks six numbers a_1, a_2, a_3, a_4, d and c. For each of the thirty time periods it calculates an 'estimate' $(\hat{S})$ of sales by adding together:

$a_1 \times$ price in that period,
$a_2 \times$ temperature in that period,
$a_3 \times$ disposable income in that period,
$a_4 \times$ the advertising (lagged using d) and adding the constant c

It then compares $\hat{S}$ with the actual sales (S) in each of the thirty periods. The computer then applies a rule for adjusting the six numbers, in such a way that, on average, the thirty $\hat{S}$s come closer to the thirty actual sales figures. It repeats this process until it has found six numbers which bring the $\hat{S}$ as close to the S as possible, in as many of the periods as possible. At this point the computer prints out the six numbers, and also a couple of statistics which summarize how close the $\hat{S}$s are to the Ss.

In this case, the computer came up with the following solution – it constructed the closest copy of the sales curve by taking $2 \times$ the temperature, adding $1.5 \times$ real disposable income, subtracting $0.8 \times$ the real price and adding $0.2 \times$ the lagged advertising (the computer chose a decay rate of 0.5 per period) and subtracting the constant 94. The numbers 2, 1.5, -0.8 and 0.2 are called 'coefficients'.

The regression equation given by the computer was:

$$\hat{S}_t = 2 \times T_t + 1.5 \times DI_t - 0.8 \times P_t + 0.2 \times A^*_t - 94$$

Where:
$\hat{S}_t$ = estimated sales in period t
T_t = temperature
DI_t = real disposable income
P_t = real price
A^*_t = lagged advertising (d = 0.5)
$= A_t + 0.5A_{t-1} + (0.5)^2 A_{t-2} + \ldots + (0.5)^n A_{t-n}$

In fact, Cassata and Clueless repeated the first three steps a number of times, inputting different variables (e.g. hours of sun) and choosing different forms (e.g. price relative to other ice-cream brands). This generated a range of alternative models. They chose the one shown above, because it explained a good deal of the variation in sales, but they rejected one that explained more on the basis that it contained counterintuitive coefficients (increasing price was given a positive effect on sales, which they knew did not happen).

The econometrics exercise complete, the gleeful ice-cream manufacturer and his intrepid agency colleague start to play with their model. They note with approval that the most significant effect on their sales is the weather, which agrees with their own beliefs, and they turn to the advertising effect.

Their advertising response function (i.e. their model of the theoretical curve discussed above) is a straight line – an inevitable consequence of the linear approach. The coefficient indicated is 0.2 which means that for each extra unit of advertising (where one unit means one unit from this bi-month, or two units in the previous bi-month, etc.) sales this period increase by 0.2 units. This response curve is shown at Figure 6.8.

The curve in Figure 6.8 shows how much extra sales will be generated for each extra unit of advertising investment. Cassata is keen to compare the cost of an extra unit of advertising (which he can work out via the lagging function) with the profit he gains from 0.2 units of extra sales, to see whether the advertising is profitable or not.

However, his calculation has rather odd implications – if the advertising is not profitable it should be cut right back to zero. If it is profitable then another unit of advertising will also be profitable, and so on ad infinitum. In fact, if the sales response is represented by a straight line, the optimal budget must always be one of those two alternatives – nothing or infinity.

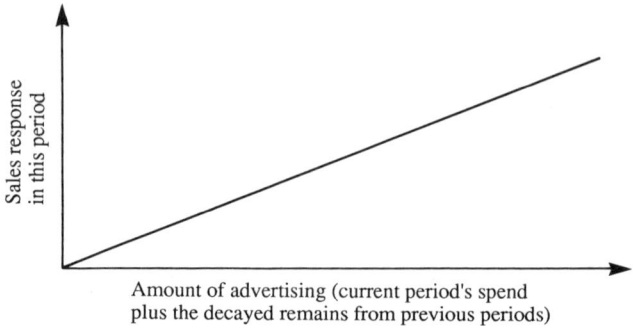

Figure 6.8   *The advertising response curve given by Clueless and Cassata's model*

This laughable conclusion leads Clueless and Cassata to ask some penetrating questions about their model and the process that created it.

In fact they are on their way to discovering the truth – their model is useless and worse, it is impossible for them to build a model which gives meaningful answers.

These are the questions they ask, and confessions they make, when they go to consult a competent, honest but somewhat supercilious statistician about their model:

C and C: We fear we omitted some factors which influence our sales. There has been a fad for a new product called Icy Mush, sold mostly by garages. It isn't ice-cream but it provides an alternative snack for hot weather. It was launched in 1986 but did most damage to our sales in 1987. This was not included because there are no systematic measures of Icy Mush sales.

Statistician: This is the problem of *completeness*. If you can't measure all the factors which influence sales, this type of modelling is liable to produce biassed results. You can check whether you have a serious problem of this nature by analysing the residual variation, that is the differences between your model's predictions ($\hat{S}$) and actual sales. If you have left out something significant you will find that these 'residuals' are not randomly distributed, as they should be in a good model. If significant factors have been left out and you can't measure them you can patch up the model in a couple of ways. You can estimate the missing variable, judgementally. You know when Icy Mush was launched and that sales were highest in 1986, so presumably you could take a stab at that. Alternatively, you can create an 'Icy Mush-craze' dummy variable valued at zero before the launch and one after the launch. You then ask the computer to choose a coefficient for it. If the craze was more extreme in 1986 you could use a combination of two dummy variables to catch the shoulders and peak of the fad. Remember though, that putting in more and more variables (of any kind) makes the model less and less reliable, for the same number of data points. As a rule of thumb I like to see six to eight data points for each explanatory variable and a minimum of thirty data points. You've used thirty data points for four variables, which is okay, but it doesn't leave much confidence to spare.

C and C: We've always felt that our distribution base has been a pillar of our success. However, since distribution did not change during the five years of the study there was no possibility of correlation with sales and this variable was left out of the regression.

Statistician: This method cannot be used to measure the effects of variables that don't vary – you must have *variation* in the data. In your case it's lucky, because you have one less variable to cope with. It's much more of a problem when one wishes to investigate a variable that has not changed much in the past. For example if advertising spend has been stable over several years, you couldn't use this method to judge whether the advertising spend was optimal, or indeed whether advertising had any affect at all.

C and C: We advertise in the summer to catch the seasonal sales and we also aim for the first heatwave of the summer for our annual price promotion. This means that seasonality affects three of the explanatory variables used.

Statistician: This is called *multicolinearity.* It is often a problem with advertising models because marketing variables are naturally related to each other in various ways. The problem you find if the explanatory variables are not independent of one another is that the computer doesn't know to which variable it should assign the explanatory power. The result is that it makes a rather arbitrary decision, say between advertising and temperature, and you can't trust the coefficients it gives, that is to say we have to put wide confidence limits on the coefficients. One solution is to group together the explanatory variables which are correlated (this can be done for say press and TV advertising) but in your case that is not much help.

C and C: The advertising has changed three times in the last four years. We think the ads used in 1986 were more effective than the stuff before or since. Is the advertising effect applicable over

| | the whole period, an average or what. How could we measure the changing response? |

Statistician: The problem of *changing elasticities* is terribly complex. Advertising agencies are understandably concerned with the subject because it is this change which would be needed to demonstrate an improvement in advertising copy, or copy wearing out etc. The main problem is that such analyses require a great deal of data to make them reliable. You would not be able to employ them with only six data points per year, and only a few years' data. If you give the computer too much freedom (e.g. by allowing it to change the advertising elasticity each year) the fit (between $\hat{S}$ and S) will inevitably improve, but the *accuracy* of the coefficients is jeopardized. This is the point I was making before with reference to increasing the number of explanatory variables. Unfortunately, I can give you little reassurance. If, as seems likely, the elasticities changed significantly during the period, your results must be considered highly dubious.

C and C: If advertising gives a return of 0.2 sales each time we buy another unit of advertising, it is profitable and so we should spend more. But how do we find the upper limit?

Statistician: To be frank, I'm amazed that you specified a *linear form* for your model of the response function. How could you possibly imagine that the response function could be linear? If you use a linear model you know from the start that it can't tell you anything about the shape of the curve you want to explore. If you had specified a concave or s-shaped function you might have obtained a credible pattern of response. Both of those functions will give you estimates of the saturation level for advertising, which you will obviously never obtain from a linear model. You should read John Little's article on advertising models[4], if you can cope with it.

C and C: We've observed that our sales increase when a new series of *Dynasty* starts, and equally ludicrous, with the number of our employees on holiday. Do these factors really cause us extra sales, or is this correlation sheer chance? Similarly, how can we be sure that the variables used in the model are really causing the sales and are not just showing the same type of accidental correlation?

Statistician: You are asking how to test for *causality*, a very important point which many debutant econometricians ignore. The 90 per cent explained variance which you mentioned, is an indicator, but not proof of causality. It is a necessary rather than sufficient condition. There are various tests for causality, such as Granger's. He suggests carrying out a regression first with all the explanatory variables except the one under question. You then repeat the regression with that variable included and take the amount of explanation of the original run from that with the extra variable to find the extra explanation achieved. You can then do an F-test to check for significance. I hope you follow what I am saying?

C and C: Another thing we need to know is how sure we can be about this 0.2 coefficient for the advertising spend? If it was 0.1 our reactions would be very different.

Statistician: For each estimated coefficient the computer will give you a standard deviation. This is a statistical measure which allows you to calculate *confidence limits* around your estimate. From your printout I see that the standard deviation for the advertising coefficient was 0.1. There is a 95 per cent chance that the true estimate lies between $+/-$ twice the standard deviation, which in this case would be 0.2. This means you can be 95 per cent sure that the true estimate is between 0.0 and 0.4, assuming that the model *is* basically sound (which I rather doubt).

C and C: According to our model the advertising from one year doesn't have any significant effect in the next year. However, we feel that the fact that ours has been the only ice-cream brand to advertise consistently over the last thirty years has given it a stature and consumer acceptance second to none. How do you explain this seeming contradiction?

Statistician: Econometrics is based on the idea of matching the variation in the variables, which works best for relatively *short-run effects*. The method can give useful information, but don't expect it to provide all the answers. It is possible to build models with more *complicated lag forms*, which might provide more information on the long-term effects, but I don't think that would be worthwhile for you. There is a theory[5], that the lag form you use does not have much effect when you calculate the profit implications of the different models. This means that though a different lagging might be interesting to you, it wouldn't necessarily change the decisions which followed. My advice to you would be not to get too bogged down in capturing the exact shape of the decay, worry more about the problems of multicollinearity, the form of the response function and causality which we discussed earlier.

Leaving the statistician's office, Clueless and Cassata feel a little down-hearted. They invested a lot of time (and credibility) in the project and had hoped that it would provide solutions to some of the problems which dogged their working lives (and prestige).

'Shame about all that' says Clueless 'but at least we know the advertising *did* pay for itself.' 'Yes' says Cassata, dubiously, 'at least we proved that before that pompous statistician put his oar in.'

Econometrics as a tool for advertising professionals

The problems with econometrics as a tool for advertising management are first data and second processing that data.

1   Data

The historical data available is often inadequate to provide the answers sought. The data has to be:

- *Complete* – it must cover all the important influences, including competitive activity and environmental influences such as growing health awareness. This is often easier for classic grocery markets than for the newer types of advertising that are becoming relatively important – business to business, retail, financial, government sponsored, political, but it is amazing how difficult it is to recover accurate and complete records of promotions, pricing and media spend by month and region even for major grocery brands and their competitors.
- *Sufficient* – a large number of data points are needed to give a reasonable level of confidence. The more complex the model (i.e. the greater the number of variables, changes in the variables, complicated forms of the variables) the more data is required to give reliable results.
- *Varied* – since the method is based on analysing past variation no infor-mation is given on variables which have not varied significantly. Fur-thermore, the input series need to be independent from one another, i.e. cannot habitually vary together. This requirement is not necessarily within the control of would-be econometricians.
- *Good* – inaccuracy or changes in the input data will jeopardize the reliability of the output. Data series spanning years often suffer from adjustments of methodology or sampling corrections. Records of price and promotions through store panels or from diaries are often vague, inaccurate and aggregated in a way designed to destroy meaning.

There are techniques for strapping together discontinuous data series, filling in gaps, using dummy variables for unmeasurable effects and substituting proxy or estimated variables for trends e.g. increasing health awareness. The problem is that each of these actions insidiously erodes the reliability of the results.

If the input data is inadequate, econometric analysis simply cannot deliver usable results. This is often hard to accept and leads to the processing of inadequate data into highly dubious results (garbage in garbage out, as the saying goes).

2   Processing

User-friendly computers will happily churn out results for anyone, but the computer has limited power to explain and caution about the results.

The first precaution should be to trust only results produced by a trained and experienced statistician, who can cope with the sophisticated models needed to handle non-linear effects and changing elasticities and, above all, who can keep sight of the receding reliability. However, even this sensible precaution does not entirely solve the problem.

In the illustration, Clueless and Cassata were left feeling that despite the uselessness of their model, the coefficient of 0.2 given for the advertising effect was usable. Somehow, once the results are printed by a computer it is much more difficult for a manager to generate a qualitative feeling for the uncertainty.

Even where the model is produced by a statistician who understands the pitfalls and limitations, it is then handed over to managers who do not. The managers either accept the risks of misapplying and misinterpreting the model, or they reject such risks and the modelling effort is wasted.

For these two reasons there are many occasions where econometrics is unable to provide a usable and useful input to advertising decisions. Few agencies are likely to find it worthwhile to provide the considerable statistical expertise necessary, in house.

However, there are ways of collecting more processable data and ways of developing models which are more robust and manager friendly. These are the ways forward and the ways in which the average advertising professional can benefit from cheaper computers.

The best alternative to trying to model the whole market, is to manipulate activities so that comparisons can be made while other variables are controlled in some way. That is to say experiments.

Experiments

Experiments generate data which are not only easier to interpret but also richer in information. Good experimental design means:

1 Holding other variables constant while the effects of the test variable are being examined.
2 Inputting many levels of the test variable, to obtain a range of readings on its effects.

The great advantage of good experimental design is that it can actually indicate and quantify causal effects.

Physicists in a laboratory are able to create near-perfect experiments, researchers in advertising have to make do with the best experimental design they can get. They then patch up the weaknesses in design by using external data, logic and past experience. This half-and-half method rarely provides actual proof or disproof, but in many cases the two approaches converge to give usable indications.

Experimental designs

The essence of experimentation is making comparisons. To set up experiments you need to arrange activities so that valid comparisons can be made afterwards. Good experimental design basically means well-matched test units (e.g. areas, groups of people, stores or whatever) and as many comparable test units as possible so that a variety of levels of input can be measured. Here six typical designs are discussed to help suggest some of the features to adopt or avoid.

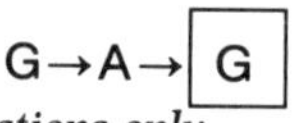

$$G \rightarrow A \rightarrow \boxed{G}$$

Figure 6.9   *One test unit, post observations only*

1 A population is surveyed after the test variable has operated (Figure 6.9). Test unit G is exposed to activity A. The box represents an observation; time is represented across the page, left to right.

   This design hardly merits the title of experiment.* It gives the current status, but no clues on causality. However, ecologists, psychoanalysts and advertisers frequently have to make use of such information, as

---

*This is the basic thesis of Milan Kundera's fashionable book *The Unbearable Lightness of Being.*[6] As an experimental design, life is lousy – man is unable to optimize his way of being.

this situation occurs whenever research results are presented without a previous, similar survey for comparison. These results can, on occasion, be made to provide usable results, though it is essential to obtain complementary information. (See 'analysis' below.)

2 Two or more comparable groups are exposed to different activities. The

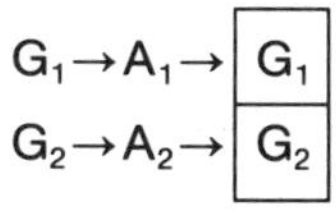

$$G_1 \rightarrow A_1 \rightarrow \boxed{G_1}$$
$$G_2 \rightarrow A_2 \rightarrow \boxed{G_2}$$

Figure 6.10 *Two (or more) groups, post observations only*

groups are observed subsequently (Figure 6.10). It is always desirable to have pre- as well as post-observations, but there are many cases when research can only be organized 'post ex facto'. This is also the design which results from using split runs in press (see below).

The key weakness in the design is, obviously, that observed differences might have existed previously, i.e. before the activity being examined. In many cases this possibility renders the results unusable. Multiple samples (for example a number of regions which experience different weights of advertising) improve the probability of readable results by reducing the chance that the differences were all attributable to initial differences. It should be ascertained that no systematic scheme was used to select the advertising activity (e.g. distribution strength, deals with retailers).

3 An observation is taken of a population, who are then exposed to some advertising activity, and observed again (Figure 6.11).

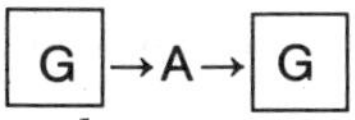

$$\boxed{G} \rightarrow A \rightarrow \boxed{G}$$

Figure 6.11 *One test unit, pre and post*

This is a very commonly-used design, despite some pretty impressive weaknesses (see below). The temptation is to attribute any change in the dependent variable (e.g. sales share) to the test variable (e.g. an advertising campaign), without having sufficient evidence to rule out other explanations. Additional controls should be brought in as suggested below.

4 Two or more populations are observed, exposed to different levels of the test variable, and observed again (see Figure 6.12).

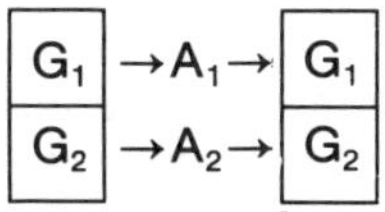

$$\boxed{G_1} \rightarrow A_1 \rightarrow \boxed{G_1}$$
$$\boxed{G_2} \rightarrow A_2 \rightarrow \boxed{G_2}$$

Figure 6.12 *Two (or more) groups, pre and post observations*

This is a popular design, particularly in the form where one group is exposed and the second is not and acts as the control. To be meaningful, the groups should initially be as closely matched as possible. This is usually checked in terms of profile (age, sex, socioeconomic group) and product/brand use and awareness. They should not be selected on some biassing procedure (for example, the test group all volunteering themselves). This design is generally more robust and more likely to generate interpretable results. Even better results are obtained if *several equivalent groups* can be exposed to *different levels of the test variable*. Several readings, showing a correlation between the input level and the effect, provide much more convincing evidence than the simple difference between an exposed and unexposed group. Test units which suffer particular accidents of history (e.g. a competitive launch) can be dropped without destroying the whole experiment.

5   Two or more pre-test stages (giving the design shown in Figure 6.13) add considerably to the reliability of an experiment, by allowing some control over the problems of regression and maturation (see below).

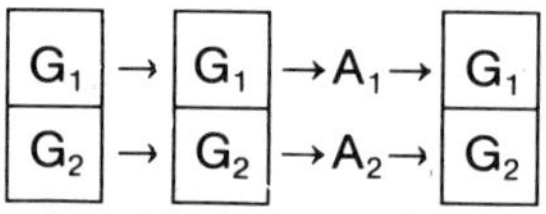

$$G_1 \rightarrow G_1 \rightarrow A_1 \rightarrow G_1$$
$$G_2 \rightarrow G_2 \rightarrow A_2 \rightarrow G_2$$

Figure 6.13   *Two (or more) matched groups, two pre and one post observation*

However, most research purchasers are reluctant to invest in multiple pre-tests (even assuming time is available) despite the favourable statistical arguments. This is one of the reasons why continuous data, not only on sales but also on attitudinal data, is very attractive to the researcher.

6   One group, several observations over time following different actions, usually including no action (Figure 6.14).

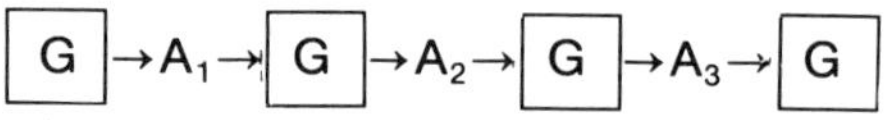

$$G \rightarrow A_1 \rightarrow G \rightarrow A_2 \rightarrow G \rightarrow A_3 \rightarrow G$$

Figure 6.14   *One group, several observations over time*

The design starts off as a one group pre and post, which as indicated above is not very robust. However, the results become more and more valuable if they are repeated regularly. Ideally, a second observation would be made while the activity continues, as shown in Figure 6.15, as this gives information on limits to the advertising effect. If the effect of advertising diminishes after a while, without this extra observation it would not be possible to estimate whether the decline was due solely to the withdrawal, or whether diminishing returns were already being found with the advertising.

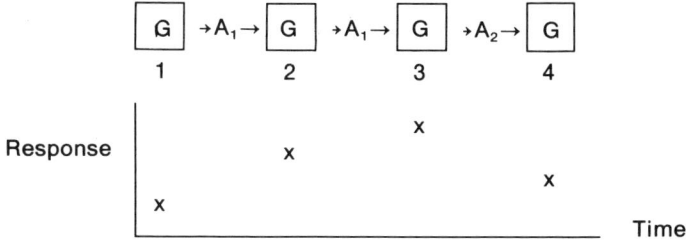

Figure 6.15   *One test unit, G, is observed before and during advertising activity, A_1. Further observations are made at the end of advertising activity, and some time after its withdrawal (A_2 is zero activity). The results show the plateauing of advertising effects, as well as the decline after withdrawal.*

Regular observations after withdrawal add to the understanding of the decline, and to the reliability of the results. As more observations are made and more activities are tried the data becomes richer and there is a better chance of being able to make a confident interpretation. This again underlines the value of continuous data.

Creating these experimental designs means grasping opportunities to create comparable test units, and then deciding and organizing the necessary observations.

Setting up experiments

Creating comparable test units means exposing defined and monitorable groups of people to different (known) advertising activities.

The four most common ways of creating comparable test units are – by area, using split copy services, by artificially exposing recruited samples and by varying advertising activity over time.

Area tests – regions or towns

No two areas are identical, but they can be used to create more or less comparable groups. Different areas can be exposed to different levels of media spend, creative material or combinations of marketing tools.

Area tests offer the possibility of measuring the effects of advertising in situations where measurement would be impossible otherwise, for example the effect of advertising on a new product launch, or long-run effects. The difficulties are in drawing clear boundaries between areas, accurate measurement and control of extraneous variables.

Matched stores/supermarkets are more practical for pricing and packaging, than for advertising response, because of the problems of presenting the advertising naturally.

Split copy

Split cable services for television (e.g. Stats Scan[7]) or split runs for press ads, create matched samples exposed to different advertising activity.

Split cable means a research company recruits a panel of consumers who agree to receive all their television channels through a cable network controlled by the research company. They either record all their purchases in a diary and/or carry an identity card (usually entitling them to a small discount) when they shop at their local supermarket. The local supermarket is equipped with scanners which record the number on the card and all the purchases made by the card-holder.

To test television advertising, the sponsoring manufacturer buys a television spot and then instructs the research company to use their cable facility to replace the spot purchased with the test spot (or spots) according to the design of the experiment. Thus a proportion of the panel can be subjected to a different advertising input from their copanelists.

Current services have been set up for supermarket products but there is every reason to expect that the method will be adapted to cope with durables and services in the future. This could be done, for example, by adapting ads to elicit a direct response (say sending for a brochure on a holiday or a new car, or a discount voucher usable against a washing machine).

The main disadvantage is expense. Provided that the panel members manage to remain representative, this methodology promises to be an extremely significant development in television advertising research.

Split runs in press mean half the editions of a magazine or newspaper are printed with one version of an ad and half with another (the coupons are coded to be identifiable), or different versions are produced by area.

Split runs teamed with direct response give a very exact impression of sales effectiveness. With a bit of imagination, even advertising not primarily designed as direct response, can be tested in this way, particularly where comparisons need to be made. For example, two press executions of an ad for a cosmetic (the old vs new campaign, say) can be modified to offer a trial sample in return for a stamped addressed envelope or a small charge, or two alternative arguments for giving to a charity can be tried out in press, before producing the television execution.

Artificial exposure (laboratory methods/hall tests)

Test units are created by specially recruiting matched samples of respondents. The sample groups are then artificially exposed to some (or no) advertising activity. The set-up can be more or less sophisticated – some research companies ask respondents to purchase subsequently from a specially constructed display, or controlled supermarket.[8] Diagnostic data can be collected after exposure or purchasing, longer-term effects (e.g. intention to repeat) can be collected in follow-up surveys.

Over time

If it is not possible to generate comparable groups, the test group can act as its own control group if repeated observations are made following changes in activity. This means that the test units are the same group of people, but at different points in time. In effect, this was the type of experiment that Clueless and Cassata were investigating.

The opportunity to make comparisons should be routinely planned-in to all advertising investments. Testing should be on the agenda along with any plans to spend money (e.g. media plans). Often the only discernable cost attached to planning activity along experimental lines is the effort involved.

Observations – the measurements to be used

The reason for introducing experiments in this chapter was that they often offer the best possibility of actually capturing sales effects. If this is the objective, then actual sales or brand share would be the key measurement. Brand share is often preferable as it helps control for global market effects such as seasonality, or long-term growth in the market.

In some cases, and particularly where advertising makes a relatively minor contribution to sales, measurement has to aim for the limit of what advertising can be expected to achieve – test drives or enquiries, or even attitude change, purchasing intentions or claimed behaviour.

Consumer panels can provide richly diagnostic data. The diagnostic value comes from their unique quality of tracking particular consumers over time. This means that the data can be used to analyse the changes in buying habits which lie behind the overall changes in sales volume. Thus one can examine whether new buyers have been brought into the market or to the brand, whether previous users have bought more frequently or whether customers have switched some of their loyalty from one brand to another. Depending on the sample size it may be possible to determine the demographics of the people who have reacted most strongly to the advertising.

Consumer interviews can give insightful data, even though actual sales are not captured. Consumer research can be designed to compare proportions of new users against all users, or type of use or weight of use across the test units, as well as attitude and preference ratings or intention to purchase.

For example, in a one-area test on the effect of television advertising for a brand of mint sweets, a pre- and post-consumer survey (matched sample of 600) showed the proportion of respondents who had 'ever purchased' to have remained exactly stable. However, the proportion of these people claiming to have purchased 'within the last fortnight' had shot up. The survey had valuable implications:

1   Sales had probably been affected.
2   The effect occurred through prompting existing users.
3   The extremely cheap off-peak television spots (bought as a bargain package by the client) seemed to have been capable of reaching the users – 73 per cent claimed to have seen the ad in the last two weeks.

Results like these are certainly better than nothing, though claimed purchasing cannot be reliably converted into volume sales. The sales effect and profit implications were only suggested.

When research has to be organized post hoc, consumer interviews offer the possibility of converting to a more sophisticated experimental design by asking respondents to look back in time. This means questions such as: 'Do you remember how you first came to try X?'

When setting up research for which no pre-stage exists it is also worth looking at past research and seeing whether any previous measurements can be replicated to create a quasi-pre-statistic.

Direct response can provide very good measures of sales effect. As described above, it can be teamed with split copy to give information on ads not primarily designed as direct response. In some cases direct response techniques can be employed to compare advertising effects across test units e.g. by measuring responsiveness to coupon press ads or direct mail shots, before and after television advertising.

The problems

The appeal of experiments is that they produce pure and rich data from which causal effects sing out. This is true if the experiment runs perfectly according to plan. However, in field experiments there are almost always complications which threaten the best-laid schemes of mice and managers. The subsequent analysis has to compensate for these effects, to isolate meaningful results.

Extraneous variables

For example, a competitor stops advertising, or puts his prices up during the test period. Far from being unlucky and unusual this almost always happens to some degree. The effects may be neutral or insignificant, but the uncertainty is enough to invalidate the experiment, unless specific efforts are made in the analysis.

Statistical regression

Values of a variable, such as yearly road accidents, naturally vary around a mean (which may itself be following a systematic trend). If one statistic, through chance or a specific cause (e.g. the weather) is well below or above average, there is a tendency for the next statistic to 'regress towards the mean'. This tendency is called statistical regression.

For example, suppose a year of exceptionally high road accidents gives rise to an advertising campaign. The advertising is very likely to show a positive result, when assessed on the subsequent year's figure. If your reaction to this example is that no one would be so stupid as to look at only the last two figures in the series, can we safely assume that you have never supported the use of a two-wave pre-post test?

The obvious antidote is a series of statistics (or, at the minimum, two 'pre' statistics) which reach into the past and establish the mean.

Maturation

This refers to changes which occur within the test units over the period of the experiment. If you gave aspirin to a sample of people with colds, the majority would be cured by the end of a week. To draw usable conclusions from this you would need either to estimate the maturation effect, using past data, or use a control group.

Surveys in the confectionery market often report a move in tastes towards less sweet flavours, based on agreement with statements such as: 'I like sweet tastes less than I used to.' This contradicts the behaviour of the market. This could be a maturation effect – as people get older they have a decreasing taste for sweetness. However, new consumers with an infantile love of sweetness are forever getting to the age when they first have pocketmoney.

Testing influences

A bias can be introduced simply by the act of asking questions e.g. making people more observant by taking pre-exposure measures in a laboratory-style test.

If the test is spread over time, there may be a systematic bias in the type of respondents who drop out (an effect known as 'mortality').

Another test bias (called 'instrumentation') is introduced if methodology or classifications are changed in any way, between observations. A rather subtle version of this problem affected a survey used by a fast-service restaurant to track its image among its users. The survey showed disappointing falls on virtually all image and satisfaction measures, during a period when sales were increasing steadily and advertising activity was high. This conundrum was eventually solved when someone realized that the pool of 'users' had greatly widened and that the later arrivals were probably less committed. They lowered the *average* image and satisfaction level among 'all users'. The mistake was to select the samples on the basis of a criterion (usage) which was not stable. The explanation brought relief, but it did not save the image data from being class one useless junk.

Equivalency of test units

Advertising experiments can never hope to create exactly comparable test units. Whether the test units are areas, matched samples of people, or the same people at different times, their equivalency is less than 100 per cent.

External validity

Strictly speaking, even if an experiment is successful in showing a causal effect, the causal effect has only been proven for that one occasion. However, the purpose of experiments is usually to provide information against which to plan future activity. The question of external validity asks: Do these results apply not just to the test sample but to other populations? (do results in large supermarkets hold in small ones, do results among weekday shoppers hold for women who work full time? People in this area react in this way, but are they typical of the whole country?) and do the results obtained in the test situation generalize to other situations (for example, from this year to next year, from artificial to broadcast exposure?)

Analysing experiments

The point of using experiments is to provide easier analysis. The basic technique is comparison, the basic objective is to isolate causal effects. If the experiment is tightly controlled and has gone according to plan, the results can be read off directly, the only confusion being normal statistical error. The fun begins if there is a need to compensate for some of the problems just discussed.

There are no simple rules for analysis, the experimenter has to tailor the analysis, and innovate depending on the data he has. The following notes suggest some useful techniques.

Time series

Time series are graphs which plot a variable (such as sales or temperature) over time. Time runs left to right along the horizontal axis, while values of the variable are measured vertically.

Time series graphs should be produced for the dependent or effect variable (sales, awareness etc.), for the test variable (e.g. advertising spend), and for any other variables that might have influenced the dependent or effect variables (distribution, promotional activity etc.).

If all the graphs, for all test units and all variables are drawn to the same time scale on thin or transparent paper (or on a computer), they can be overlayed on one another for easy comparison. This simple graphical technique is invaluable for making visible the possible effects of test and other variables, and spotting the differences between test units.

The dependent variable, the one being explained, can be presented in different ways. Since the problem is usually that this variable (e.g. sales) is affected by several explanatory variables (seasonality, competitive activity) choosing a different 'form' for the dependent variable can simplify the task by removing one of the explanatory variables from the analysis. So, for example, it may be plausible to take out seasonality or the effect of market growth by plotting brand share rather than straight sales. Similarly, plotting sales in the form of a ratio comparing sales in the test area with sales in the rest of the country can control for competitive activity (if the competitive activity has been national). This process can continue – plotting the ratio of brand share in the test area over brand share in some other area of the country, may be a way of removing seasonality, market growth and competitive activity.

These more complicated forms are usually suggested sequentially by the initial plots. An initial plot of sales against temperature may indicate seasonality. Brand share is then shown to nullify this effect and is thus preferred. Brand share is shown to be sensitive to competitive activity, which can be removed by taking the ratio of the test area with another comparable area not receiving the test influence, but still experiencing the competitive activity.

Time series are a powerful tool. As a rule of thumb one can say that if results are not visible in the time series plots, then they are probably not provable by more sophisticated methods.

Scatter plots

Scatter plots, or cross plots, are created by plotting two corresponding values for each of the test units. For example, if the test units were different areas, advertising spend during the test period might be plotted on the horizontal axis and change in sales in the period after the activity might be plotted on the vertical axis (See Figure 6.16).

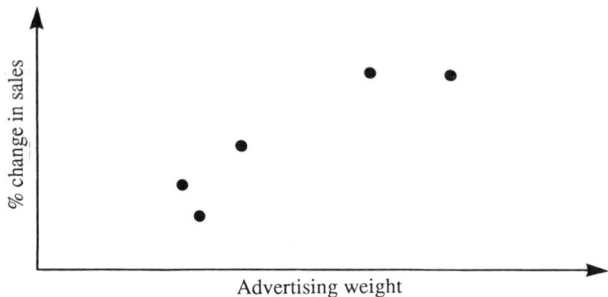

Figure 6.16   *A scatter (or cross) plot of advertising weight against change in sales for five different areas. The points correspond to the test units, areas in this case. There is clearly a positive correlation betwen advertising weight and sales change*

Scatter plots visualize the correlation between the two variables plotted. Figure 6.16 shows a positive correlation between advertising weight and sales change.

In Figure 6.16, change in sales was plotted, rather than absolute sales. Processing the variables in this way brings in more data and helps to control for extraneous variables, or initial differences in the test units. For example, a further step would be to plot changes in brand share rather than volume sales. This would help to compensate for certain extraneous variables such as seasonality or a growing market. In the same way it may be revealing to compare the demand curve (i.e. scatter plot of price against sales) in the different areas, subject to differing advertising inputs. This refinement would help to control for the extraneous variable price. Obviously plotting 'price relative to competitors' vs 'brandshare' compensates for even more extraneous variables (by bringing in more and more extra data).

Scatter plots can be plotted for experiments which run through time – in this case the points plotted will be different times, and the two values readings taken at that particular time.

Looking for signatures

Signatures can strongly suggest causality, where simple correlation cannot. Hence, if pre and post results for an 'extended use' campaign recorded a marked increase in sales, in itself this would be suggestive but not convincing (in any two periods sales are likely to go either up or down). However, showing that after the 'extra uses' campaign users were more frequently claiming to use for the new uses, would suggest that the extra sales were indeed being caused by the advertising. Similarly, spotting a signature may make it possible to redeem results from a good experimental design which has become confused by extraneous variables.

Looking for causal links in a one-off survey is not a hopeless task, if one can find a 'signature' which links effects to one particular cause. For example, if repeat buyers of a new product recall a specific message from the advertising while lapsed trialists do not, one could generate the hypothesis that the message was instrumental in encouraging commitment.

Using non-affected non-test variables

If the results concern several test units, it is often important to establish what differences existed between the test groups, before exposure. One way of arguing that the initial groups were comparable is to compare the groups on any available statistics other than that of interest and those that are unlikely to be affected by the exposure e.g. age, sex, wealth.

Dropping data

Depending on the experimental design it might be possible to drop some results while still having a workable portion. This is justifiable if some test units or time periods are known to have been significantly affected by an event (e.g. a strike). This practice is also justifiable if one result on the time series or scatter plot seems well out of line even without any known cause. Such points are called 'outliers' and risk strongly distorting conclusions if they are processed with the other data, and are for some reason in error.

A technique to avoid

It is sometimes tempting when analysing the effect of an advertising campaign, to compare all those who claim to have seen the advertising with those who claim not to have seen it. The mistake is then to attribute differences in buying behaviour and attitudes to the experience of having seen the advertising.

This is, of course, a twentieth century 'chicken and egg'. Which came first – the buying behaviour or the decision to notice the advertising? This correlation is, however, a favourite red herring in agencies. Served up lightly cooked and with appropriate sauce to their clients, it can, to the untrained palate, be mistaken for the true flavour of causality.

Introducing extra data – creating models

An experiment which runs over time is almost always affected by extraneous events. One extraneous event can ruin a simple pre-post test, but repeated tests are more robust and can often be interpreted intelligently by using extra data on the extraneous variables. This data could be corresponding time series such as the weather or the retail price index, a 'seasonality' variable, surrogates for trend (for example the proportion of brown to white bread sales, which is monitored by government statistics can be used to give an index on the 'fibre' fashion, which is a factor in the breakfast cereal market), or estimates of parameters, such as the decay of ad recall, calculated from other experiments. It is also possible to use some of the sound experimental information to estimate the effects of the extraneous variable(s).

This was demonstrated in the Clueless and Cassata illustration where extra data was brought in on the weather and disposable income. In fact econometrics is an example of a sophisticated method available for handling rather unruly data produced by poor experimental design.

Although the analysis of experiments can become very involved, the objective of experiments is to create better and clearer data. If the experiment has become confounded for reasons beyond the advertising team's control, it is often more realistic to shrug and hope for better luck next time.

The advantage of sticking to simpler techniques is that the managers who design the experiments can carry out all the analyses themselves (hopefully on their own desktop computers). They understand the results thoroughly and they will therefore use them confidently. A very important, additional advantage is that the process of analysis itself, as against the final results, gives the experimenters a 'feel' for the effects they are monitoring.

Furthermore, understanding the problems of analysis, and the gaps in understanding, is a useful input into the design of the next round of experimentation.

Turbo-charged guesswork

There are still going to be cases where the advertising response curve remains unmeasurable, so that important decisions such as setting the ad budget have to be based on the manager's best estimate. Given this situation it is sensible to get serious about guessing. This means becoming more conscious of the guesses (also called 'implicit assumptions') currently being made and asking whether there are systematic ways of improving the quality of these guesses.

In fact, considerable effort has been devoted to analysing and formalizing the judgement of managers. There is even a glamorous name for it – decision calculus.

These are some examples of the tools and the ways they can be used:

Aggregating answers

If you ask a hall full of people each to estimate the length of the hall and average the answers, the group estimate will be more accurate on average, than the estimates of the individuals. This is because some people will over-estimate and some will underestimate and the errors tend to cancel each other out.

In the same way, asking the managers involved in a project each to give estimates, and then averaging, should achieve a better estimate than that from one individual or even the consensus of a committee which has adopted one particular set of errors.

This technique can be applied to estimating the advertising response curve.

Ask the executives involved (say between five and ten), independently, the following five questions:

1   What sales would you expect next year if advertising was dropped to zero?
2   What sales would you expect next year if advertising was dropped to half the current rate?
3   What sales would you expect next year if your ad budget is kept the same as this year?
4   What sales would you expect next year if your advertising is increased by 50 per cent?
5   What level of advertising would you estimate to give saturation? What level of sales would you predict for that spend?

The five (averaged) estimates so obtained can be plotted to give the team's best estimate of the advertising response function. Perhaps none of the participants will believe the curve they generate (s-shaped or concave?) but they will be interested to see it appear before their eyes for the first time.

Decomposing questions

Suppose the treasurer of a bridge club needs to estimate its expenditure for the next year. Rather than directly estimate the total he is more likely to decompose his estimate. He lists all types of expenditure (new packs of cards, stationery, rent, Christmas party), makes separate estimates for each item and then sums the estimates. The advantage of this technique is that it helps the decision maker(s) make full use of all available information.

Turning to marketing applications, consider the task of estimating a new product's sales, before the launch. The question can be decomposed into level of trial and rate of conversion to first and subsequent repeats. These in turn can be related to say, media reach, interest on seeing advertising, distribution and satisfaction after trying. These factors can be estimated individually, perhaps using specially designed research, and by studying the media and trade promotional plans.

Such a decomposition not only improves the final estimate, but also focuses the manager's attention on the sensitivity of sales to the various elements in his model. The model also provides a framework against which to assess the actual results when they become available.

The complicated choice algorithm

When a child has trouble choosing one cake from a plateful, he can be helped like this: Pick two cakes at random and ask which of them he prefers. Retain the preferred one and compare it with a third and so on. Such paired choices are easy compared to the enormous task of choosing one best option from a large range, and soon the optimum is reached (or rather eaten).

A similar system can speed up the choice of candidate brand names from a large list – consider the candidates in pairs, choose one, drop both or pass both. Each time through the list should roughly halve it. A team of three can select ten names from 500, painlessly, in half an hour.

Conjoint analysis, the method introduced in the bleach manufacturer example in Chapter 2 (see page 38) exploits this ability to make simple paired comparisons. In that example it was used to investigate consumer preferences between product characteristics, but it can also be used to help managers reveal their implicit values.

For example[9], take the problem of allocating a marketing budget between a selection of marketing tools (e.g. consumer and trade advertising, consumer and trade promotions, trade fairs, conferences, sales force incentives). A comprehensive list of alternative combinations is created, say nine options at each of three budget levels. The twenty-seven options are then given to a selection of managers, who rank the options according to their estimated effectiveness, disregarding price (a task which only requires paired comparisons).

Computer analysis of the ranking will reveal quantified values for the worth put on each tool by the managers, as it did for the product characteristics (viscosity etc.) in Chapter 2. It thus gives the relative worth of each of the tools which can then be compared to the actual cost.

Back of an envelope and probability calculations

One of the themes stressed in this book is that advertising professionals have to make decisions under uncertainty. Sometimes doing a range of calculations which consider the possible outcomes of a decision, can help a manager cope with his lack of definite knowledge.

For example, a manager feels that a substantial increase in his advertising budget would lead to increased profits, but it is only a feeling. Instead of forcing himself into a yes/no judgement on the issue (which he finds difficult) he can try to assign probabilities to the possible outcomes. These probabilities represent his level of uncertainty. He can then use these probabilities to calculate an expected value and work back to the implied decision, like this:

Double ad budget, cost X
Probability that sales increase by 20%? estimate: 0.3
Probability that sales increase by 10%? estimate: 0.5
Probability that sales increase by 0%? estimate: 0.2
Expected sales increase $= 20\% \times 0.3 + 10\% \times 0.5 + 0\% \times 0.2$
$$= 11\%$$
11% increase implies Y extra revenue
marginal profit rate is y
Compare X and Y/y

Sales increases can be related by further back-of-an-envelope calculations to ad strategy – it means so many new users or so many extra purchases per year by current users. Does this seem realistic?

Calculations like these often help one become more conscious of the relationships between brand size, marginal profit, sensitivity to advertising and the profitability of advertising.

It might seem worrying that the people involved in judgemental decisions are not disinterested. This is true, and may be unfortunate, but it does not counterindicate the use of turbocharged decisions – the same bias would influence any decisions the team makes. In some cases it is useful to have the process administered by an independent agent such as a market research or consultancy company.

Similarly, it does not matter if the managers are making complete guesses, i.e. have no hard data whatsoever to back up their estimates – the complete guesses would have been made anyway.

Becoming explicit actually encourages managers to think up ways of obtaining the missing information.

Computers for all

Each of the turbo-charged guesswork examples above (estimating the response curve, estimating a new product's sales, allocating a marketing budget, and estimating the profit implications of different outcomes) involved building a simple model.

Models make the world more comprehensible. They simplify and collate information. They are formed by taking the most important characteristics common to the real objects under consideration.

A model of how a friend behaves allows us to work out who our friends are, and how to be a friend. When a new experience arrives concerning something for which we have a model (e.g. a friend borrows our car without asking) reference back to the model leads to one of two outcomes, either:

1   The model helps us to process and question reality (... is this person in fact a friend?), or
2   the model is altered to cope with reality, and thus becomes truer and more helpful (friendship also means putting up with some invasion of privacy and autonomy).

In the same way models of advertising response or new product sales help managers process reality. If reality does not fit the predictions of the existing model questions can be asked to pinpoint the cause of the discrepancy. Alternatively, the model may be improved and a richer level of understanding attained.

The models described above were all so simple that (with the exception of the conjoint analysis example) they could be handled with pencil, paper and calculator. However, changing the parameters to try out slightly different scenarios takes time with paper and pencil. They can be made faster and more enjoyable if the models are fed into a personal computer.

Five years ago, the idea of a manager in an ad agency or marketing department handling this sort of activity on a computer would have seemed unreal. Currently it is no more than avant-garde. Computer programs are becoming genuinely usable by non-computer trained personnel, and cheap computers now have the power to provide rapid data analysis and good graphics.

The advantages of bringing the data handling and modelling into the hands of the involved managers are significant. The creation of (judgemental) models makes managers more aware of the gaps in their knowledge and increases their desire to experiment and learn. The models can then be validated or modified by the results of those experiments. This tends to imply a very active, motivated use of the experimental data.

In turn, managers are able to bring better intuition to the judgemental modelling as their understanding deepens and becomes more accurate through experimentation and handling data.

These benefits only accrue if the modelling and data handling are the responsibility of the management team, and not some more qualified, but more remote specialist. The information revolution is better used bringing mildly sophisticated techniques to people who can really act on the results, than bringing mindblowingly convoluted analysis to some department which fails to communicate with the people at the sharp end.

Developing a model of how advertising works in the marketplace is the key aim of feedback. Rocking backwards and forwards between these two techniques, experiments and decision calculus, is probably the most realistic way of getting there.

Notes and references

1   Bogart, Leo and Lehman, Charles, 'The Case of the 30-second Commercial', *Journal of Advertising Research*, vol. 23, no. 1, Feb/March 1983.

2   Such as Thomas, Angus et al. 'Dettol: A Case History', in *Advertising Works*, Broadbent, Simon (ed), IPA, 1981.

3   Such as SPSS – Stats Pack for Social Sciences from North Western University.

4   Little, John, 'Aggregate Advertising Models: The State of the Art', *Journal of Operations Research*, April 1979

5   Bultez, Alain V. and Naert, Philippe A., 'Does Lag Structure Really Matter in Optimizing Advertising Expenditures?', *Management Science*, vol. 25, no. 5, May 1979.

6   Kundera, Milan, *The Unbearable Lightness of Being*, Harper & Row, 1984.

7   HTV provides Stats Scan, demographically matched samples in South Wales.

8   Stewart, David W., Furse, David H. and Kozak, Randell P., 'A Guide to Commercial Copy Testing Services', *Current Issues and Research in Advertising*, vol. 1, 1983; Carefoot, John, 'Copy Testing with Scanners', *Journal of Advertising Research*, vol. 22, no. 1, 1982.

9   Adapted from Naert, Philippe A., Weverbergh, M., Verswijfel, G., *Subjective Estimation in Integrating Communication Budget and Allocation Decisions: A case study*, Working paper 85–108, Centrum voor Bedrijfs economie en Bedrijfseconometrie Universiteit Antwerpen, August 1985.

7 Endwords

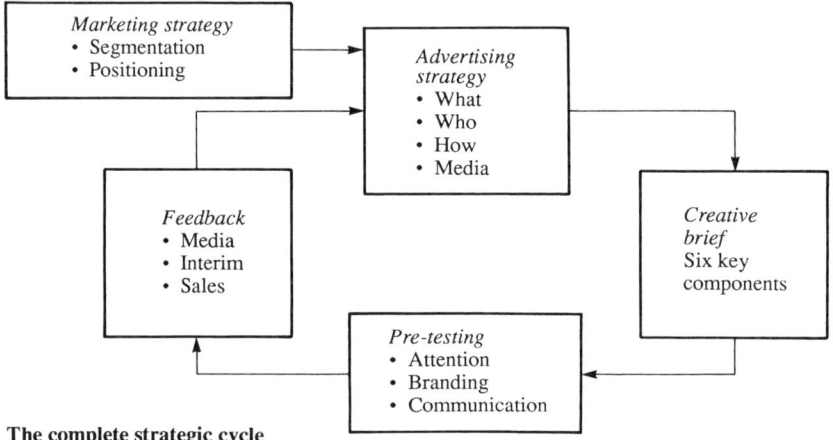

The complete strategic cycle

The theory and techniques described so far for developing strategic advertising, are not revolutionary or particularly subtle. Not many advertising professionals would disagree with them. The difficulty is usually in applying them systematically.

Advertising development is inevitably an established activity in all advertising companies and agencies. The challenge is to improve the execution of some very basic functions. In many ways this is more difficult than introducing completely new ideas.

This, last, chapter presents a few thoughts on applying the theories described in this book, in practice.

Delicate strategy

Strategic thinking has been described as 'important' rather than 'urgent' and as 'compressible' rather than 'incompressible', terms which well capture its vulnerable nature.

Suppose an advertising executive starts his week intending to go through the (rather scattered) reels of competitive advertising in preparation for writing the advertising strategy. Suppose he also has to make sure that 100 copies of a photo from the current television ad are delivered to a hotel in Cardiff in time for the sales conference on Friday.

The first task is important, the second is urgent. He will be scalped if the photos miss the conference, probably nobody will ever know for sure whether he has reviewed the competitive ads or not.

As preparation for writing the advertising strategy he also intends to read the qualitative post-test of last year's ads and on Wednesday he is booked from 9 am to 6 pm to give the new assistant research manager a briefing on all his brands. The first task is compressible (he just reads the summary) the second task is incompressible by definition.

Strategic thinking needs to be protected from the urgent and the incompressible – somehow it has to be guaranteed the attention it deserves.

Strategic thinking is also a creative process – actual ideas are demanded. On the whole we have a tendency to avoid such tasks. Creative teams have to know that they have got to do something before they can begin to concentrate. Many people find they actually need the pressure of a deadline, necessity being the mother of invention.

Creating the culture that encourages strategic thinking

Most advertising professionals already recognize the need to develop a fertile culture with respect to one area of advertising development – the creative process. They already try to provide an encouraging, even slightly protective environment for the creative personnel. They try to provide them with precisely-defined tasks and to suspend evaluation of their output in order to develop, rather than kill, half-formed ideas.

The same managers are generally much less careful about creating a positive culture in the rest of the development cycle. However, improving strategy means becoming more 'creative' outside the creative department.

Strategy is usually a logical rather than tangential mental process, but the logic still needs to be creative. Logical solutions are ideas which themselves need to be innovative and original. Encouraging strategic thinking means encouraging creativity. The need for better ideas to feed to the creative department implies improving the culture or environment in which strategic ideas are expected to grow.

Creativity has an interesting parallel in humour. Humour involves originality and making unexpected connections; humour is a widespread human trait though some people are undoubtedly wittier than others; humour can be encouraged or discouraged by circumstances and experiences.

The parallel is interesting because advertising people are generally expert at cultivating humour. They do it like this:

1   Jokes and wit are valued and praised. Being funny is a way of being liked and admired.
2   The penalties of failure are kept small. It is good to be a funny guy and it is good to give positive feedback in the form of hearty laughter. It is frowned on to be a killjoy. The joker is treated gently on the occasions when he fails to be funny.
3   There is a friendly conspiracy to build on other people's jokes. Everyone wins when everyone laughs, a joke is 'shared' and the repartee belongs to everyone who joins in.

In contrast, strategic ideas often get a less nurturing reception. This imaginary conversation between a joker/strategist and his five cynical colleagues, illustrates the point:

JS: 'Hey, I've got an idea for the new fruit drink.'
CC1:   'Oh yeah?'
JS: 'What about: the winter fruit juice to supplement your diet in the months when you miss the sunshine and eat less fresh fruit?'
CC1:   'It's rather restrictive, the client's brief specifically says: "delicious health drink for everyone, for everyday and for *all seasons*" '
CC2:   'It's not very brand-specific either, why couldn't JaffaSplash say that?'
CC3:   'Anyway, I'm not sure we'd have the right to say diet supplement.'
CC4:   'Quite honestly, I don't think there is a solution for a complete me-too like this one.'
CC5:   'Yes, on this one it's really up to the creatives, we just need something really zany and full of impact.'
JS: 'Yeah, stupid idea. How about "contains vitamins that haven't even been discovered yet" or "does you good even though you can't feel it?" '
CCs together: *Raucous laughter*

This *is* an imaginary conversation, but very much based on real life. The cynical remarks sound quite reasonable and innocent, but quietly and destructively contradict several sound ideas of marketing and advertising strategy.

Cynic 1 fails to grasp that strategies *have* to be restrictive (see Chapter 2). Segmentation and positioning imply making the product more specific. You have to say goodbye to some customers, if you are going to serve another group more closely.

Cynic 2 feels happy using the term 'brand specific' without understanding what branding is. Branding means *attaching* some specific imagary to the product.

Cynic 3 makes the brutal mistake of jumping on the form i.e. the words, that JS used to convey his idea, and not its content. What he should be trying to do is take the content of the idea and build and develop it – as he would a joke. Instead he bludgeons a genuine idea with a brick wall of pedantry.

Cynic 4, who doesn't believe there is a solution, and calls the product a complete me-too, is falling into the trap of believing that the positioning exists within the product. These guys have the responsibility for thinking up the marketing and advertising strategies, but Cynic 4 *does not realize it*. The objective of the task which he does not recognize is to save the product from being a complete me-too, by positioning it uniquely.

Cynic 5 does not recognize his responsibility to simplify the task for the creatives. In a sense he is right – the advertising strategy is going to be a pretty arbitrary decision, and creative punch is going to be extremely important for a launch in the fruit juice market. However, the creative team would settle down to work much more quickly on 'the winter fruit juice for when you miss the sunshine' than on 'something really zany and full of impact'.

Finally a chorus of cynics rewards JS for being funny. But he does not get any incentive for coming up with another candidate strategy.

There are several simple rules for creating a more fertile atmosphere for strategy development:

Well-defined task and responsibility

Very few ideas come to people who are not looking for them. On the whole, the better defined the problem the easier it is to find solutions. The team has to become more aware of the need to generate ideas and solutions and not to leave it all to the creative department or senior troubleshooters.

The contents of this book, starting with an understanding of the marketing strategy, recognizing the need for an explicit advertising strategy and creative brief (Chapters 2, 3 and 4) suggest the questions which need to be posed.

There is no risk in asking juniors to propose solutions which still have to be approved up the hierarchy. If responsibility is not pushed down it will creep back up the organization until it swamps those key people who do not feel they can pass the buck.

Positivism, teamwork and mutual support

This means learning to nurture strategic ideas by applying some of the 'creativity-enhancing' tricks that are already applied to the creative department.

Advertising people tend to be the products of high level, academic institutions. This type of education tends to emphasize evaluation, criticism and finding the one correct solution rather than imagination, appreciation and exploration (also answering questions rather than discovering them).

The analytical skills so developed are useful in the second, evaluative stage of creativity but often hinder the first, generative stage.

The rules for the first stage are often contrary to those of the second stage:

- Suspend judgement – all ideas are good ideas, ask what is good about this idea and how it can be improved,
- Ignore the negatives, there will be time to deal with them in the future, and only if the idea survives.
- Forget errors quickly, do not ridicule.
- Aim to generate several possible solutions rather than one perfect version.
- Question assumed constraints such as 'the client won't like it' or 'the market norms'.

It often seems natural to have one person creating ideas and six people knocking them down. It is more efficient to have six creating and just one censuring.

Rewarding strategic ideas

Laughter reinforces the desire to make jokes. Stated appreciation, attribution and acclaim for strategic as well as creative ideas, reinforces the motivation to produce those ideas. (Money helps as well – creative salaries depend on delivery and so should those of strategists.)

An indicator of the value an agency puts on its strategic ideas is its attitude to presenting them to its clients. If a brief is taken from the client and the response is the presentation of creative work it is clear that the agency does not feel its strategic thinking is worth much. If the agency feels a distinct need to present, discuss and seek approval for its advertising strategy before proceeding to creative work it believes in the importance of strategy.

Once there is an acceptance of the conceptual division of the ad into two parts, the strategy and the creative vehicle, the emphasis and value put on the pre-creative ideas is natural and highly beneficial to the morale and motivation of the people who are expected to have those ideas.

These attitudinal requirements naturally reflect the description of the 'market-led philosophy' described in the introduction, i.e. the cultural stance needed to ensure the success of strategic advertising is a market-led philosophy.

However, describing the culture is a long way from getting there. Company cultures can be compared to people's personalities – they are hard to pin down but very real, very individual and extremely hard to change!

Physical support material

Agencies favour the informality and spontaneity which are in sympathy with their creative role. It would be ludicrous to try to impose a rigid, mechanical system for producing advertising. However, establishing the need for a few key 'stages' and demanding the production of certain specific documents can help to install good strategic practices, without demanding any significant increase in the existing, or essential, administrative tasks.

Typically these documents would be:

1 *Advertising strategy document* – produced in response to the client's original briefing or request for an advertisement. Presented to the client for approval as the basis for the creative brief. Even if the ad is of little significance the strategy document should summarize the four points detailed in Chapter 3:

   • Purpose of the ad
   • Target
   • Message/content
   • Media choice

2 *Creative brief* – produced as the formal request to the creative department for work. Agreed between agency and client it also forms the basis for reacting to the subsequent creative work. In the case of major new campaigns a draft version should form the subject of a meeting with a suitable authority within the agency before the ad is briefed (e.g. creative director).

3 *Proposal for pre-testing creative work* – produced and presented alongside creative work, as the first stage of client approval. The document is complementary to the agency's 'sales pitch' for the ad, outlining what is not known or is considered risky about the work. In explaining what the agency want to investigate about its proposed creative solution, a research proposal sets a more realistic tone for a creative discussion than one where the agency simply 'sells' and asks for client approval (see Chapter 5).

4 *Proposal for feedback research* – presented along with any media plans. This is essential if experimental designs are to be well thought out. For the most enlightening feedback, testing possibilities have to exist in the media plans.

The purpose of a system of formal documents is to ensure that certain issues have been considered. Hence the key to its success is to keep the documents brief and simple, rather than dismissing their usefulness on occasions when an extensive document is not required. A contact report summarizing the creative brief or why no pre-test or feedback proposal was felt necessary, may suffice.

A secondary reason for demanding the latter two documents (proposals for pre-testing and feedback) is the need to budget for the extra cost of better data.

Research investment

Greater emphasis on strategy demands greater investment in research, testing and data handling. Unless current research is seriously underused, greater out-of-pocket expenses on research are absolutely necessary. The benefit of the extra data should amply cover its cost, but the agency should take the trouble to present well thought-out proposals to justify such investment.

The generally increasing willingness to invest in information is apparent from the increasing amounts of money spent on research each year.

Keeping good records

Marketing departments tend to be lax in keeping good records of their thinking, and ad agencies are twice as bad. Junior personnel move from account to account and from one job to another so rapidly that the incentive to keep good files over the years is marginal and the resulting waste is frightening.

The data and experience needed to produce strategic advertising builds up over years, and has to be cared for. The chapters on pre-testing and feedback stressed how difficult it is to obtain norms against which to compare test results, and the importance of past data for understanding relationships and causal effects. Given that a high turnover of staff is likely to remain a reality, a priority for anyone hoping to create a more strategic orientation in a company or ad agency must be to systematize and harmonize the data storage systems on the various brands. At least then a changeover of executives would not have the familiar effect of washing the account's memory.

One way to preserve and organize the research and past thinking that has been accumulated would be to keep a strategy book or diary. The diary would simply be a standard looseleaf file, kept up-to-date in line with a few simple rules. It would contain copies or summaries of the advertising strategy document, creative brief and summaries of research. The objective would not be to create a massive filing system, but to keep a chronological record of the thinking on the account and present it in a coherent and readable form.

The strategy book would provide the ideal briefing document for newcomers to the account and a precious record of the research documents which exist. The book would also be helpful to agency management interested in monitoring the strategic work being carried out and to younger employees wishing to learn through reading about real examples.

Strategy reviews

Top management already concerns itself with the quality of the creative output. Creative work is often reviewed in board meetings or at separate creative review committees. In a similar way top management should formally keep a check on the advertising strategies developed by the account teams. At the very least a summary of strategy and the creative brief should be demanded and reviewed at the same time (and as a basis for) reviewing creative work.

If top management adopt the attitudes summarized in this chapter, the tangible effects will appear rapidly. Pressure from the top to have a strategy, interest in creative briefs and not simply the resulting creative work, respect for research, encouragement for innovative strategic ideas all pass down the line of command. If senior management can themselves honestly accept the cultural changes outlined, the cultural change will have been largely achieved throughout the organization.

Over to you

Advertising is about having ideas. Ideas which sell, ideas which communicate, ideas which stick in the memory. In the introduction I boasted that this book gets as near as a book can to helping you find original advertising ideas. Maybe that was puffery, and the truth is that no system or logic can churn out genuine inspiration – you cannot rely on my ideas for your ideas. What I hope I have done, is help you organize your understanding of advertising, in a way that frees you to have better ideas.

As advertising becomes more sophisticated and competitive, and methods of evaluation become more reliable, a re-orientation towards the market and a specialization of the resulting, market-led tasks seems inevitable. Despite the difficulties, more strategic work and sophisticated research programmes seem set to become the normal practice in advertising development. Companies and agencies which succeed in putting greater emphasis and expertise behind the strategic tasks are likely to be more consistently successful with the creative task.

The fundamental premise of this book (in case you have read to the last page without noticing) is that advertising depends on two ideas, and that it is possible to get more systematic in the way we look for the strategic ideas. I cannot end without admitting that this is not altogether true. Pontificate as one might, there is no denying that the out-of-the-blue stroke of originality is still the salt of agency life. It is not even worth arguing that the inspiration comes to those who have first diligently done their homework. Advertising is not fair like that.

Index

Page numbers in italics refer to plates